Tell It Like It Isn't

Tell It Like It Isn't

The definitive guide to surviving in a deceitful world

DR. LORI L. BADURA

ARCHWAY
PUBLISHING

Archway Publishing books may be ordered
through booksellers or by contacting:

Archway Publishing
1663 Liberty Drive
Bloomington, IN 47403
www.archwaypublishing.com
1-(888)-242-5904

ISBN: 978-1-4808-1159-1 (sc)
ISBN: 978-1-4808-1158-4 (hc)
ISBN: 978-1-4808-1160-7 (e)

Library of Congress Control Number: 2014919469

Printed in the United States of America.

Archway Publishing rev. date: 11/21/2014

For John,
who taught me to always tell the truth, even to myself.

By doubting we are led to question, by questioning we arrive at the truth.

—PETER ABELARD

All truths are easy to understand once they are discovered; the point is to discover them.

—GALILEO

A lie can travel half way around the world while the truth is putting on its shoes

—CHARLES SPURGEON

CONTENTS ═══════════════════

Part 3: Truth, Lies, and Videotape: Deception Run Amok in Mainstream Culture

Part 4: Epilogue: Breaking the Cycle

INTRODUCTION ====
The Many Faces of Deception

My purpose in writing this book is to bring public attention to an epidemic that has been growing in our country for generations, quietly invading our thinking and mindset with insidious ease. It starts in childhood, grows in strength and effectiveness as we mature until it becomes an integral part of our existence even while remaining largely beneath our notice. We seldom see it within ourselves, and yet we revile it in others without ever recognizing the contradiction or the dependency it represents. Success for many is based upon it, while others are condemned and punished for exhibiting it. Its effects are felt through every aspect of our lives—the state of the economy, the actions of the government, expressions of culture, practices of social groups, the nature of religious beliefs, and the structure of our legal system. Not a single day goes by where we are not either exposed to it or found guilty of it ourselves. It is pervasive, communicable, and, while publicly denounced, it is functionally embraced at all levels of society. As such, it is the single greatest challenge to our continued health and wellbeing as a culture unless we start to take stock of its rampant influence on our lives.

No, I am not talking about a virus. I am not referring to terrorism, or crime, or climate change. I am not pointing to obesity, diabetes, or an obsession with reality TV shows. I am speaking of the explosion of lying, distortion of truth, and disingenuous behavior displayed daily across all relevant aspects of life that have now become accepted aspects of social interaction.

If you just shrugged and said "Oh, is that all?" you have just made my point. It is not so much that the failure to tell the truth goes unnoticed—you have only to watch any cable news network to see dozens of examples being discussed during your morning coffee. It is that lies have largely become an accepted part of how we interact. To be honest (pun intended), most people no longer care—unless of course a lie from someone else puts us personally at a disadvantage, at which point we rave and bleat about it like mad. We have by and large become numb to the flurry of unfounded accusations that fly back and forth in politics, the news, and popular culture, much to our own detriment.

The idea for this book was born out of recognition of just such ennui surrounding blatant and very public examples of dishonesty. I had just sat through more than a year of political posturing and chest beating via the Republican primaries, and now we were starting the final push to the 2012 Presidential election with a series of nationally televised debates. I had already heard some of the most outrageous claims and policy positions I had ever experienced within a single party. Now we were expected to somehow erase all of that from memory and watch the titanic clash of the two major parties with an eye to choosing the individual we thought could best move the country forward. To do that, we had to understand the true nature of the issues, the facts underlying the state of the deficit and the economy, the global challenges we faced in trade and in peace and security, and obstacles facing our ability to work, have access to healthcare, and maintain or purchase a home. In other words, we needed to know the truth about the things that really matter to us all every day of our lives in the real world.

What we got was a shameful series of lies and sleights of hand, accusations, name calling, and distortion of facts. We got personal attacks and vague statements made ever more firmly and definitively, and yet devoid of real information, as the campaign progressed. It was bad enough to be bombarded by unfounded rhetoric during endless hours of television ads, but now we had to watch them play the political game in person instead of actually standing up and saying something true and relevant. I was already at the tipping point when one camp made the now infamous statement "We won't let our campaign be dictated by fact checkers." Now to watch these two gentlemen vying for the highest office in the land regress to a barely civil exchange of unfounded and wildly inaccurate jibes and misinformed assessments, well, that was just too much. I literally threw my hands up in the air and said I had had it with the both of them. Shouting "That's not true" at the TV wasn't going to solve anything. If only, I thought, their podiums could be wired up to electrical boxes so they could be zapped into submission every time one of them knowingly uttered a false statement. Or electronic dog collars for that matter. What a boon it would be to the nation if there was some consequence, some behavioral deterrent to the disgraceful, offensive, and downright insulting state of affairs that our political process has become.

And so was born the idea for this book. I realized that politics is only the most public and obvious arena, and that such deceitful behavior has actually become commonplace in our everyday existence. I decided I had something to say about it, and could encourage a way of thinking that might impact on the prevalence of lying and deceit going forward. Not that fact checkers are not readily available. Groups like Politifact.com (on whom I will rely heavily in this book) do an admirable job of researching the truth or falsehood of various claims and making the information available to the general public for your own evaluation. What I wanted to talk about was not just specific examples of "pants on fire' or "four Pinocchios" but rather the appalling fact that, as a society, we accept such behavior way too readily. My years spent as an academic in the Psychology field made it easy for me to understand why lying exists, but did not so easily explain why it is so tolerated. Acts of evasion, dodging the true question, and making outright false statements aren't secret–we see them on the news every day. But our society has reached the point where our ability to discern fact from fiction has waned at the same time, so that we now attend more to the spin put on a statement than to the substantive content thereof. That is the true tragedy, and the stimulus that drove me to conceptualize the premise of fostering a personal process of deductive reasoning as a means to creating a world where people are actually accountable for what they propagate.

The underlying premise of this book is that each and every one of us is capable of developing and honing our ability to distinguish truth from falsehood by using a simple process of deduction and logic. The inherent process of reasoning that is available to all of us provides a framework from which to both judge the veracity of any information to which we are exposed, as well as providing a basis for our reactions to the nature of that information. This rationally-based tool of judgment is a personal cognitive process that you can apply to virtually any situation to increase the chances of making an accurate and truthful assessment, even in reference to your own internal dispositions. Using the fundamentals of scientific empiricism, you can easily learn to apply rigor and skepticism as inherent principles of judgment across the entire range of personal and social situations covered in this book. The goal is to make you a better and more effective consumer of information.

The Convoluted Anatomy of Deception

Research shows us that the average person tells at least six falsehoods on any given day, a number that many of us tend to underestimate. In fact, many types of lying go unnoticed or are considered acceptable parts of human interaction. Most people would admit to telling a falsehood or stretching the truth on at least some occasions and some social mores may require certain types of deception in order to promote harmonious interaction and/or self-preservation. Any husband who has been asked how his wife's new outfit makes her look is more than familiar with the concept of telling it like it isn't! However, we do not like to think of ourselves as liars by nature and we tend to overlook many deceptive behaviors because we have lost some of the factual distinction between truth and lying in daily practice. We find it convenient to focus on prohibitions against "word lies" while ignoring the malicious spirit of less well articulated types of behavior nevertheless designed to mislead, deceive, and misinform. To understand the true extent of this phenomenon in our society, we must first consider the different forms lies may take and their respective functions, as not all deception is created equal in our eyes.

In its most basic form, a lie is defined as an untrue statement told with the intent to deceive (Mirriam-Webster Dictionary). A lie can also be described as "a statement meant to make a false or *misleading* impression." Already we start to get into a gray area. Technically, one can say something that is factually correct but, through omission of certain key data or through emphasis on words, the statement can still be misleading. Some people feel that this latter example does not count as lying, since the words stated were in fact correct. Nonetheless, the *intent* was to create an assumption not supported by the full range of facts, therefore it is still a lie. This can be achieved by omission of key elements, altering or constraining context, and altering the emphasis of portions of a statement to purposefully draw attention away from contradicting information. Historically, deceptive techniques of this kind have been termed "contextomies" and date back at least to the time of Aristotle. In essence, the meaning of statements are altered or even reversed through removal of important contextual cues.

For example, our esteemed second US president, John Adams, has historically been accused of anti-religious sentiment for many generations, largely as the result of a quote taken from a letter he penned to Thomas Jefferson in 1817:

> *This would be the best of all possible worlds, if there were no religion in it!*

On its own, there is no way to interpret this statement other than that John Adams had a negative view of religion. Interestingly, addition of the full context around the statement reveals quite the opposite interpretation:

> *Twenty times, in the course of my late Reading, have I been upon the point of breaking out, "This would be the best of all possible Worlds, if there were no Religion in it"!!! But in this exclamation I should have been as fanatical as Bryant or Cleverly. Without Religion this World would be Something not fit to be mentioned in polite Company, I mean Hell. (From Lester J. Cappon, [Ed]1988, The Adams-Jefferson Letters: The Complete Correspondence Between Thomas Jefferson and Abigail and John Adams)*

It is impressive how much the full context alters the derived meaning of the statement, and also obvious how useful such a tactic can be for misleading an audience by distorting context. It is not surprising that this technique is used quite frequently in political contests whenever it is a goal to influence the voter and create a negative impression of the opponent.

Similarly, exaggeration and embellishment are forms of lying that many people fail to notice in everyday life, even the perpetrators themselves. The "fish that got away" tactic is often used to purposefully create excitement and enthusiasm, to make the story appear bigger in the telling than it was in reality. While that in of itself constitutes deceptive showmanship, it is also possible to distort the truth in a more unconscious fashion due to the effects of passing time and the accumulation of slight embellishments to the thread. For example, I had a close encounter with a 15 foot hammerhead shark when I was a student while diving in the Caribbean. I told the story in good faith for many years before I ran across an old diary I had kept during that period. Imagine my absolute shock to discover that the monster fish I had run across was actually only 7 feet long (still a big fish in its own right mind you)! The story simply grew over time without me being aware I was adding a foot here and there for the effect of the story. Nonetheless, the tale became of a work of fiction whether I intended it to be so or not.

As previously mentioned, lying typically involves the intent to deceive, and when we do so consciously, it is termed "tactical deception." As an example, a spouse who leaves out the incriminating parts of the story about why they were so late coming home is in fact being untruthful without lying outright. Many people feel they have a certain leeway in this area and are able to sooth their consciences by emphasizing that they did not actually say anything untrue. However, this does not really stop what they say from being disingenuous and misleading—creating a false impression that obviously serves to benefit the teller at the expense of the listener.

We also need to be clear about the distinction between purposeful deception and the statement of someone's opinion, as these are often confused in practical terms. Opinions are not bound by truth or facts and do not require the burden of evidence to support them. The best opinions, of course, do have a factual foundation that can be checked out by any interested party for accuracy. But even an opinion based on no facts at all cannot really be classified as lying, as long as it is clear that it is simply an opinion. And just because someone thinks, believes, or wishes an opinion is true does not make it so. The problem is that people do not seem to be able to effectively distinguish between opinions and facts when they are exposed to them, and as a result, many unfounded theories get perpetuated throughout our society, particularly in public forums like the media.

Take this example of a statement made by Rush Limbaugh on his popular radio program, *The Rush Limbaugh Show*, on August 12, 2005:

> *Feminism was established so as to allow unattractive women access to the mainstream of society.*

This statement reflects Mr. Limbaugh's opinion. As such, he is entitled to make such a claim without providing supporting evidence to back it up. It also happens to be wrong. However, neither of these facts indicate that he was telling a lie. For us to come to that conclusion, we require more context around the intent and the available facts. Therefore it is important to be able to judge the underlying motivation for any incorrect statement before concluding intent to deceive. It is not only possible to inadvertently say something untrue simply because you have not gotten the facts straight, but it is also something that happens frequently to every one of us. While this behavior may be unfortunate, and might even lead to unexpected negative consequences, it is not construed as lying in the absence of intent to deceive. As we shall see, it is not always easy to identify intentional from accidental untruths, and thus there is a growing need for more effective means of judging the quality of the information around us.

Benefits and Consequences of Deception

It is often obvious what factors motivate behaviors like lying, distorting the truth, and spreading misinformation. Most often the driving force is either self-promotion or avoidance of unpleasant events. The child who denies having tracked mud into the house seeks to avoid being reprimanded. The criminal who lies about culpability in a crime seeks to avoid jail time. The politician who professes to be blameless in a scandal seeks to avoid loss of votes or status. Therefore, the psychological and personal benefits of manipulating the truth are usually easy to understand.

What is less clear is the consequence of lying on a sociological level, including economic, legal, and cultural aspects of our lives. Compared to investigations around the etiology and function of lying, relatively little research to date has focused on the ramifications of deceptive behavior for the broader society. Personal bias and various psychological factors inherent in the individual can profoundly impact the thinking of the group, and belief systems promoted by the group can feed back on the thinking of the individual. Emerging evidence on the interplay between individual and group dynamics suggests we could all benefit from a better understanding of how sociological and cultural factors shape our interest in the truth and our reaction to deceptive behavior.

Finally, it is important to understand that lying perpetuates most strongly under conditions where the behavior is not met by negative consequences. Children may lie to avoid punishment, but children who receive stronger punishment for the lie than the original offending act tend to grow up to behave more honestly in general. Clearly delineated consequences for deceptive and dishonest behavior are a key attribute to discouraging such behavior across many aspects of our culture. Our legal system has profound penalties for lying to police or in a court of law designed to discourage behaviors that block the framework of justice. A job applicant who is caught lying or misrepresenting themselves on a resume is punished, at the very least by not getting the job, and more dramatically, by becoming unlikely to be hired for any job. In some cases, such as falsely representing medical or educational credentials, lying by these individuals may even be punishable by law.

Why is it then that we can be so blasé about lying during political campaigns? How can we sit through media presentations that demonstrate profound bias, contextual distortion, and other mechanisms of misinformation without being insulted by what they are trying to pull over on us? They get away with it because there are no consequences significant enough to alter the behavior. We continue to listen to and vote for political candidates who have knowingly tried to mislead us. We continue to tune into the news shows despite the obvious bias and factual distortions inherent in their broadcasts. In essence, many forms of lying and deception in society do not give rise to negative consequences and thus are relatively free to flourish. The final section of this book will focus on opportunities to rectify this lack of consequences if we hope to avoid the continuing degradation and undermining of our societal mindset.

How effective are the measures we take to punish lying and reward honesty in our society? What can we do to promote more truthful interactions at both the local and national level? Imagine a world in which political candidates risk being zapped in public if they tell a lie or otherwise misrepresent the truth during a political debate. Not only would this perhaps provide an unprecedented level of entertainment for the millions of viewers glued to the TV, but I cannot imagine that any politicians who have seen a colleague literally zapped for lying would not try and stick to the high road themselves.

While it is not likely we will see any truth-saying panels with real power of punishment during political exchanges in the near future, there is no excuse to passively accept a system that is obviously devoid of appropriate checks and balances. The answer must lie with the consumers of information themselves. Every person has the ability to develop and apply a process of judgment that allows them to more critically evaluate the information to which they are exposed, and foster conclusions based upon fact rather than emotional appeal. Furthermore, we, the listeners, have the duty to modify the behavior of the teller by virtue of our response to the accuracy of the information they impart. The aim of this book is to explore the biological, psychological, and societal bases that underlie deception in order to consider the possible options by which we can achieve a higher standard of truth. Each of us has the potential to improve our ability to identify and react appropriately to deceptive behavior, thus making it much less prevalent in our daily lives. To effectively tell the truth, one first has to understand the human propensity to *tell it like it isn't.*

═══ PART ONE ═══
Gold Standards of Judgment

I n order to make judgments about the nature of any given statement, situation, or observation, it is necessary to have a fundamental understanding of what constitutes the truth. This is more difficult than you might imagine. Consideration of any event must be objective and reflect criteria agreed upon by all reasonable parties. The truth cannot shift to suit our whims or opinions. Truth should not change depending upon ones upbringing, the culture in which you live, or your gender, age, and skin color. Therefore, we need to establish clear criteria for judgment that are consistent, factual, and unbiased.

In a perfect world, this would never be in question. But as we shall see, a myriad of tangential factors influence our judgments of what is true and what is false. In this section, we will define the principles of a cognitive process of judgment that provides a framework from which to evaluate any source of information in a way that satisfies the criteria of objective assessment. The fundamentals of this approach are based upon universally held definitions of the nature of truth. Therefore, we will start our exploration with a review of some of the most accepted sources of factual judgment we have–the scientific approach and our legal system of justice. It is to these gold standards that we will align our personal measure of judgment as we consider the topics discussed in this book.

Furthermore, evolutionary pressures have shaped our very biology to promote deception in social situations. Rather than standing as an aberration of morality, it may well be that society would never have advanced to modern day without our ability to lie and deceive those around us. The mechanics of lying are indelibly written within our own physiology. In fact, the functional activity of the brain when a person lies contains a cognitive roadmap–a neural "signature"–associated with deception. It may soon be possible to create a lie detector with an unprecedented level of accuracy using emergent technologies like functional neuroimaging.

CHAPTER 1

Scientific Truth:
Foundations of Empirically Based Evidence

T hroughout our history, we humans have always been avid observers of our environment and the consequences of actions within it. This very human propensity to understand the world around us is the key factor underlying our success as a species. It is not our ability to walk upright, an attribute we share with most birds and some higher primates, nor is it the opposable thumb and the unprecedented increase in manual dexterity and manipulative ability. It is primarily our big brains that make these other features so useful, as we can decide when, where, and how to interact with our environment in ways not accomplished by any other species on the planet. We can learn by observing rather than solely through experience. We can conjecture about how altering circumstances might impact outcome. We can project, predict, deduce, and contemplate before ever we act, thereby allowing us to choose the best course from among a variety of options. This is beneficial in a world where "flight or fight" is the typical totality of response. It also allows us to take what we have learned from our observation and apply it in ways that alter our environment to preempt various undesired outcomes–clothes and houses protect against weather and extremes of temperature, refrigerators allow food storage all year round, and planes, trains, and automobiles allow us to move quickly and efficiently from place to place. Our minds give rise to art, music, literature, and theater. We invent technologies, medicines, and caffè lattes. There is no doubt that the expressions of our intellect are likely boundless in their potential for significant impact on our lives and the world around us.

This amazing mental agility is molded through the processes of conjecture, testing, and doubt. We develop understanding of the world first by observation. We see what things are around us and observe how they behave. We look for cause and effect— we notice how actions (both our own and those of other actors in our environment) lead to outcomes and we form hypotheses about what that relationship might mean. We seek evidence that explains what we observe and logically describes the relationship among all potentially contributing factors. Sometimes we are able to directly test our premises–we purposely manipulate one or more variables and see how it affects the outcome. Other times, direct testing is not possible or practical, so we collect multiple observations looking for a pattern and/or exceptions to a rule. For example, I have seen young children who are a bit wary about going down a playground slide for the first time wait and watch several other children go down before making the decision to try it. The observation that playing on the slide occurs in the absence of bodily harm and evokes the obvious delight of the other children provides evidence around the nature of the experience.

Interestingly, the foundation of science is based upon the fact that it is easier to refute than to confirm–that is, it is easier to prove something is false. You only need one example where the predicted relationship didn't hold up and you are able to rule it out as untrue. It only takes the observation of one child toppling off the jungle gym or crashing into their face at the bottom of the slide for a child to refute the premise that it is a safe thing to play on, even when that child might have previously observed dozens of other children play without injury.

Consistent results are suggestive of a true relationship, but since it is difficult to test a theory under all possible and necessary conditions, we can seldom be certain we have identified all of the key factors that affect the outcome. To address this, we construct plausible explanations based upon the prevailing evidence and then seek to refute them through rigorous testing or observation, making modifications as we go. The child who has learned that the jungle gym is not always a safe plaything can consider various factors that might influence when a sliding board is safe and when it is not in order to account for observations of both jubilance and catastrophe, rather than reject it out of hand as a dangerous experience. As such, we develop theories about the world as a matter of course and approach them with healthy skepticism until a definitive link between events can be demonstrated. Interestingly, while scientific truth is by far the strongest measuring stick for understanding the reality of the world around us, it is important to know that it reflects the truth as best we understand it at this moment in time. Evaluating truth through the fundamentals of this scientific method is thus a living process designed to alter over time as our knowledge and understanding increase.

The Fundamentals of Scientifically Defined Truth

All scientific research across disciplines shares certain basic underlying tenets for arriving at truthful conclusions. Scientists therefore need to understand and abide by the characteristics of the scientific method in order to conduct good research. However, the non-scientists in our society can also benefit from some knowledge concerning how experiments are conducted and how conclusions are validated, as we are all exposed daily to summaries of scientific findings through media and news reports. Here is an example:

statistics show that cigarette smoking may be hazardous to your health. But what exactly does this mean? In this case, the term *statistics* is used to indicate that certain health problems appear more frequently in association with the behavior of smoking (i.e., they are *correlated*). However, at least in humans, true experiments have not been conducted to test the cause and effect underlying the relationship.

As opposed to correlative epidemiological approaches, an experiment is a rigidly designed and controlled investigation of the impact of one or more variables on another. To conduct a true experiment on smoking's effects on human health, one or more groups of people would need to be exposed to identical quantities of smoke for the same period of time, while another group would not experience smoke. The people in these groups would need to be matched on a variety of factors—age, race, gender, weight, exercise level, and family history of health problems—to name just a few. The purpose of matching people in the smoking and nonsmoking (or control) group is to try and have as few other possible explanations for differences in the health outcome as possible. In this way, if the people in the smoking group showed a higher incidence of health problems, this could be attributed to the smoking itself, as all other conditions between groups would be relatively equivalent.

Certainly, experiments of this type with laboratory animals have indicated detrimental health effects from smoking, but ethical considerations preclude doing this type of study in humans. Therefore, the statement about the potential impact of smoking in humans must remain correlative, meaning there appears to be a relationship between smoking and certain health problems that resembles those seen from experimentation in animals, but causality has not been directly proven. How can it be that something so clearly related might not be causally linked? Consider the following facts. The incidence of heart attacks has been shown to be higher in those who smoke. Smokers also often score higher on scales of anxiety. Anxiety is also linked to the prevalence of heart attacks. So, do smokers have more heart attacks because they smoke, or do they both smoke and have more heart attacks because they are anxious? Correlation implies a relationship exists but cannot necessary prove the direction of causality in that relationship (Note: therefore both smoking and anxiety are good things to avoid if you are worried about heart attacks!).

While I am not arguing that smoking is healthy, I use this example only to illustrate the difference between general health statistics used in our society and the statistics arrived at through true scientific methodology. While the correlation between smoking and heart attacks may in fact be causal, the link has not been arrived at by careful experimentation in the human population. Understanding the nature of the scientific method is thus important for interpretation of the information we receive through media sources, and for deciding upon the proper response to this information. Here is a current and rather poignant example—there has been a recent attempt to ban sugary soft drinks of sixteen ounces or larger in New York City in an attempt to address growing societal concerns about obesity and related health problems, such as diabetes. It is a scientific fact that sugars are high in calories and that unused calories (i.e., calories we take in through food and drink that are not immediately used for energy expenditure and metabolism) are converted into fat stored within the body. However, a ban on sugary drinks is a rather myopic attempt to address the problem and is not done in a manner that gets at the scientific basis of the truth underlying the health issue.

Firstly, the ban would only address the purchase and consumption of large containers of sugary drinks, but not put a limit on overall consumption (i.e., you can buy and drink as many smaller containers as you would like). Secondly, sugar from these large drinks is only one source of sugar in our potential diets—no bans on candy, ice cream, cookies, or any other sugar-packed delicacy have likewise been imposed. Thirdly, sugar is only one form of high calorie food available for ingestion. As many, if not more, extra calories can (and will) be imbibed through pizza, bagels stacked with cream cheese, and foot-high corned beef sandwiches across the greater New York City area. Therefore, as an intelligent response to scientific fact and health-related statistics, this approach at intervention makes a mockery of the truth underlying the obesity epidemic and could never stand up to the rigorous standards of the scientific method.

What then are the characteristics of the scientific method, and what types of information should you be on the lookout for when you hear about scientific facts and government statistics on the cable news network of your choice? The following represents some of requirements that must be met for research studies and scientific results to fulfill the requirements of sound methodology:

1) <u>Empiricism</u>: Empiricism refers to the fact that any conclusion drawn from the data in an experiment must involve *verifiable* and *objective* evidence obtained through systematic observation. This means that the hypotheses you create must be testable, the proposed relationship must be measureable, and the conclusions you draw from the results must be reasonably expected under similar conditions and circumstances. You can test the relationship between sugar and obesity and you can measure how much sugar intake results in weight gain. However, the relationships are only empirically valid for the conditions under which they were tested. As a result, it is an empirical fact that too much sugar can make you fat, but it is not an empirical fact that limiting the size of drinks you can purchase in the greater New York City area will have any impact on reducing obesity.

2) <u>Rationality</u>: Any conclusions drawn from the results of an experiment must be derived logically and rationally. In other words, conclusions should clearly represent the facts as they have been demonstrated in a given experiment and in the context of

available knowledge. Objective interpretation must be freed of one's opinion. While you can have an opinion about anything, an empirical factual result must arise from something that is measured and quantified in a controlled fashion regardless of your desire for the outcome. Bias reflects a situation where one's preconceptions can skew the design of an experiment in such a way as to presuppose an outcome, or conversely, to influence the judgment of the results in favor of one interpretation over another (i.e., the results come out the way you hoped they would because you had an eye for certain aspects over others). In addition, potential confounding variables–factors that may affect the outcome even though they were not meant to–must be identified, controlled, and accounted for as much as possible in the experiment. For example, a study designed to evaluate the effects of limiting the size of drink containers without limiting how many small containers can be consumed is not likely to give rise to rationally derived results since there is no actual restriction on sugar intake.

3) <u>Rigorousness</u>: All good experimental data are the result of carefully and rigorously designed studies. This means that the results should be valid and replicable under a variety of circumstances. Validity refers to the correctness of the variables being studied. Internal validity means that you are in fact measuring what you think you are in a given study. When internal validity is violated in a study, the results will often be highly misleading. Consider the example of a soft drink taste test between two major brands of cola. Volunteers across the country taste-tested the two cola brands in blinded cups (one was marked with the letter Q and one with the letter M). In a first experiment, the results showed an overwhelming preference for one cola brand over the other. Unhappy with the results, the losing company asked for a repeat, and this time the results showed no difference. As it turns out, the cups for "cola 1" were labeled with the letter M in the first test and "cola 2" was labeled with the letter Q. When the experiment

was repeated, this time alternating between labeled cups, there was no preference of one over the other. This result shows that the experimenters were actually testing preference of the letter M over the letter Q, not the taste of the two different colas as they had originally thought!

Another critical type of validity is external validity—the generalizability of the results of your experiment to the general population or world at large. An experimental finding that only occurs in one circumstance under a specific set of conditions at one moment in time may be a true result, but it does little to contribute to our understanding of the world outside that specific situation. A good example of an impactful (and embarrassing) violation of external validity occurred during the presidential election between Harry Truman and Thomas Dewey. The results of polls that were conducted before the election, as well as the early exit polls on election day, so overwhelmingly favored Dewey that the Chicago Tribune newspaper (November 3, 1948) printed the headlines "Dewey Defeats Truman" in the morning edition of the next day's paper, before the final results were in. Obviously, history showed that they were wrong in their interpretation of the polling results. Partly what they failed to consider in arriving at the prediction is that much of the polling was being done by telephone for the first time and telephones, being somewhat of a luxury during that period in history, were found more often in wealthy homes. Since more wealthy individuals were Republican, what they were actually doing was selectively sampling Republican voting for the Republican candidate.

Scientific Foundations of Judgment

The preceding discussion of the characteristics of the scientific method likely appears somewhat irrelevant to the life of an average American. However, scientific thinking should not be restricted only to those with advanced degrees working at institutions of higher learning, and it is in fact a capability and way of approaching the world that is hard-wired in to all of us. Humans consider life from this perspective even without laboratory benches, fancy equipment, and grant funds. From the time we are children, we tend to approach unknowns in a way that seeks evidence to satisfy our desire to understand how a given thing works. Even without formal training and education, children will set up scenarios where they test *what happens if I do this...?* Kids try things out, they apply explanations to things that seem to make sense, and then discard them for new and better ones when those fall short. In other words, they evolve theories about life that are modifiable—things that do not hold up are discarded and explanations are expanded as new data are added (albeit it sometimes very creatively!). This process matures throughout our lives and ultimately leads to a *personal truth* or individual life view about how the world works and one's place within it. Thus, employing empiricism and rationality is natural to humans and represents the greatest tool in our historical search for truth.

Constructing a Scientifically Valid Measure of Judgment

The ability to think rationally forms the basis of all deductive reasoning. All new information is always automatically weighed up against what we understand about the world so far. When that information seems to fit with our current understanding, we tend to view it as truthful. When it diverges in any marked way from our expectations, we react with skepticism. It is here that the scientific process comes in handy for those seeking the truth. Being skeptical about something is not a negative thing. Often our gut reaction arises from an unconscious recognition of a larger inconsistency. Instead, it should be a motivator to find out more about the contradiction or inconsistency apparent in the new information. We stand to learn the most about those things that surprise us or do not fit in with our preconceptions. Rather than reject the contrary information out of hand, investigate it! Check out the source of the information and determine on what basis the claims were made. How credible is the source? Is it an authoritative or respected source of information? Is there a possibility of bias? Can the facts be interpreted in other ways? Is there research that supports the view? What explanations exist for why what you previously believed is incorrect? These questions give rise to the basic series of steps underlying the principles of deductive logic:

> **Step 1:** Evaluate the new information to see how well it fits with what you already know. Does it support or conflict with existent information?

> **Step 2:** If it conflicts, determine the sources of the contradiction and evaluate the degree of credibility. Does the information originate from a respected and accredited source?

> **Step 3:** Weigh the validity of the methods that generated the data—is there verifiable evidence to back up the claim?

> **Step 4:** Form a judgment about the new information—true or false?

> **Step 5:** Update your mental rolodex to reflect the judgment.

Following these simple steps creates the basis of a process of judgment that you can apply to just about any situation. Here is an example: Recently I was discussing government spending with a friend of mine, and he cited a statistic to back up his assertion that tax payers are footing the bill for things we do not want. He told me that there have been over 65 million abortions in this country over the last decade, nearly 750,000 of them in the last year alone. I immediately raised an eyebrow and started to question him. Firstly, the math was questionable. These are numbers that did not seem to fit with my understanding of population statistics. There are just over 300 million people living in the United States at the moment. If the incidence of abortions he cited is correct, it would mean that there is one abortion for every five people in this country, and more abortions than there are live births! Furthermore, if there were just under one million abortions in the last year, there would have needed to be six to seven times that many every other year in the past decade in order to make up the total number he postulated. The information did not fit with what I knew to be facts and did not seem mathematically plausible.

Secondly, the friend in question is an enthusiastic individual with a strong political viewpoint who has a history of having bought into somewhat exaggerated claims in the past, and was known to believe circulating rumors about a number of fantastical claims (aka, conspiracy theory enthusiast). Therefore, his past history of gullibility did not add weight of evidence to his claim.

Thirdly, the information in question was readily available from respectable and scientifically accredited sites on the internet (e.g., The National Data Book and Center for Disease Control). It turns out that he overestimated the claims by an order of magnitude— there were roughly 6.5 million abortions across the past decade, not 65 million, with a fairly steady annual rate of around 750,000. In this case, the misplaced decimal makes a huge difference to the point being put forth.

I rejected the information my friend had supplied and chalked the inaccuracy up to inflation that occurred somewhere along the way as the story propagated through his social circles. I did not need to update my mental rolodex to incorporate this new information because I found it to be untrue. As you can see, this process was simple, required little time or effort, and my healthy skepticism resulted in clarification of facts that hopefully will encourage him to be more careful when he shares information in the future (I have no doubt he will be, at least with me). Noticing potential discrepancies and applying this type of critical and rational thinking does not require an advanced degree and can have a huge impact on your ability to judge the accuracy of all kinds of information to which you become exposed in the process of daily living.

Subverted Science—Frauds and Imposters

Despite serving as a gold standard for our judgment of truth, science is no stranger to fraud and deception. The same intellectual potential that allows us to develop a framework of rationale judgment unfortunately also allows us to deceive, distort, and alter information to support our own ends, sometimes without even consciously being aware that we are doing so. We have a long history as a species of trying to avoid or subvert scientific fact if it challenges our world view. In some cases, scientific falsehood is perpetuated purposefully—individuals will falsify results in order to gain prominence in a field, access to grant funding, or personal fame. This is typically not tolerated by the scientific community and the consequences are harsh—loss of job and position, loss of funds, removal from the field as a whole, as well as ridicule and condemnation by the scientific community. In other cases, unconscious bias by the experimenter (or the subjects themselves) can skew research data and lead to erroneous conclusions that give a false picture of cause and effect. Typically, these conclusions end up being refuted over time when other researchers try to replicate the results and fail to do so, leading to a rejection of the theory derived from such data. In short, scientific truth is still susceptible to fraud and deception in the absence of unbiased rigorous evaluation, and thus it behooves even the non-specialist consumer of information to be capable of assessing the logic and accuracy of scientifically-based claims.

We began this chapter with a discussion of how scientific empiricism is the primary means by which we set the gold standard for truth in this world. It is normal for us to believe that the individuals who are actually responsible for using this method to develop the facts and knowledge of our world must also be unbiased and truthful in their reporting. Unfortunately, numerous examples of scientific hoaxes, fraud, and medical imposters occur each and every year in this country. How then can the average consumer of information make judgments about the veracity of information coming from those they have trusted to provide the best in unbiased, objective, factual claims? Luckily, the same process of logic deduction we have been discussing so far is usually the undoing for those who attempt to pervert it. In this section, we will review some blatant and very public examples of scientific deceit and medical fraud of recent times.

To most scientists, it is not only intellectual curiosity that drives their scientific careers, but also the desire to achieve prominence in their field. The various disciplines within science represent microcosms of research endeavor, little societies populated by hard-working laborers and a few elite individuals at the top whose achievements and vision have elevated them to superstar status. These people not only get their share of federal and private funding, publications, and conference presentations, but they are also often invited to provide keynote lectures, be interviewed for newspapers and TV, and receive many other forms of public acclaim.

Within the highly competitive world of physics and nanotechnology, one of the brightest rising stars in recent times was *Jan Henrik Schön*, a German-born physicist who was hired straight out of his graduate program by Bell labs in New Jersey in 1997. Schön turned heads within the scientific community for his work on field-effect transistors, publishing an astonishing number of articles over the next few years in top journals in the field. His data were exciting, spectacular, and well beyond anything that had yet been demonstrated in the area. Unfortunately, no other researchers could replicate his results. Trust me, this is one of the greatest worries for legitimate researchers in all fields. It is bad enough to be wrong despite all of the best intentions and efforts to be accurate, but lack of replication always raises the specter of suspicion about data falsification whether it is warranted or not. We all breathe a sigh of relief when other researchers corroborate our findings and theories.

In this case, subsequent investigation by a Bell Labs committee revealed a number of instances where the results from different experiments appeared to include the same data (a practice not tolerated in legitimate scientific work), and others where the data appeared to be derived from mathematical functions that were instead reported as real time results. Schön could not provide the raw data for review as he did not keep laboratory notebooks (cardinal sin #1) and he had erased all of the electronic copies from his computer hard drive (cardinal sin #2). Based upon the results of the investigation, the committee found numerous instances of scientific misconduct and Schön was relieved of his position. Furthermore, the University of Konstanz, who had awarded him his doctorate, stripped him of the degree for dishonorable conduct in 2004. Thus, in less than seven years, Schön went from rising young superstar to discredited outcast. Not only that, he left behind a trail of embarrassed colleagues who had worked with him and put their names on the research articles, and journal editors who had published the fictitious results.

Falsifying data for publication purposes is only one means of deceiving the scientific community and having a negative impact on the public sector. The drive to obtain grant funding through federal or private sources is enormous. Many scientists only retain their faculty positions as long as they remain funded, and for all researchers, it is difficult (if not impossible) to maintain a lab and train students without a funding source (research is extremely expensive!). As you might imagine, the competition for funding is extreme and success in academia is directly linked to one's ability to master this task. Therefore you can imagine the horror and anger most scientists experience when they find that one of their colleagues obtained a much coveted source of research funding through fraudulent means.

Dipak K. Das was a notable member of the faculty at the University of Connecticut and the Director of their Cardiovascular Research Center. He became known for his work on the health benefits of resveratrol, a chemical found in small amounts in red wine that has been reported to promote heart health, lower cancer risk, and have a number of other positive effects. He published 117 journal articles on the subject, was well funded for his work, and was a spokesman for a number of companies that market the product. That is why it came as such a shock when, tipped off by an anonymous accusation of misconduct, the University of Connecticut commenced an investigation resulting in a report to the federal Office of Research Integrity that found 145 instances of data fabrication, falsification, and inappropriate manipulation of images. The University subsequently started dismissal proceedings, froze Das' research, and returned two federal grants worth nearly $1 million to the funding agencies. But the nefarious impact of his misconduct is much farther reaching than the punishment and public humiliation he received. All who worked in his laboratory now carry the stigma of association with a fraudulent scientist and will likely experience suspicion around their potential culpability in the scandal. Furthermore, the publicity around the case cast doubt on the legitimacy of claims around potential health benefits of resveratrol. Although other independent research has supported evidence for health benefits of the chemical, there will likely be a financial impact for those companies who employed Das in their marketing campaigns. It is hard to believe the claims of a company that associates with frauds and cheats, even if their claims are true.

While a small percentage of scientists will cheat and lie in order to obtain standing within the scientific community or resources and funding, an even smaller number use science as a way to gain a broader popularity within secular society. Scientific hoaxes have long captured the public imagination, largely because there is a deep seated public desire for the outlandish and inexplicable to be true. Take for example the scandalous story of the Piltdown Man hoax, where scientists and the public alike were fooled for over 40 years into believing that bone fragments taken from a gravel pit in East Sussex, England were evidence of a hitherto undiscovered early ancestor of humans (it was actually an orangutan jaw bone and part of a modern human skull). It would seem laughable now, as we would expect modern forensic and technological capabilities to easily see through such a ruse, and it is much harder to fool a discerning public with such ready access to information sources and internet communication. Or maybe not so difficult after all...

In 1971, the world reeled beneath the exciting news that a small tribe of Stone Age humans (about 20 individuals) was discovered by *Manuel Elizalde* to be living on the tiny Philippine island of Mindanao. Supposedly isolated for countless years from other members of the human race, the Tasaday tribe was reported to be living in caves, to possess a unique language, to use stone tools, and to dress and interact with the characteristics of an early human culture. The story created a sensation across the world, becoming the subject of television and news headlines, making the cover of National Geographic, and inspiring a documentary, "The Last Tribes of Mindanao," that was aired in the year after their discovery. Small groups of anthropologists were allowed to visit and observe the tribe for short periods of time until the Philippine President, Ferdinand Marcos, closed off the caves and surrounding land in 1972, turning it into a preserve and banning further visitation from the public. But not before some suspicious questions began to be raised. For instance, the tribesmen were well fed and yet they appeared to exist on foraged foodstuffs (roots, vegetation, insects, etc.) that would have been insufficient to sustain them. Their elaborate burial rites were said to involve placing bodies under layers of leaves on the forest floor to decay, but no evidence of human remains was found anywhere in the vicinity. The caves were very clean, showing no signs of accumulated refuse or other debris common to human habitation. Lastly, there was a modern village only three hours walk from the cave site and yet the foraging Tasaday had reportedly never come across their neighbors.

After the Marcos government was overthrown in 1983, the Swiss anthropologist Oswald Iten took a small team to visit the cave site, only to find it abandoned with no sign of the tribe. Around the same time, Manuel Elizalde allegedly fled the Philippines with millions of dollars stolen from a fund ostensibly established to protect the Tasaday. Subsequently, two young men who were part of the alleged tribe said in an interview for the 20/20 documentary, "The Tribe That Never Was," that there was no such tribe and that they had merely played out a ruse perpetuated by Elizalde. These individuals did in fact live in modern dwellings, farmed and traded with neighboring groups, wore modern clothing, and spoke in the local dialect. Furthermore, these same tribesman later confessed to lying during the interview because they had been bribed by the translator to do so. So the "Tribe That Might Never Have Been" continues on, leaving behind a disappointed and disillusioned public who would have preferred the extraordinary to mendacity, fraud, and deceit.

The apparent impropriety of the Marcos government is not the only such entity of State to be rocked by claims of scientific wrong-doing. In 2011, German defense minister, *Karl-Theodor zu Guttenberg*, resigned his post when it was discovered he had plagiarized portions of his doctorate thesis in law from the University of Bayreuth. He allegedly copied various sections of the thesis from popular sources and the work of other students. To his credit, Guttenberg admitted to the improprieties and requested that the University revoke his degree. However, that did not save the German government, under the leadership of Chancellor Angela Merkel, from international scandal. Imagine the impact, then, of another allegation of plagiarism for a high ranking government official in the same government only a little over a year later. Germany's Education Minister, *Annette Schavan*, resigned in February of 2013 after her doctoral degree was revoked as a result of alleged plagiarism as well, an event even more embarrassing because of Schavan's role of overseeing university education for the entire country. Schavan is currently denying the allegations and has lodged an appeal with Dusseldorf University, but that will not save her reputation or that of the German government.

Finally, even more revered in human society than scientific truth is the faith we place in those whose calling is to heal and repair us—medical practitioners, especially doctors and surgeons. We instinctively trust these individuals and look to them for help in crisis and trauma. No one stops to question the individual who rushes up to the wreckage of a car accident shouting "I am a doctor!" We move aside and give that person the space and assistance they need to ply their skills. But what if that person is not a doctor at all? As hard as it is to believe, there are cases every year where people are caught lying about their medical credentials, sometimes putting the public at risk by engaging in activities without appropriate training and knowledge. Most of the time, such acts are committed out of a desire to gain status, income, and a lifestyle without having to put in the hard work, long hours, and grueling training.

Take for example the strange tale of *William Hamman*, a United Airlines pilot and supposed cardiologist who for 15 years balanced his flying career with an avid passion for educating other medical practitioners using technology that allowed training on simulated medical emergencies. Hamman was known as an excellent speaker, a frequent presenter at Continuing Medical Education conferences, and an innovator in this aspect of medical training. Through his association with Western Michigan University and Beaumont Hospital in Royal Oak, MI, he helped set up applications for millions of dollars in research funding, he was paid consulting fees, and he drew salary around this work. He also conducted Grand Rounds for the hospital on a number of occasions. However, during a routine background check associated with a grant application through Beaumont Hospital, it was discovered that Hamman did not have medical credentials at all. In fact, he also never earned a doctorate and did not have experience as a cardiologist (but he was, thankfully, a fully certified pilot)! Administrative staff and medical colleagues alike were shocked to discover the charade, as Hamman had consistently come across as knowledgeable and exceptionally competent. Even more oddly, neither the medical credential or research degree he claimed he had were even required for him to have conducted the medical simulation exercises for which he became so well known. Why then did he perpetuate such a ruse? It is unclear why he took such an unnecessary risk, but as a result he suffered public disgrace, was fired from his pilot as a job with the airline, and subsequent investigations are underway to ascertain whether he published any materials that are tainted by the credential fraud. Luckily, he never practiced medicine directly and so did not put patients at risk. As it stands, the simulations he developed are still in use and highly regarded, even while he is not.

The take home message from these examples is that, while the scientific method itself provides access to the fundamental truths of our world, the people who employ the scientific approach can have the same human propensity to distort the truth for their own gain. This is all the more reason for each of us to understand how to go about ferreting out the truth using our own wits and logic. It is crucial in making a judgment about credibility of information to consider the nature of the assertion itself, how it was arrived at, and the methods used to verify it—not just rely on the credentials and status of the source of the information.

Deception as a Scientific Tool

Not all scientists who deceive come under fire for misleading others. Having just emphasized in the preceding sections how fundamental scientific empiricism is to uncovering truth, and how unacceptable it is for those doctrines to be violated, it might come as a shock to learn that deception is a tool sometimes employed for legitimate purposes in scientific research. The most notable and widely recognized scientific discipline that uses deception to promote research goals is that of Psychology. In fact, most psychological research would be impossible without deception.

The biggest problem with conducting psychological research using humans as subjects is that it is very difficult to remove the impact of bias and expectation. Human subjects are aware that they are in an experiment, and they can easily, either inadvertently or purposefully, behave in ways they think reflect the needs of the experimenter rather than how they might spontaneously react in the real world. This is especially true for research done at universities where much of the human subject pool is derived from Introductory Psychology students. These individuals know just enough about the field of Psychology to try and second guess the true purpose of the experiment, and this can have profound negative effects on the results. Thus, it is common practice for experimenters to hide the true purpose of the experiment, often by making the subjects believe there is a different purpose, in order to try and get unbiased responses. While this might seem unethical or run contrary to the spirit of the scientific method, it is an essential approach where humans with their clever intellects are involved. Of course, that doesn't mean that there are not checks and balances on how the deception is employed.

Ever since the now infamous work on obedience to authority done by the American psychologist, Stanley Milgram, in the 1960's, ethics board approval is always required before deception can be used in a human study in order to guarantee that it is not likely to cause harm. Milgram conducted research to investigate what factors influence when a person will follow instructions from an authority figure, especially when they may go against the individual's personal moral beliefs. He deceived the subjects by saying that they were assisting in research to detect the effects of punishment on the learning process. They were told that another "subject" was waiting in a separate room that was monitored by audio. In reality, the person in the other room was actually part of the deception and not a real subject at all. The real subjects were asked to apply what they believed were varying levels of electric shock to the "learner" every time they gave a wrong answer. The electrical voltage appeared to be increased for every additional shock they received, and the "learner" made sounds of increasing agitation (even to the point of screams) as the supposed current was delivered.

Surprisingly, all of subjects were willing to apply some level of electrical shock when instructed to do so. About 90% of the subjects were actually willing to apply what they believed was extreme shock, and an incredible 60% of the subjects still flipped the switch when the voltage was believed to be potentially lethal! These findings were shocking (pun intended) and demonstrated that, at least in our culture, apparently normal people are willing to engage in actions that might result in serious, perhaps even mortal, injury to a fellow human, simply because they were instructed to do so by an authority figure.

While the results of Milgram's work may provide insights into our understanding of behaviors like conformity and coercion, the point that is relevant to the current discussion is the impact of the deception he employed on the people who served as subjects. While no one was physically hurt during the experiment, the subjects obviously did not know that. Some of them suffered mental and emotional trauma as a result of what they thought they did in the experiment. Many experienced shame to learn that they would actually blindly follow instructions that could have caused serious harm to another. We must therefore question whether the value of deception outweighs the costs to the subject. As a result, it is no longer permissible for subjects in psychology experiments to be exposed to events or procedures that are likely to cause them undue stress. There is universal requirement for Institutional Review Board approval, a form of ethics evaluation, before an experiment can be conducted using human subjects, even in instances where deception is not employed. All experimenters must demonstrate, prior to starting their research, that no harm is likely to come to their subjects, and when deception is employed, that the individuals are debriefed and given the opportunity to lodge a complaint or receive counseling if they are disturbed by the treatment. The bar is set pretty high on the review, but rightfully so. Although it may be important to fool the subject to some degree in order to get them to react without bias, the tools of research should never become mechanisms for harm.

The Impact of Culture on Empirical Rationality

The truth and accuracy of scientific knowledge can be skewed and distorted by means more subtle than outright manipulation of research findings. Although scientific facts are largely immutable, scientific interpretation is modifiable by culture, especially when the theory itself is treated as falsehood or heresy by the target audience. Because of religious doctrines, Copernicus' theory that the earth revolved around the sun was met with controversy and derision by many, despite the compelling evidence that his calculations of the movement of planetary bodies supported a heliocentric model. Luckily, the fact that he was not believed by many did not make his conclusions untrue or else our calendar system as well as our space exploration programs would look very different than they do today!

Historically, scientific understanding is of necessity influenced by the current state of our understanding of any field. Great achievements of truth are rarer than those approaches that we view, in retrospect, with ridicule and derision. For nearly 2000 years, medical experts explained everything from personality to illness in the human body in terms of the internal balance of four circulating "substances" (known as humors). Even as recently as the early 20th century, this philosophy predominated in explanations of disease, mental illness, and personality traits such as avarice and melancholy. It wasn't until more modern understanding of the brain-behavior relationship and the basis of microorganisms and immune system function underlying disease were developed that this approach was discarded.

History gives us a multitude of examples of visionaries meeting derision, ridicule, and often even death when faced with the task of presenting new and contrary evidence to the face of public thinking. One has to wonder if today, in the form of the debate over climate change, we are seeing yet another chapter in the playbook that is fact versus fiction.

At least a portion of the global warming controversy arises from the uncomfortable circumstances of correlative science versus empirical science. It is impossible to submit the planet itself to controlled experiments with different levels of carbon and greenhouse gas production to evaluate changes in temperature over time. Thus, we must rely upon careful observation of the changes in the global environment across historic periods, information from core samples whose analysis gives a record of climate changes over many thousands of years, and results from laboratory experiments designed to empirically evaluate the relationship between small subsets of climate variables, to arrive at the truth. Therefore, the truth is potentially compromised by the impact of bias—those with a vested interest in maintaining a high burn rate of fossil fuels will continue to disagree violently with those whose world view focuses more on concern about our carbon footprint.

So what does it matter to you? In fundamental ways, the

human ability to seek truth and identify falsehood remains a fine balance between objective evaluation of data and facts with logical application of the current state of knowledge. We are bombarded daily by information from the media, internet, and our social groups. All purport to represent the true interpretation of the events central to a variety of things important in our lives, and yet few are actually based upon the fundamentals of empirical rigor. Even the scientists themselves are capable of deception and distortion of facts, adding another layer of fog to the glass of truth.

Based upon what you now understand about the scientific definition of truth and the factual means by which it is pursued, I hope you at least entertain the possibility that not all of the information to which you are exposed is based upon sound scientific principles. You should accept that, at times, truth is distorted by louder voices to maintain a *status quo*, and that biased interpretations often go disguised as facts. I hope you will pause to consider whether the information you encounter every day represents a sound interpretation based logically upon factual data or whether you are experiencing a personal, and possibly uninformed, opinion. I challenge you to think about the sources of information to which you are exposed, look for areas of bias, potential violations of validity, lack of rationality, or conclusions not based on empirical fact. When you come across any of these, I encourage you to spend some time thinking about what it means for how you evaluate the truth or falsehood of what you are hearing and that you adjust your opinion accordingly. In essence, I hope you will construct a rational process of judgment of your own and apply it to at least some of the questionable information that comes your way.

In my house, as much as we respect each other, my husband and I seldom take each other's word without proof in a debate. Daily, one of us will purport some fact or piece of information to which the other scoffs (in fact, skepticism may well be our favorite hobby and the glue that holds our relationship intact). Thanks to the advent of modern technology, we are never out of reach of a smart phone, tablet, or laptop, and are forever reaching for the information highway to provide the dazzling factual gems that make our case or not (unfortunately, I am wrong way too often for my own liking, but hey, facts are facts!). Therefore, you have no excuse for lingering in ignorance in this day and age. At the very least, when faced with a piece of new information that is important to your life and wellbeing, I hope you will pull out some resources and FACT CHECK before you arrive at a conclusion.

CHAPTER 2 ========

Legal Truth:
Veritas aut consequential

t is a widely accepted premise that truth and the law go hand in
hand. It can be a crime to lie or deceive others. We swear an oath
in a court of law to "tell the truth, the whole truth, and nothing but
the truth." We are threatened with grave repercussions for lying to
the police or other law enforcement representatives. Legal truth
is simply and clearly defined as 'a completely accurate account of
the facts' (*Webster's New World law Dictionary, 2010*). Therefore,
it should be a simple matter to define truth and lying by legal
standards, and to have readily applied legal consequences for
violating such, right? Absolutely–NOT! As it turns out, there are
many ways to consider truth from a legal standpoint, and it is often
difficult to tell when something is true and when it is false. And
this is further complicated by the fact that the prevalence of lying
in legal settings is very nearly the same as in any other area of life,
despite our universal opinion that it is illegal and reprehensible.
So much for our belief in truth and justice!

What is notable is the fact that dishonesty is so prevalent

in human interaction that legal codes are required to define numerous distinct categories of wrongful and deceitful behavior along with guidelines for punishment and recompense. Let us start by examining some of the different definitions and exploring how they are dealt with by our legal system.

The Law of Lying

1) <u>Perjury</u>: "The willful assertion as to a matter of fact, opinion, belief, or knowledge, made by a witness in a judicial proceeding as part of his evidence, either upon oath or in any form allowed by law to be substituted for an oath, whether such evidence is given in open court, or in an affidavit, or otherwise, such assertion being known to such witness to be false, and being intended by him to mislead the court, jury, or person holding the proceeding" (*Black's Law Online Dictionary 2nd edition*).

This rather verbose definition simply means that the key criterion for lying about facts (i.e., relaying false information) requires that the deception be material to a case and therefore have potential impact on the verdict reached by a jury or judge. Lying that has no bearing on the outcome of a case is typically not considered perjury and is largely ignored, both legally and punitively (although it will speak to the credibility of the testimony of course). While it would seem a fairly simple matter therefore to identify when a witness has perjured themselves, the nature of the legal system itself renders this more difficult than it might appear. For example, in cases where material evidence is sparse or lacking and the truth is being ascertained based solely upon the statements of key witnesses (who likely have wildly diverging views of what transpired), the judge or jury must make a decision about who is being truthful based upon factors other than factual evidence. Jurors typically have no formal training in determining truthful or deceitful behavior, and while judges have practical experience seeing such behaviors daily in their profession, their credentials are typically not based upon this ability. Thus we are asking the unskilled to judge truth largely in the absence of evidence.

The very structure of court proceedings also adds to the confusion about when perjury has legitimately occurred. Both the prosecutor and defender in a trial have the goal of winning the case, which means dealing with testimony from witnesses in a way that best supports their desired outcome. Information that is not supportive is suppressed if possible, either by lodging an objection to prevent its entry as evidence, or simply by avoiding questions that would promote the information being exposed. Witnesses are typically asked simple yes or no questions that do not allow them to answer in their own words and thus the information being imparted is led by the questioner rather than an actual description of fact. As such, the witness may be answering truthfully, but the very nature of the questioning leads the judge or jury to draw a different interpretation of events than the whole truth. The witness is not perjuring themselves, but could appear to be when the whole context is taken into consideration. In other words, the prosecutor and/or defender create a "truthful fiction" that best supports their case rather than acting in the interest of unveiling the whole truth.

In the final analysis, perjury is a crime that usually goes unpunished, except in examples where the perjury itself has an untoward impact on the verdict in a trial, or when an obvious wrong-doer will go unpunished for other more serious crimes. I recently heard a story about a man who was found guilty of perjury during his murder trial that was pleased that the time served was a lot less than that for the murder they could not quite pin on him. Proving perjury is often difficult, and it may even seem unreasonable to punish it under some circumstances. For example, in a divorce trial where the husband and wife give completely opposing testimony about the circumstances underlying the suit for divorce, it may be obvious that one of them must be lying. However, it might be difficult to determine who is telling the truth, and little may be served by fining or incarcerating the liar even if it could be ascertained. There are even those who argue that the entire court system would be overrun with perjury cases if an actual attempt was made to punish all instances of the behavior.

2) Fraud/Deceit: "Some deceitful practice or willful device resorted to with intent to deprive another of his right, or in some manner to do him an injury" (*Black's Law Dictionary Free Online legal Dictionary 2nd Ed*)

Fraud is the basis of virtually all scams and cons perpetuated in our society, with varying degrees of criminality based upon the extent of damage imparted. For example, there is a phone scam currently harassing thousands of Americans on a daily basis. The phone rings (at any hour of the day or night) and an automated message says "There is nothing wrong with your current account. We need to talk to you immediately about your credit card balance. Press 1 to talk to an agent, or press 2 to be removed from our calling list." If you press 2 to be removed from the list, they will keep calling back because your response lets them know your number is actively in service. If you speak to an agent, they will tell you that they have a special relationship with your credit card company and can negotiate reduced interest rates on your behalf for a small fee. According to the Federal Trade Commission (FTC), most of these calls are scams and either seek to provide you with services you could do yourself for free, or make inappropriate use of your credit card information once you give it to them over the phone. While the FTC and state agencies have been trying to shut down scams such as these, they are too widespread and result in relatively too small an impact to warrant the enormous effort such an undertaking would require. Your best recourse is to be able to recognize these scams when you come across them.

Similarly, the internet provides a ripe hunting ground for fraudulent predators amongst the unwary. Most of us have received emails with the exciting news that we have won millions in an international lottery (that we of course never entered), and have only to pay a small processing fee to collect our winnings. We've all received emails from Americans stranded in foreign airports after losing their passports who now need money wired to them so they can get home. There are the Craigslist scammers who purchase an item from you and then send a money order accidentally made out for too much money, which they ask you to cash and send the extra back to them—and when the money order turns out to be bogus, you foot the bill. And of course we've all heard from the terminally ill Russian woman who wants to share her fortune with you for a small fee, or the British Barrister who is trying to settle the estate of someone with the same last name as you and wonders if you'd be willing to accept the inheritance (again, for a small processing fee). Even the most vaguely worded of entreaties is likely to snare a few unsuspecting victims, as with this example I just received in my email inbox today:

The Regional Manager,
Barclays Bank of Ghana,
Tema Branch.

Dear Friend,

I wish to contact you on a good business which I want you to assist me, receive this fund into your bank account in your country and I believing that this will really workout between both of us.

I am the manager of Barclays Bank of Ghana Ltd in Tema branch, a family man and a man of peace. I discovered this money Five million, Five hundred and Forty thousand united state dollars (USD$5,540.000.00) On the course of the last year 2011 business financial report. I have packaged this transaction in a way that it will be of mutual benefit to us. As the regional manager (Tema branch) it is my duty to send in a financial report to my head office in the capital city Accra at the end of each business year and I have placed this funds on what we call Escrow Call Account with no beneficiary.

As an officer of this bank I cannot be directly connected to this money, so my aim of contacting you is to assist me receive this money in your bank account and get 35% of the total funds as commission. This business will be a bank-to-bank transfer. All I need from you is to stand claim as the original depositor of these funds who made the deposit in my branch so that my head office will order the transfer to your designated bank account.

If you accept to work with me on trust I will appreciate it very so much. Email me with the above email address so that we can go over the details.

Thanks for your co-operation and I wait to hear from you soon.

Sincerely Yours,
Mr. James N.kojo.

These are extremely cost effective means of bringing in fraudulent dollars—the internet access and tracking system employed by these criminals are relatively inexpensive, and although the hit rate is very low, even a few foolish takers provide an enormous return on investment. Furthermore, they tend to avoid getting caught, as the perpetrators of these crimes are typically safely ensconced in some foreign venue with multiple methods to cover their electronic footprints making them difficult to track down and bring to justice. Although you would think that anyone would be suspicious of such gifts of good fortune to begin with, or at the very least would raise an eye brow at the appalling grammar or the "too good to be true" promises. Notice that the names at the heading and closing of the letter above don't even match. Nonetheless, many people fall prey to such deceitful practices every day.

On a much larger and more damaging scale, the now infamous Ponzi scheme debacle perpetuated by Bernie Madoff might be the largest securities fraud paradigm in our history, estimated as affecting nearly three million people at a cost of over $60 billion. As appalling as the fraud he carried out may be, it is even more astonishing that he got away for so long. He actually lied on numerous occasions to the Security and Exchange Commission (SEC) investigators who were looking into his business activities for several years in the mid 2000's. Despite clearly conflicting stories and contradictions of testimony, the 2007 SEC investigation found no evidence of misconduct or requirement for enforcement action, despite the fact that lying to the SEC itself is a felony crime.

Of course we know that, just a year later, the top blew off the Ponzi scheme ultimately leading to Madoff's incarceration and imprisonment on a 150 year sentence. But how could such an enormous act of malfeasance, with so many clear indicators that something was amiss, go unchecked for so long? How could trained investigators not identify and react to blatant falsehoods and a cover-up of this size? In fact, at one point all the investigators needed to do was check the trading records for Madoff's account number with the Depository Trust Company and the game would have been up, perhaps saving countless victims their life savings. The failure to react to suspicion of lying in a case as obvious as this underscores the challenges inherent in investigating and bringing such criminals to justice.

3) Libel/Slander—"To publish in print (including pictures), writing or broadcast through radio, television or film, an untruth about another which will do harm to that person or his/her reputation, by tending to bring the target into ridicule, hatred, scorn or contempt of others. Libel is the written or broadcast

form of defamation, distinguished from slander, which is oral defamation" (*Law.com legal dictionary*)

Fundamentally, libel and slander are equivalent to defamation of character. It is important, and often difficult, to distinguish libel/slander from a simple statement of one's opinion, resulting in massive opportunity for wiggle room when it comes to prosecution. It is the consequences of the action that ultimately constitute the key aspects of the legal definition. You can have a negative opinion of someone and even put that opinion in a speech or in a written editorial. That opinion can even be untrue and misleading in its content. However, if there is no irreparable harm done as a result of the statement, there may be no grounds for a defamation suit. The basis of judgment centers upon the malicious nature of the comment, opinion, or statement as indicated by this excerpt from the Legal.com legal dictionary on slander and libel:

> *While it is sometimes said that the person making the libelous statement must have been intentional and malicious, actually it need only be obvious that the statement would do harm and is untrue. Proof of malice, however, does allow a party defamed to sue for general damages for damage to reputation, while an inadvertent libel limits the damages to actual harm (such as loss of business) called special damages. Libel per se involves statements so vicious that malice is assumed and does not require a proof of intent to get an award of general damages.*

For example, the radio show host, Rush Limbaugh, recently received national notoriety for his harsh criticism of Sandra Fluke, a female law student who testified before Congress in support of mandated health insurance for oral contraception. His vocal condemnation of Ms. Fluke was centered on an assumption that promiscuity served as the basis for the needed birth control. The underlying assumption of the link between frequency of sexual behavior and the manner of taking oral contraception was patently untrue (a woman takes an oral contraceptive once per day, every day, regardless of whether she is engaging in sexual behavior or not). The statements were highly derogatory about her personal character, and one would think might serve as the basis for a law suit. Limbaugh's comments could be considered slanderous if they can be interpreted by any reasonable person as a significant enough defamation of Ms. Fluke's character that proof of intent is not needed.

To my knowledge, Ms. Fluke has not accused Mr. Limbaugh of slander, despite the fact that her reputation was impugned and many followers of his radio show accepted the premise that she was wantonly promiscuous and grasping. I recently met a Limbaugh fan who informed me with great enthusiasm that Sandra Fluke, and women like her who "have sex dozens of times a day, should not ask for his taxes unless he is in on the action" (he believed Limbaugh's claim that Fluke and her friends were hypersexual). Obviously Limbaugh's comments impugned Ms. Fluke's reputation in the general public. What is unclear is whether such defamation would warrant legal recompense based upon damages. However, if she subsequently gets dismissed from her academic program, is unable to find employment, or is otherwise discriminated against as a result of negative impressions created by his statements, she would likely have had a strong case to take him to court.

Who is the Judge?

In the preceding section, we considered examples of lying and/or deceitful behavior across a range of consequences from that which goes unpunished to that which earns life imprisonment. What are the factors that dictate whether and how lying will be punished, and who is the authority that makes that decision?

There are three main sources of judgment when it comes to

prosecuting and punishing untruthful behavior: the judge, the jury, and the court of public opinion. The role of the judge and jury are fairly obvious. When something comes to formal trial, the judge and/or jury have the responsibility of following the letter of the law, and this includes identifying and reacting appropriately to false behavior like perjury, fraud, or making judgment in case of libel/slander. They are the embodiment of rational judgment in a legal forum.

But what about the myriad of ways in which lying can be perpetrated in a less obvious fashion? How qualified are judges and jurors to detect truth within the vast mix of information that comes from testimony? As previously mentioned, most judges and jurors are not formally trained in lie detection or psychology, and thus have only a superficial ability to read the body language and tone of voice of victims, witnesses, and alleged perpetrators. Therefore, when possible, trials include testimony by expert witnesses and the presentation of confirming or refuting evidence to back up claims made in the court room. Under conditions of clear contradiction, it is easier to identify perjury and therefore bring due process if warranted. For situations where such concrete evidence does not exist, the likelihood of accurately detecting truth or falsehood becomes tenuous at best.

The *court of public opinion* is a less tangible influence on our ability to detect untruthful behavior. The more outraged the public, the more likely it is that the hunt for the truth will be taken seriously. For example, events around the September 11 2012 attack on the US embassy in Benghazi and the death of four Americans inspired a massive rallying of opinion around how events were communicated to the public. UN Ambassador Susan Rice delivered a press statement on several morning news shows on September 16, 2012 claiming that the attacks were the result of spontaneous protests inspired by an anti-Muslim video. Subsequent investigation revealed that the attacks were planned and executed by terrorists, and public opinion held that this information either was or should have been known to the Ambassador when she made her public statements. Interestingly, even though the White House and several other sources stated that Ambassador Rice spoke based upon the intelligence report with which she was provided, the clamor from the court of public opinion resulted in formal investigation into whether she knowingly made a false statement to the public. The voice of the people holds sway over where the legal eye turns.

Obviously, increased interest in finding the truth in a criminal situation benefits everyone—but when the court of public opinion is fueled more by emotion than by thirst for the facts, the investigation can emolliate into a witch hunt fueled by cultural truth rather than legal truth.Truth in the law is inviolable regardless of whether it lines up with your cultural, religious, or personal beliefs. Someone is not guilty of a crime because you think they have behaved immorally or because they have different beliefs than you. A heinous crime is not scrubbed clean because a sufficient number of heads have rolled in retaliation. Therefore, care must be taken to clearly and correctly apply the legal recourse according to the appropriate factors of judgment.

Nonetheless, we cannot separate the impact of changing cultural perspective on our legal system and how laws are interpreted. The law itself is not inviolable–it is subject to continual review and adjustment as our society grapples with changing times. Even the US Constitution is a living example of the impact of this change, with the addition of multiple amendments over time designed to address issues that were not in the minds of our founding fathers at the time the document was first written. Behaviors that once were viewed as crimes often become acceptable in the court of public opinion over time, and the laws eventually change to accommodate this (albeit it not without controversy and clashing in the process). Most notable amongst such examples are the legal views on marijuana use and homosexuality.

Use of marijuana for religious, medicinal, and recreational

purposes has been around for generations and, until recently, was viewed as a crime in all US States, although with varying severity based largely upon the quantity possessed. Nonetheless, marijuana as a medicinal therapy and as a recreational drug continues to be widely used across large strata of the population. This widespread use has over time has given rise to more tolerance of the behavior, culminating recently in the legalization of recreational marijuana use in Colorado and Washington, and its decriminalization in several more states. This cultural shift will not be a smooth one and time will tell how the contradiction between federal classification of controlled substances interfaces with state laws It is clear that the impact of public opinion on the legal approach to marijuana use will undoubtedly continue to influence legislation in other states over the next couple of years.

Likewise, societal views toward homosexuality and gay rights have been steadily changing over the past few generations, and challenges to the legal definition of marriage continue to be entertained across states and in the US Supreme Court. Cultural views are extremely important here, as homosexuality has become more accepted as its expression has become more public. In 1973, the American Psychiatric Association formally removed homosexuality (as regards sexual orientation) as a mental disorder from its diagnostic roster, thereby in an instant transferring a segment of the population from classification as ill to normal. This opened the door for more public expression and acceptance of the lifestyle, culminating today in civil rights advocacy for equal opportunity in marriage and partnership. The Defense Against Marriage Act was recently reviewed by the US Supreme Court for its constitutionality (and overturned), and nine States currently legally recognize gay marriage. Obviously, the court of public opinion has enormous clout and influence in defining our cultural values.

Since our legal definitions of right and wrong change and adapt over time, we must consider that legal aspects of lying (perjury, fraud, libel, slander) will likewise be affected by changing cultural values. While we can safely assume that the distinction between truth and falsehood is strongly colored by social context, it is equally likely that our societal attitude toward punishment for dishonest behavior will change with the times. Even in law, *Tempora mutantur, nos et mutamur in illis*—times change and we change with them!

Punishment for the Crime

So how well does the process of deductive reasoning apply when it comes to the legal judgment of lying and deceit? The incidence of punishable acts of deception is quite low in the US, compared with other types of crimes. Out of 80,539 federal offenses in 2011, only 57 (0.1%) were for fraud/deceit charges and 50 (0.1%) were for perjury (*US Sentencing Commission, Use of Guidelines and Specific Offense Characteristics, Guideline Calculation Based Fiscal Year 2011*). This incredibly low incidence of lawsuits likely reflects a basic reticence to prosecute these offenses, rather than a clear reflection of their frequency. Certainly, perjury is a fairly common occurrence in family law courts, filings with the IRS, traffic violation cases, and the like. Convicted murderers who testify they are innocent in court have by definition perjured themselves. So why then are perjury convictions relatively rare?

There are three main factors that determine whether, and in what manner, lying will be punished: the impact/consequences resulting from the behavior, the nature of the crime, and the likelihood of success. Incidents that do not meet one of more of these thresholds typically go unpunished, either due to a lack of interest by the parties involved or because the acts are viewed as minor and not worth the time and resources it takes to prosecute.

The Bernie Madoff fraud case mentioned previously is a good example where the magnitude of the penalty was based upon the impact of the behavior (fraud). Although Madoff was in his seventies when he was sentenced, the judge still chose on principle to assign the maximum possible penalty–150 years in prison. In addition, his estate (estimated $1 billion in assets) was seized to help settle the claims against it (unfortunately in total over $7 billion). The nature of the individual punishment was the direct result of the extent of damage perpetrated on the victims in this case, being so devastating in effects that no amount of reasoning would allow for a simple slap on the wrist or a looking the other way.

What about the nature of the crime–does it have an impact on when and how the principles of judgment will be applied? This was seen recently in the Jerry Sandusky child sex abuse scandal, when perjury charges were levied against the Penn State Vice President and the Athletic Director for false and misleading statements made before the grand jury. It is common for such acts by tangential persons to go unpunished, but the heinous nature of the charges against Sandusky and the impact on the reputation of the university likely insured that the strictest enforcement of all laws and processes would be in effect during the investigation.

The final factor governing whether lying, misinformation, or other deceptions will be tried and punished is whether some other, more significant offense, will go unpunished. In the recent highly-publicized trial of the murder of Caylee Anthony, her mother, Casey, was acquitted of the murder charge itself but was convicted with four counts of lying and providing false information to the police (1 year and $1000 for each count). These charges were successful because of the well documented contradictions in testimony to police during the initial investigation, leaving no room for doubt about the veracity of the verdict. Such perjury charges are often overlooked in criminal and civil court cases, except in situations such as this where the primary charges themselves could not be made to stick. Interestingly, on January 25, 2013, the 5th District Court of Appeals in Florida overturned two of Ms. Anthony's convictions for lying to the police stating that they amounted to punishing her for the same offense more than once and thus constituted double jeopardy under the law.

Lying as a Tool of Justice

While police, detectives, government agents, and other members of law enforcement are sworn to uphold the law, the norms and standards that comprise the enforcement code of ethics is by necessity somewhat disparate from that of the rest of the general population. For example, some degree of deception or trickery is a common method employed in police and detective work, ranging from misrepresenting information pertinent to a case during an interrogation, to posing as a criminal during undercover work. While one might argue that such behavior is dishonest, most would also agree that it is imperative for uncovering the truth and accurately identifying perpetrators of crimes or would be crimes.

This type of deception is distinct from entrapment, a practice that is recognized as unacceptable by law. Entrapment occurs when a person is "induced or persuaded by law enforcement officers or their agents to commit a crime that he had no previous intent to commit" (*USLegal.com*). Posing as a prostitute and accepting money for a sexual encounter to foster an arrest is not entrapment, as long as the undercover agent did not solicit or persuade the individual to commit the crime. It needs to be clear that the act originated from the perpetrator himself or herself through no overt action of the enforcement agent.

It is not always easy to tell the difference. We have all seen the sting operations on TV designed to capture would be child molesters and statutory rapists in the act of attempting to commit a crime. While it may be entertaining to see the target lured into a meeting expecting to hook up with a teenage girl and instead find a dozen law enforcement officers waiting to take them away, many of these operations walk a fine line with the entrapment law. For example, the 1992 case of *Jacobson v United States* found in favor of the defendant with regards to entrapment in a child pornography case. In this instance, the defendant did purchase child pornographic materials through the undercover sting exercise. However, he successfully argued that the behavior did not reflect an inherent predisposition toward child pornography, but was rather the result of repeated exposure to, and pressure to take, the opportunity to purchase the material over a 26 month period. In other words, "they talked him into it."

Such dramatic examples aside, deception is an everyday part of much of law enforcement work and the tolerance of such behavior is largely dependent upon the context in which it occurs. On the more accepted side, making false statements to a suspect during investigation to evoke a reaction is a fairly well tolerated and even expected behavior. Typically, the officer or agent is feeling out the situation and may be looking at how the person responds to a false statement to get at a greater truth. Misleading the suspects about the true nature of what they are doing or looking for is the key to the success of the investigation.

In contrast, it is unacceptable to cover up improprieties or breaches of conduct that would preclude the rightful arrest of the individual and that deprive him or her of the due process of law. For example, the police may know they have correctly identified the perpetuator of a crime, but also know that a procedural problem will allow that person to get off on a technicality when the case comes before a judge. Thus, they lie about or cover up the inconsistency in order to go ahead with the arrest and prosecution. This could include altering the arrest record to give a different report of events, planting items on an individual that make an arrest possible, attributing words or actions to the suspect that were not true, and the like. While these actions may serve a greater purpose of getting a guilty individual into custody, they violate the Constitutional rights of every individual to due process by law and thus should be subject to the same anti-perjury laws as every regular citizen. Likewise, lying during testimony is seldom tolerated under any circumstances and is typically subject to the same perjury sanctions as any other witness in court or grand jury.

It is difficult, if not impossible, to estimate the frequency of such behaviors across law enforcement functions. Seldom are such behaviors prosecuted, and even less so punished. Officers and agents are unlikely to self report such behavior due to the consequences for their careers, as well as implications for the prosecution of those arrested. And our tolerance of such behaviors is influenced by the cultural pressures of the times. We are more tolerant of deceptive practices when homeland security is involved than we have been in the preceding decades. It is important to get the job done so we can feel secure and safe in our daily lives. Nonetheless, the boundary between acceptable and unacceptable deception is a fluid one where justice is concerned, and certainly bears watching as our society faces increasing pressures on our right to freedom, both at home and abroad.

Truth and Consequences

It is obvious that, while our legal system is built upon the tenets of truth and justice, legal process by these standards is far from simplistic. Successful execution of legal processes depends upon both the ability to identify truth from dishonesty and the means by which to enforce legal doctrines. In addition, the contexts in which potential falsehoods are committed dictate the acceptability of such behaviors.

The ramifications of this complex socially-based standard of judgment are that inconsistency in the application of law is prevalent across all strata of our daily lives. Criminals who lie and cheat may go free due to competing priorities or due to a lack of resources for enforcing punishment. Individuals who are caught engaging in relatively minor lies may receive harsh retribution depending upon the mindset of the judge or jury. Law enforcement agents may use deception and falsehoods to expose dishonesty in a suspect. Clearly, the ability to depend upon the legal definition of lying as a gold standard is weakened by the inherent flexibility in the conceptual basis of truth within the legal field.

As such, the judicious application of our own inherent process of rational judgment to issues of legal truth could serve to streamline and simplify many of these issues. The rigorous empirical standardization of legal due process and evaluation would obviously increase the facility of legal agents to identify and prosecute lying and wrong doing. However, the fact that we live in a societal context necessitates the inclusion of exceptions and latitude in our treatment of deceptive behavior. In other words, the scales of justice are tempered by a very human interpretation of truth, without which we would not be able to maintain a dynamic and just culture.

CHAPTER 3 ═══════════

Biological Constructs:
The Brain Behind the Curtain

N either the scientific nor legal standards of judgment just discussed would be possible without the complicity of the large, convoluted, and incredibly complex organ that lurks so unceremoniously beneath your skull. The human brain is top of the tree within the animal kingdom in its ability to deceive, and such an attribute would not likely have evolved unless it conveyed some advantage to the wielder. In fact, many would argue that the ability to deceive and prevaricate is indisputably linked to all forms of creative expression, including art, literature, and drama. Thus, it is not surprising that sociobiologists and cognitive neuroscientists alike have grown increasingly interested in, not only how the brain assesses and evaluates the truthfulness of information surrounding us, but also how it functions when generating lies and falsehoods.

Evolutionary and Biological Bases of Lying

Deception is by no means unique to the human species. Many animals (and even some plants) are equipped with the means to fool and mislead the living things around them. The most common forms of deceptive practice are *innate* deceptions–those that are a natural and usually involuntary form of protective sleight of hand, like camouflage or mimicry. In these cases, the individual can either change its visual coloration (as with the chameleon) or has physical characteristics that allow it to blend in with the surrounding environment (e.g., stick insects and rock fish), effectively hiding it from predators or potential prey. Some organisms have even evolved particular physical characteristics that mimic prey, allowing them to ambush their would-be meals (e.g., the angler fish). In other cases, the organism's very appearance resembles that of another species that is free from predation because of toxins or other protective traits (e.g., viceroy butterfly mimicry of the poisonous monarch butterfly). These types of innate deception have evolved because of the very obvious advantage they confer upon the organism for survival.

Tactical deception is a much more complex behavioral adaptation that depends upon cognitive processing to achieve a goal. Such behaviors typically involve using common signals in a misleading manner in order to misdirect others about the nature of a given situation. A very simple example is the well know ability of the opossum to lie completely still when threatened, feigning death in an effort to fend off further attack. Other animals use calls and displays to fool competing members of their own species. For example, some frogs will employ mating calls that mimic females in order to lure other males to a location, and then attack them in an effort to drive off competition. Some species of birds will engage in diversionary tactics, such as using the signal for a located food source in a place where no food exists in order to distract other members of the flock from the real location.

Across the animal kingdom, the extent and complexity of tactical deceptive behavior does seem to correlate very well with the level of brain development. Primates are the most developed on the mammalian phylogenetic tree in terms of brain function and mental capacity, so it is not surprising that both anecdotal and scientific reports of deceptive behavior are most common in the higher primates like chimps and other great apes who share the Order Homindae with us humans. The most notable (and relevant to this discussion) differentiator between primates and most other mammalian species is the extent of development of the telencephalic portions of the brain.

Telencephalon literally means *end brain*, and it is so called not because it resides at the back or bottom of the brain, but because it is the most recent portion of the brain to have evolved. The most obvious structure in the telencephalon is the neocortex that covers the surface of the brain and is highly convoluted to increase surface area and pack more tissue into the small space of the skull. In a human, the cortex would cover several square feet if it was removed and unfolded. Within this region lies the phylogenetically recent addition to our brain known as the frontal lobe, which resides in the front of the skull behind the eyes. This region is considered one of the most important areas of the human brain, as it gives rise to consciousness and executive control, allowing us to consider options and make judgments. Thus, it is not surprising that emerging studies of brain function related to lying focus on this region, particularly the prefrontal cortex that is known to regulate higher order cognition and decision-making. It is the development of the brain in this region in particular that appears to correlate with facility to deceive amongst animal species.

In fact, researchers Richard Byrne and Nadia Corp from the University of St. Andrews in the UK postulate that the ability to deceive is specifically related to the size of the neocortex in primate brains. Collecting data from 18 different primate species, ranging from prosimians through apes, they evaluated the frequency of tactical deception behaviors in relation to the volume of various brain areas. Their results quite clearly showed that the larger and more developed the neocortex, the more extensive the occurrence of deceptive behaviors across species. Considering the fact that humans have the most developed neocortex of all primates, it is no wonder that our ability to deceive is legion.

It has been theorized that the social nature of higher primates is at the root of the evolution of both our more complex brain function and our widespread capacity for deception. As hominids developed socially, our brains became more and more primed to evaluate events in terms of value to self versus value to the group. Living in social groups obviously better protects us from external threats and creates a culture of shared responsibility, but it also gives rise to challenges in terms of resources that may not benefit the individual. Those individuals who are more capable of tipping the cards in their favor in a way that is not obvious to other members of their group are thus more likely to gain the greatest benefits from the social environment for preserving individual advantage. For example, the member of society who hides access to a rich cache of food by leading their neighbors to a less resource rich location to forage gets both the advantage of sole access to better food and the perks of being viewed a contributing member of society. And of course those who have better, more evolved brain function are more likely to succeed when it comes to such deceptive practices.

But there is an obvious caveat in terms of committing disingenuous behavior within a society—the benefits of deception must balance out with the consequences of getting caught. Some researchers, like Jonathan Rowell of the University of North Carolina at Chapel Hill, have been constructing mathematical approaches to deception based upon evolutionary game models. His work looks at the frequency of signals within animal populations that are either true (they represent the actual state of the organism or environment) or false (they are misleading in some aspect of context) in terms of benefits to the individual and costs to the listeners. It is clear that the interaction between the deceiver and the listener favors a balance where dishonest behavior is infrequent or occasional, and thus likely to reap the highest benefit with the lowest risk of consequence. In other words, habitual lying is counterproductive because the response of the listening network will not promote reward—we tend to ignore the boy who cries wolf—whereas the occasional deception tends to be overlooked. As we shall see later in this book, this is the very premise upon which most political campaigns depend.

In terms of humans, deception goes one step beyond what is typically seen in the rest of the animal kingdom. We are not only good at fooling others for our personal gain, we are capable (and often very successful) at deceiving ourselves. Self-deception is the creation of a personal fiction of which we are not aware (this phenomenon will be discussed in depth in Chapter 4). From a personal stand point, self-deception serves multiple purposes that enhance the experience of the self. These include internal emotion-regulating functions such as enhancing the ego and sense of self-esteem, reducing stressful responses, and creating a better sense of belonging and social context.

But self-deception has also likely evolved to promote a social advantage. Since advantage can be gained within a social group only by practicing deception that is not obvious to others, it is critical for an individual to be successful in hiding the deceptive behavior. Humans are adept at reading subtle signs in voice and body language that can give the deceiver away—therefore, and individual who can actually come to believe their own deception will have reduced visibility of the cues that can be read by others about false intent. Bill von Hippel of the University of Queensland in Australia and Robert Trivers from Rutgers University have postulated that such a framework of self-deception could only have evolved in the presence of an *unconscious mind* that allows for a dissociation of psychological process. In their model, self-deception is not only a defense mechanism against uncomfortable beliefs about the self, but also serves as an offensive strategy that facilitates the deception of others. As such, humans have evolved the capacity to deceive both the self and others because it confers a significant advantage to those individuals capable of playing out the ruse, and the means by which such successful deception occurs is the highly advanced neocortical areas of our brains.

Windows of the Mind: Behavioral and Physiological Evidence of Lying

In order for interpersonal deception to be achieved, the individual must have a fully functioning *Theory of Mind* perspective—one in which they are able to understand that their own beliefs represent mental and emotional constructs that may vary from those of others around them. It is a crucial functional component as it accounts for the ability to consider another's view and create a fiction that will be a convincing. To put this in simple terms, to intentionally deceive another, you must be able to consider your own goals and desires, how someone else might perceive the situation, and imagine what you could do to create a fiction that the other could believe. Therefore, it is not surprising that Theory of Mind ability occurs only at developmental stages where neural connectivity among key brain regions is sufficient to generate such thought processes. Interestingly, these brain regions overlap with those that are associated with lying and pretense.

By its very nature, a lie is a complicated process within the brain, requiring the coordination of various cognitive processes that partition truth from fiction in very concrete ways. In all cases of deception, there is a conflict set up between the inherent understanding of reality and the fictitious scenario the perpetrator aims to use to deceive. Furthermore, it triggers a complex cascade of psychological and behavioral processes that are crucial to the successful perpetuation of the lie. The individual must be able to inhibit certain responses that do not fit within the fictional context—for example, emotional responses that do not support the deception. They must also be able to anticipate and infer a wealth of information about the other person or people involved in the social exchange—for instance, their relative knowledge of the area, their inherent beliefs, personalities, goals, and so on—in order to judge how the lie is coming across and make adjustments as necessary, The detection of conflict and the inhibition of normal responses are not only achieved by active circuits within the brain, but they also lead to the coordinated activity of various brain regions involved with formation of memory. After all, if you are going to create a fiction, you will need to remember it for future reference and respond to it as if it were real in order to minimize body language markers and other telltale signs of deception. Therefore, a successful liar needs to set up a *false memory* in order to create continuity. As it turns out, the coordination of these behavioral requirements and the establishment of an alternate reality are mediated by very specific and distinct regions of the brain.

The earliest explorations of how the brain functions during deception have come from studies using electroencephalography (EEG) technology. EEG employs highly sensitive surface electrodes positioned on the skull to detect and record small electrical pulses in the brain during a variety of tasks and cognitive processes. By using advanced computer software, the researcher is able to determine real time changes in localized brain regions and this has allowed us to begin developing a better understanding of how various brain areas respond during different cognitive processes, including deception. These approaches have been complimented and extended by the advent of advanced imaging technologies, such as functional magnetic resonance imaging (fMRI) and positron emission tomography (PET). Functional MRI detects the shift in alignment of spinning atoms (often located within water molecules) within the brain when exposed to intensive magnetic fields–active brain regions yield a different signal pattern than areas at rest. PET imaging relies upon the use of radioactive tracers (often attached to a form of glucose molecule since that is the major fuel source of brain cells) that are differentially present in tissues during times of activity and rest. These technologies provide much higher resolution than EEG in terms of identifying the specific brain regions that contribute to any given cognitive event, thereby allowing us to begin parceling out the circuitry involved with honesty and deception. However, they also give us a window into more subtle cognitive processes that underlie our ability to deceive, including detection of conflict (and its resolution) and distinction between lies pertaining to the self versus those pertaining to others.

In order for a deception to be successful, the individual must to be able to: 1) detect an opportunity for deception, 2) judge the likelihood of success based upon the social situation and knowledge of the listener, 3) inhibit responses that would compete with the deceptive statement or behaviors, and 4) create a false memory that supports the deceptive construct. It is thus not surprising that various brain regions subserve each of these conditions in distinct ways. The earliest studies of brain function during deception identified the involvement of specific areas known to be important for memory formation and consolidation, especially a region of the cortex known as the dorsolateral prefrontal cortex. Likewise, those brain areas that are involved with executive control–the ability to make judgments, decisions, and inhibit responses (i.e., the ventrolateral prefrontal cortex and anterior cingulate)– are also clearly active during all deceptive events. Subsequent research has revealed that lying carries with it an emotional processing aspect related to social interaction as evidenced by the involvement of brain regions responsible controlling emotional responses, (amygdala) and those involved in processing sensory information(parietal cortex).

Furthermore, successful deception requires the coordinated activity of these various neural components in order to create a sense of fluidity and plausibility to the deception. Such coordination requires a lot of communication between various brain regions. Whereas the so called *gray matter* of the brain relates to the regions containing brain cells themselves (the engines of deception as it were), it is the white matter–bundles or conduits of neural processes that run between brain regions–that serves as the communication line between the various parts of the brain. Interestingly, individuals who have been described as habitual or pathological liars have significantly increased amounts of white matter in the prefrontal cortex regions, indicating that frequent acts of deception can have a profound effect on brain development and function. Their brains actually appear to adapt to a physical state that allows for better creation and execution of lies.

The brain uses extra energy when we try to lie to someone else–this isn't at all surprising considering the fact that lying is essentially the creation of a fictional reality that needs to exist side by side with the facts. What is perhaps an unexpected finding is that the amount of effort required to lie about oneself is much greater than when lying about anything else. Many cognitive neuroscientists have postulated that lying about information relevant to the self involves a distinctive pattern and level of brain response. Certainly, the neural *signature* of activity differs in terms of areas recruited into the deception. For example, the memory consolidation areas of the brain are active on functional neuroimaging scans whenever a general deception is being evoked, largely because of the need to access relevant memories for comparison with the emergent falsehood. However, distinctly different areas of this brain region show activity in response to self-referential lying, suggesting that the task of lying about oneself involves different cognitive requirements. Areas that control the processes of interference and inhibition of response also become involved during deception, reflecting the interplay of interpersonal domains and levels of experience (people require different effort when lying about themselves than about non-self topics). Furthermore, when people lie about themselves, additional areas of the brain that are involved in retrieving and processing autobiographical information are recruited in order to create plausible fictions.

Summarizing the scope of research in the area, a few key points emerge as themes.

- Different regions of the brain control different types of cognitive, behavioral, and physiological functions.

- When those brain regions are used, they have a *signature of activation* that can be detected using various technological methods.

- The regions that are involved differ when someone lies compared to when they tell the truth.

- When people lie about themselves, the pattern of activation is somewhat different than when they lie about other things.

From these findings, it is clear that the brain itself leaves a roadmap that shows when we have been truthful or deceptive, but how accurate is the evidence? Is it possible to create a truly infallible lie detector that can obviate the need for lengthy and often costly legal and law enforcement proceedings when we need to understand the facts around a transgression or questionable event? In the next section we will examine whether brain imaging technologies can prove effective as truthsaying devices and whether we will likely see such approaches used to weigh the truth in the public arena.

The Truth about Lie Detection

The human desire to possess a means of lie detection extends throughout recorded history, and probably well beyond. As previously mentioned, humans evolved the ability to lie as a means to promote survival and access to resources at the expense of the group. Therefore, it makes sense that members of the group would likewise seek to develop ways to pierce the fabric of fiction and at least return things to an even playing field. Nonetheless, despite behavioral training, advent of crazy contraptions, and application of hi-tech devices, the ability to accurately detect lies effectively enough to use as a standard of legal judgment remains elusive.

The earliest attempts around lie detection involved honing the ability to read body language in order to detect physiological and behavioral changes typically associated with deception. Visible endpoints such as shallowness and rapidity of breathing, flaring of nostrils, dilation or constriction of the pupil, direction of the gaze, facial expressions, posture, and limb movements (such as unconscious rubbing of the hands or touching of the face) have all been used to one extent or another for determining whether a given individual is being truthful. The more familiar you are with the individual in question, the more accurate such assessments can be, since frequent exposure allows one to recognize what is normal behavior. For example, most parents have an innate understanding of this, having developed their own techniques for judging when a child is lying or being truthful. Likewise, the longer a couple is married and the closer their relationship, the more difficult it becomes to carry out a ruse of any kind, even a positive one like the planning of a surprise birthday party!

However, this does not work as well in a court of law, since most jurors and judges will not have experience with any given individual called to the stand to testify, and such signals of deception vary wildly from individual to individual. In addition, a variety of other variables can have a profound impact on the signals a person gives off during interrogation, including how anxious they are about the process of questioning itself. And of course people can learn to control their behavioral expressions through training—ask any actor who has cried for an audience.

Therefore, it is not surprising that we have repeatedly turned to more and more involuntary measures of physiology to try and separate truth from fiction. And of course, potential advances in such efforts have gone hand in hand with the development of technologies and medical devices. One of the first such efforts was made in the late 1800's, when an Italian medical doctor named Cesar Lombroso attempted to employ blood pressure measurements to uncover deception in accused criminals. While his approach met with some success, we now know that it is possible to consciously control blood pressure through approaches such as biofeedback. In addition, any type of anxiety-provoking situation can induce elevations in blood pressure and thus the utility of this approach was severely limited.

A few decades later, an American law enforcement officer named John Larson succeeded in designing and employing the first polygraph—a device that used both breathing rate and blood pressure measurement combined to increase the sensitivity of the device for detecting falsehoods. Over the next few decades, improvements were made to this device, including the measurement of the galvanic skin response, a signal that reflects changes in the electrical conductance of the skin that is impacted by moisture levels (such as sweating), and which is regulated by unconscious (and thus involuntary) responses of the sympathetic nervous system. The idea here is that combining various measurements and looking at the output of them all as a profile would be more indicative of state of mind than any single measurement alone. As it stands, the polygraph remained virtually the same (with the exception of upgrading to a computerized form) for the next 60 years, and was considered the gold standard for lie detection.

Nonetheless, the polygraph has been viewed skeptically by legal process, and polygraph results have largely been considered inadmissible in a court of law due to issues with reliability. There is just too much scope for gaming or beating the system and too many instances of false positives to rely on such a method when questions of guilt and innocence are at stake. While such devices are still used in general law enforcement actions and in counterintelligence and security applications, attempts to make such results admissible in court have been repeatedly denied–for example, the 1998 Supreme Court hearing of the U.S. v Scheffer which upheld the long standing ban on use of polygraph results as evidence.

More recently, other potential physiological indicators of deception, such as voice stress analyzers, have been evaluated as lie detectors. These acoustical analysis devices are extremely sensitive to levels of psychological and physiological stresses represented within the speaking voice, and have been successfully employed in scenarios where it is important to predict the level of stress an individual is experiencing. For instance, one type of voice acoustic analyzer can detect small changes in the voice patterns of pilots indicating they are tiring well in advance of any psychological recognition of sleepiness. However, the ability to successfully distinguish the source of stress–whether it is anxiety, fear, pain, or deception– remains less clear and thus this technology has not caught on for use as a lie detection standard.

So what about the signature our brain displays when areas associated with deception get detected with neuroimaging technologies–is this the unbeatable measure of truth detection for which we have been looking for so long? Certainly, the activity of various brain regions is beneath our awareness and thus almost impossible to control by design. Or is it...

It seems the underlying brain signature of deception may not be as free from conscious intervention as we might have hoped. Recent research has shown that neural signaling associated with lying can indeed be altered with repeated training on giving deceptive responses. Furthermore, individuals who create a false memory–one in which they actually come to believe the fiction through repeated telling over time–have neural signatures virtually indistinguishable from those who consciously tell the truth.

Unfortunately, this may be a case of the technology has advanced faster than our understanding of the signals. While neuroimaging technologies have certainly improved in sensitivity and resolution, our understanding of how the brain functions in generating cognitive processes, including those associated with deception, is still lacking the required depth to allow us sufficient accuracy in determining a truth from a lie. There is still much we need to understand about the functioning of various brain regions and the interrelatedness between them before we can correctly identify the presence of a lie to the degree that is required for legal (an ethical) judgment.

Significant improvement in reliability and standardization of lie detection devices will be also required before such approaches could gain applied use, but it should be noted that advances in both neuroscience and neuroimaging technology are happening at a rapid rate. As the technology and our understanding of brain function improve in the next few decades, it may become possible to develop a validated instrument for measuring truth.

PART 2

Let the Games Begin: Sources of Mud in the Water of Truth

As we all know, truth in real life can be fairly hard to recognize, despite availability of facts and processes designed to assist the making of judgments. This is because we do not live in a clinically sterile world of reasoned thought. We are driven by emotions, needs, desires, and other intangible forces that impact the very nature of what we perceive. It is rather important to understand these influences before we submit someone's statements to the rigors of our personal process of objective judgment, lest we fail to consider important mediating factors. How can we be certain that someone's claim, whether under oath or just in good faith, actually represents truth or falsehood? What if they are saying something untrue, albeit without knowing or with intent to deceive? Do these extraneous factors merit consideration when forming the conclusions we draw about the level of honesty inherent in any statement or action?

To understand the poorly defined boundary that exists between truth and falsehood, we first need to understand the personal and cultural factors at play in each and every one of us. No one lives completely independently of those around us. We all have individual beliefs and social and cultural doctrines that color our thinking in ways most of us never notice, and many of these exert a huge impact on how we determine the truth of anything in our daily lives. So, let us take a look at some of the major factors that impact the nature of our cognitive abilities and see how well some key examples hold up to the principles of objective and deductive reasoning.

CHAPTER 4

Psychological Truth:
Personal Fictions in a Perceived Reality

The fundamental tenet underlying psychological truth is that we exist in a *perceived reality*. While there are concrete facts, occurrences, needs, and laws of nature in the world, every single one of us creates an interpretation of events based upon our observations and experience, and these interpretations can (and often do) vary wildly from individual to individual. It is a difficult concept for most people to accept that our individual view of life and self is in fact only one version of reality. Nonetheless, each of us goes through life learning about the world and our place within it, observing and experiencing the relationship between action and reaction, and ultimately creating our own personal fiction around life and self. By personal fiction, I do not mean a fantasy ungrounded in reality (although sometimes it can be!). I mean instead that the way in which we view ourselves and all aspects of life is the end result of our own innate characteristics, our cultural upbringing, the views to which we have been exposed, our personal experiences in the world, and the ways in which we have been taught and educated.

This perceived reality reflects a hierarchical milieu of factors to which we attend in explaining our personal experiences of life. No two of us experience all of the same events and influencing factors while growing up, and thus no two of us have exactly the same view of life. Yet every one of us has a strong compelling belief that our own view is real and correct, even when it is not supported by the full range of facts. This is not a function of some form of moral relativism where one's views and beliefs dictate reality and therefore the way things must be, but rather an example of personal biases coloring the *interpretation* of reality. This single fundamental explains why witnesses to the very same event will have different views of what transpired, and why individuals can look at the same evidence and come down on opposite sides of the opinion table. It is also not a function of the strength of belief in the veracity of the information upon which a view is based. A narcissist will believe in the accuracy of their perspective without question, even in the face of massively contradicting facts. Therefore, psychological truth is by definition a personal phenomenon that may or may not accurately reflect the whole truth underlying any given situation or principle.

For example, at varying times throughout US history, we faced dissension between political parties about one important public issue or another. Most recently, this has been reflected in the economic crisis around reforming entitlements and the tax code. All parties agree that reform is necessary, but there appears to be little or no willingness to compromise on the view of how to solve the problem. Despite the impending threat of fiscal cliffs, sequestration, and other examples of financial and economic crisis, each side has staunchly held to its views of cause and effect, solution and revolution. For example, recent debates had liberals insisting that allowing the Bush era tax cuts to expire on the wealthiest individuals would be the right way to generate increased revenue. Meanwhile, the conservative side emphatically disagreed and refused to allow tax increases on the top two percent, citing historical evidence that raising taxes on the wealthy inhibits economic growth. This represents completely opposite views of the same historical facts. Both sides cannot be correct, and yet both sides passionately believed they had the right interpretation of the facts.

This same type of polarization characterizes virtually every debate, disagreement, conflict, and war throughout human history. How do we explain such apparently irrational behavior from a psychological perspective? In the next section, we will examine some of the processes that underlie *implicit psychology*, or the theories each of us constructs about the world which we view as facts despite a lack of empirical evidence.

Attentional Processes

We are bombarded by millions of pieces of information every day. Very little of that information is actually processed and formulated into awareness and memory. Instead, only the pieces that are personally relevant to us undergo storage for later retrieval and use. Thus, attentional processes are critically important for determining which information in the complex mix we experience from minute to minute is subject to interpretation. This also means that, right from the very start, we pick and choose what information we think is important and therefore open the door to selective attention and a potential for skewing of the truth.

All humans have a tendency to apply certain decision-making tools to help make judgments under ambiguous or novel situations. It is common for decision-makers to make use of readily available external characteristics about a person in making judgments about the internal dispositions of that person, whether they reflect the truth or not. Errors in judgment arise from the disconnect between expectation and reality—for example, expecting that the nerdy guy wearing the thick glasses at the gym is a wimp instead of a national judo champion, or that the large bosomed blonde sitting next to you on the train is a ditz on her way to modeling school instead of to the university course she teaches on theoretical physics.

Importantly, the main contributor to creating and maintaining these false views, even in the presence of contrary evidence, is that we preferentially attend to information that confirms our expectations and ignore information that does not. This means that how we interpret and remember any given situation may or may not reflect the truth of that situation, calling into question everything from eye witness testimony to our recollections of what was said in a recent conversation. All of us are certainly familiar with the wildly diverging interpretations that can arise between spouses regarding "who said what," but attentional effects have an even more insidious impact on how we view life events in general.

Preconceptions influence how people interpret and remember information. Consider the following research finding as an illustration. People were asked to view a series of pictures demonstrating particular events, and later to recall the content of those images. Many of the participants misremembered key pieces of information based upon their inherent views, including cultural stereotypes. For example, in a scenario showing a black business man being robbed at knife point by a homeless white man, a majority of the participants remembered a black man robbing a white man. This has been explained by the fact that common racial stereotypes would predict the role reversal, and thus people ignored the contradictory information in the scene and attended only to that which aligned with their preconceived views. Shockingly, a substantial percentage of black research participants also made the same error, indicating that stereotypes can even influence the views of those in the stereotyped group.

Attributional Theory

Psychological truth reflects an intuitive state that satisfies our inherent desire to categorize and explain the world around us. To do so, we rely upon a rich milieu of internal and external observations and experience to construct a reasonable explanation of the events. At the root of this process is our pattern of attribution–the way in which we judge the causes and effects underlying behaviors in others and within ourselves. For instance, most of us would agree that it is very difficult to change a first impression. The behaviors that we each present to the world are believed by those around us to reflect stable personality characteristics, regardless of situational factors. Thus even the nicest of people can be labeled as hostile if seen in the wrong situation the first time around. These types of views are difficult to alter and usually require long exposure to an alternate set of behaviors before they can supplant the original impression. Take for example the long-running trial by media of Richard Jewell, the security guard falsely accused of planting the pipe bomb during the Atlantic Olympics in 1996. In truth, Jewell was responsible for discovering the device and saving many people from death or serious harm. Nonetheless, it took years and admission of guilt from the actual party responsible (Eric Rudolph) to clear the black mark on Jewell's name. Once branded, it was extremely difficult for people to change their initial opinion even in the face of sound evidence of his innocence.

Attributions are typically based upon two different categories of traits: *dispositional* versus *situational*. Dispositional traits refer to characteristics inherent in the person being judged, and are what we believe are giving rise to the behavior that we are witnessing. In contrast, situational traits are those that are specific to a given situation, not the person themselves. Attributions to either are influenced by the familiarity with the individual being judged. Interestingly, in cases where the person being judged is unfamiliar, most people attribute causation to the dispositional traits of the person, even when they have a great deal of familiarity with the circumstances. Take this example of attribution error I witnessed between two friends of mine who had previously not met. One friend (Harry) was scheduled to interview with the other (Susan) for a job in her department. On the day of the interview, Harry had a family emergency in the morning that resulted in him rushing out of the house without some important documents, and then a minor accident on the way to work that caused him to be late. By the time he got to the interview, he was disheveled, distracted, and anxious. Even though he was by nature one of the most punctual and focused of individuals, Susan's impression was that he was too disorganized to provide value to her group. The propensity to arrive at a dispositional explanation for the behavior outweighed any consideration of how the situation might have played a part in this specific instance.

The reverse can be true when the individuals in question know each other well. I know of two friends who got on well for years, despite the fact that one was habitually late to everything (even the other's wedding) and sometimes even would not show up to an appointment, usually without calling to give a heads up. This often caused significant difficulties for the jilted friend, but because she knew and liked the other, she spent years attributing her behavior to the various situations that got in the way, rather to an inherent deficiency in her prioritization and organizational abilities. Finally, it took a total stranger to ask "And this woman is your friend WHY?" before she got enough perspective to start considering dispositional factors as the underlying cause. These methods of judgment are very hard to alter. Even when faced with contradictory information, we tend to believe our initial attributions reflect the truth. They are compelling because they explain the situation to our satisfaction in a way that aligns with our beliefs and experience, and therefore appear irrefutably real. They are emotionally satisfying–if it *feels* real, it must *be* real!

Sources of Attributional Error

Because of our tendency to make judgments based upon the degree of familiarity we have with the situation and the people involved, it is common for us to make errors regarding the true cause of any given event. These sources of error go unnoticed, thus perpetuating a false sense of personal accuracy. The *fundamental attribution error*, defined as an overestimation of the importance of dispositional cues (those internal to the person), is one of the most common. Part of the reason we believe so strongly in the veracity of our attributions is that we tend to believe that everyone gets what's coming to them. This "Just World Hypothesis" underlies most judgments we make without us ever being consciously aware of it. How many times have you hurt yourself bumping into something and questioned "what did I do to deserve this?" Have you ever withheld sympathy for someone who got fired because you felt they were "asking for it?" This type of unconscious thinking serves to protect us from a sense of powerlessness in an unpredictable world by preferentially attributing dispositional causes in negative events. For example, jurors in a rape trial might find blame in the victim –believing she dressed or acted provocatively, or that she foolishly put herself in a dangerous situation–in order to avoid accepting the premise that bad things can happen to innocent people, including possibly themselves.

Another source of error arises from the fact that people tend to perceive their opinions and views about life as being representative of the majority perspective, even when that is not the case. This tendency toward *false consensus* is particularly evident in the world of politics where every candidate believes quite strongly that they reflect the view of what the country wants. In the wake of the 2012 presidential election, Republicans still rally around the idea that majority of the country desires social conservatism, despite the fact that they lost the election running on this very platform. False consensus is perpetuated by the fact that the more popular a view appears to be, the more truthful it appears. However, regardless of how loud the crowd cheers, and no matter how much we believe a thing, false is false.

There are also a number of *motivational biases* that lead to misjudgments. Motivational biases are the subconscious factors that influence our view of the world, even though we are not aware of them. The three most common forms of motivational biases are *outcome, relevance,* and *personal causation fallacy.*

Our understanding of the *outcome* of an event, particularly when it involves attributions relevant to the self, can be a major source of error. A person's pre-existing self-concept (either positive or negative) and understanding of the difficulty of the event will dictate how the person attributes cause for the success or failure. A person with a strong positive view of their own skills will attribute success to hard work, effort, and/or smarts in how they ran the race. Likewise, if they lost, they would likely explain it in terms of the superior skill level or better training practices of the winner. The success would be attributed to an internal factor and the failure to an external factor. In contrast, someone with a negative self view would do exactly the opposite—winning the race would be attributed to luck or a problem with the better runners in the race, and a failure would be explained in terms of their lack of talent as a runner. A friend of mine with very low self-esteem never enjoyed the years of success he had as a cross-country runner (including winning the State Championship) because he considered every win to be the result of luck in one way or another. The role of personality becomes more apparent as the stakes in the event increase, so something like winning the New York City marathon would spotlight the influence of personality style better than winning the three-legged race at a company picnic. However, identifying these types of influences is often difficult because they reflect an inherent bias in perception that is not readily observable to either the individual or to those around them.

Another source of potential error in attribution arises from the *relevance,* or normalcy, of the behavior being observed. In other words, the behavior being judged is inescapably done so in relation to the normal behavior of the individual. Using the Lewinsky-Clinton sex scandal as an example, your judgment of whether the inappropriate behavior occurred would be influenced by your pre-existing opinions of both Clinton and politicians in general, regardless of what situational factors might be present. Many people believed that President Clinton willfully and knowingly engaged in inappropriate sexual contact, even when he denied it. Their explanations for why they did not believe his denials ranged from views they held about his personal conduct from other publicized scandals with women to more general and impersonal ones reflecting a belief that most politicians (and people in power) behave in such a way. As it turned out, those individuals were in fact correct, but their assertions still were based upon bias and speculation rather than on evaluation of factual evidence. What is important to understand is that they would not likely have changed their opinions even if he had turned out to be innocent. An individual who makes judgments based upon the full array of facts will be more likely to change their minds when faced with contradictory evidence, whereas someone who judges the truth solely upon their expectations seldom changes their view. Truth is determined by what they expect the person will do rather than what they actually did. This is a major root cause underlying the propagation of misinformation through the media and internet that we will discuss later in this book.

Finally, our judgments about cause and effect, as well as the underlying truth of a given situation, can be affected by a psychological construct known as *personal causation fallacy*—the belief that our actions are more important in causing some event than they actually are. This belief can be strong and will persist even in the face of contrary evidence. For instance, someone who has a person close to them commit suicide often blames themselves, even if they played no part in the events that led to the tragedy. They may feel that the victim would still be alive if they had only done something differently, failing to take into account the overwhelming fact that suicides usually result from a large number of contributing factors, many of which they have no ability to control. Such a life view extends from childhood when we are seeking to understand how the world works and our place within it. Most of us grew up around the concept of "step on a crack and break your mother's back." It was years before I could walk normally down the pavement for fear that I would inadvertently send my mother to the hospital! Luckily, we outgrow many of these subconscious influences, but there can still be an impact on our life view that more subtly influences our judgments when it comes to determining truth and falsehood.

Impact of Learning

Everyone readily accepts the concept that human beings are learning organisms. From birth, we are exposed both directly and indirectly to opportunities to collect information and develop an understanding of how the world works. There are a variety of sources of such information—parents and family, teachers, clergymen, authorities, peers, media—who may have either a sanctioned or an inadvertent role in the teaching process. Some learning is overt—we are taught to speak and read and write, to drive a car, to understand science and memorize history and learn geography. We are taught to eat with a knife and fork, to adhere to our family values, and the meaning of right and wrong. We are directly taught truth as our parents or other authority figures see it— religious beliefs, cultural mores, and proper societal behavior—without necessarily having empirical facts to back it up. Therefore, what we view as truth is based upon an individualized compilation of perspective, belief, and memory.

Other times we form concepts unconsciously as the result of experiences in our lives, and we are uncertain how we came to believe what we do. We may learn by subtle example rather than formal demonstration. A parent who tells a child it is wrong to steal and then engages in stealing themselves is saying one thing and doing another, with the likelihood that the child will follow their example. Parents who lie in front of their children are directly teaching that it is ok to do so. For example, lying to the police when pulled over for speeding, lying to one's spouse about how much something cost, or lying about one's age when buying a movie ticket are all examples that impact a child's view of the importance of the truth. Worse yet, parents who pull their children into collusion with the lie reinforce that it is acceptable behavior even more strongly. Many of us have been asked to engage in support of a lie around one event or another—"Don't tell your father about...." or "your mother doesn't need to know this...." may seem harmless enough, but such demands place a child in the untenable position of engaging in either deception or disobedience. Reconciliation requires one competing side give, and it is the side of truth that caves in all too often.

Many people are raised in an environment where the truth is often bent to the breaking point, ostensibly to avoid an argument or to justify hiding something they know would otherwise cause a problem (e.g., the true cost paid for an item they wanted). Without ever noticing it, children adopt these same tactics and believe it is perfectly appropriate to tell *little white lies* across a whole range of situations. It is hard to recognize these types of ingrained behaviors in our personal expression, and even harder to root them out once we become aware of their existence. And it is even more difficult to uncover the subtle and insidious impact that such learning by example has on our overall approach and the attitude we have to life in general.

Attitude Formation

An attitude is a predisposition to view someone or something in a positive-negative fashion without the need for facts or understanding of the actual truth involved. Historically, attitudes have been very difficult to study for a number of reasons. Attitudes are actually *hypothetical constructs*, internal to the individual, and thus are not directly observable or provable. As such, we must infer someone's attitude based upon their behavior or what they say that they believe about a given situation. Unfortunately, attitudes are seldom indexed by a single behavior or statement, instead representing a constellation of behavioral patterns, the expression of which is dictated both by the specific situation and the goals of the individual. For instance, a police officer might have a very negative attitude toward a particular social ethnic group, but may behave in a very positive and professional fashion towards a member of that group because they do not want to be brought up on charges of misconduct. I know an attorney who treats ethnic clients with the highest regard in public, but maligns them horrifically in private. If you were to observe only his public behavior, you would erroneously conclude that his attitude toward ethnic minorities was admirable.

In a similar fashion, the expression of an attitude might be subsumed by a larger belief system, and therefore it is difficult to judge the true nature of the attitude itself. Take the example of a female defense attorney who avidly defends a rapist. Her behavior might suggest that she does not have a supportive attitude toward victimized women, when in fact her larger belief in the fairness of the American judicial system might override the expression of her personal beliefs. This conflict of behavior and attitude is extremely common in the legal system, as attorneys are required by law and by oath to defend the rights of their clients without regard to their own personal beliefs.

Finally, the expression of attitudes is strongly influenced by social desirability factors. In other words, fitting in with the crowd is a strong motivator for some individuals, particularly teenagers, and thus they may behave in ways that appear wildly at odds with their true attitudes. This type of peer pressure is particularly evident in situations where the individual in question does not feel competent to face the social task before them. For instance, a high school student may have a negative attitude about drinking alcohol, and also have a strong need to be popular and part of the "in crowd." Thus, the person might drink heavily at parties even though it goes against their personal beliefs. Judging such individuals based upon this single expression of behavior would thus lead to a false view of their inherent attitude.

Peer pressure and conformity can mask the true nature of someone's attitude, both to outside observers, and even to oneself. It is common for such conflicting behaviors and beliefs to set up an unconscious state of *cognitive dissonance*–an uncomfortable state of imbalance between internal belief systems that seeks resolution of the conflict. As such, the individual will attempt to rationalize their behavior in such a way that allows them to maintain the most important belief structure. For example, a woman who has been sexually abused and now harbors a deep seated fear of sexual intimacy might, ironically, become very promiscuous in her sexual attitude. Because the sexual assault created such a profound state of dissonance between her belief that she is a "good girl" and the view of herself as being disgraced, she might unconsciously resolve the conflict by overcompensating toward hypersexuality. Of course, another person in the same situation might go the opposite direction and avoid all sexual contact, resolving the imbalance by pushing away all opportunities for intimacy. Either way, the victim seeks a means by which they can diffuse the underlying dissonance and the result will seem like a natural expression of attitude, when in fact it may not represent the a true attitude at all.

The take home message is that attitudes form the basis of our larger belief systems about ourselves, other groups with whom we interact, and the world in general. These beliefs are extremely strong and are viewed as personal truth. However, as previously discussed, there is a range of ways in which we can distort and misrepresent information that forms the foundation of our beliefs, and thus our personal truths can become personal fictions.

Personally Judging the Truth

The biggest difficulty in judging the nature of human behavior is that it is seldom clear even within ourselves where the truth lies. The mechanisms that give rise to understanding are governed by the objective level of the person expressing it and are unconsciously colored by inherent personal bias, cultural influences, and the effects of experience. In other words, our ability to detect the truth is the product of a learned perspective that varies across individuals in terms of how capable we are of stepping back and viewing our own motivations and unconscious goals impartially. Most of the things I have described in the preceding section occur largely beneath our awareness, and it is only with hard work and experience that we can start to see their impact on the pattern of our thoughts and behaviors.

Our sense of truth is undeniably influenced by our upbringing, the beliefs of our friends and family, and by the copious information assailing us from the world around us. Some children are raised such that they are more successful in keeping an open mind, to consider all sources of information before coming to a conclusion. These individuals will grow up to be more analytical in their approach to any situation, to look for evidence for and against, to hear all sides of an issue before ascertaining the underlying truth –an inherent predisposition toward rationality. In the best case scenario, individuals who are able to step back and distance themselves enough from the emotional aspects of a decision also tend to correctly identify the impact of their own motivations and goals in defining truth. It is hard for most of us to admit that we are often biased before we even start to evaluate information. However, there are some steps that any of us can take to try and insure that we are making the best informed and most truthful judgments.

Roadmap to Objective Assessment

1. Collect data from as many sources of information as possible.

2. Distinguish factual information from opinion–discard that which is based solely upon opinion.

3. Fact check the remaining information–discard that which is not supported or makes no empirical sense (be cautious about the sources used for the fact checking procedure–look for bias and distortion in the agent)

4. Sort the remaining information into evidence for and against (or any other relevant basis for judgment)

5. Identify and compensate for any subtle internal impactors (e.g., personal desires for outcome) and external drivers (e.g., social motivators)

6. Identify the most parsimonious and explanatory relationship among the facts

7. What is left, whether it suits you or not, is most likely the truth!

Ok, so how does this work? Remember, we are really talking about psychological truth, and I have already indicated that we can lie to ourselves and distort information unconsciously for our own personal aims. It is not a simple thing to traverse the tumultuous landscape of our psyches to thwart unconscious defense mechanisms. These have evolved to keep our perception functioning in a way that perpetuates the best case scenario for our mental-emotional balance and thus are fairly resistant to detection and alteration.

Here is an hypothetical scenario that will help illustrate how the steps above can help improve our understanding of our true psychological motivators and belief systems. Please note that, while it is possible to do this on your own, it is certainly a massive effort for all of the reasons I discussed in the previous section. If you are serious about finding your own personal truth, consider engaging a good (and highly objective) friend to assist you, someone with thick skin and who you will be likely to forgive no matter what truth they are instrumental in helping you uncover.

Situation

Cynthia has been moving from position to position within the same company for over ten years. In every role, things seem to go well at first until she runs into one or more individuals who seem bent on causing her problems. They don't respect her opinion, they cause trouble for her with the boss, and she ends up getting downgraded on her performance evaluations for not getting along with her colleagues. No matter how hard Cynthia tries, there always seems to be someone who undermines her efforts. Finally, she meets with the Human Resource department where she is told that she has been identified as a difficult person with whom to work and not a team player. Cynthia is shocked—she has always prided herself on being likeable and an enthusiastic member of the team. She feels victimized and believes the real cause of the issue is that she is always partnered with troublemakers on teams.

She considers quitting the company. Before doing so, however, a friend suggests that she take a closer look at both her behavior and that of the people with whom she has difficulties working in order to see if she can identify the true cause of the issues with her co-workers.

Approach

1. Information gathering—Cynthia receives the reports lodged against her with details about times, places, and events. She also solicits anonymous reviews from a cross

section of peers specifically describing the pros and cons of her behavior and approach over the years.

2. Evaluate the data—Cynthia evaluates all of the information specifically based upon what is fact and what is opinion. She considers subjective phrases, such as "Cynthia was pushy in the meeting" as opinion, and ones that describe actual behaviors or events, such as "Cynthia arrived 30 minutes late for the meeting and insisted she deliver her presentation immediately, despite the fact that another was already in progress" as pieces of factual evidence.

3. Ascertain the validity—Cynthia then fact checks the objective material. Anything that is not supported by evidence is discarded. For instance, a description of behavior for a date on which Cynthia was not at work is suspect and likely false. A similar description of a behavior put forth by several individuals, even if Cynthia has no recollection of the event, is deemed to be true.

4. Sort the data—Cynthia then divides the evidence into two groups, one that reflects negative behavior and one that reflects positive behavior.

5. Identify motivators—Cynthia then reviews the data across the two assigned groups looking for any entries that might reflect motivated behavior. For instance, an entry from the "positive behavior" group showing Cynthia going out of her way to assist her team leader with a task on the day before performance evaluations occurred might be considered motivated by a desire for a good rating rather than an intrinsic characteristic of how Cynthia normally behaves. Likewise, a complaint lodged about her leadership style on a project by someone who lost out on getting the job assignment might be motivated by jealousy or desire to make her look bad.

6. <u>Identify patterns</u>—Are there more entries remaining in one category than the other? Do certain behaviors seem more prevalent than others? Are there any factors associated with the most common behaviors (e.g., they occur in times of stress, or around people with certain traits)? Are they associated with particular situations, or do they trend across scenarios? Do the people who complain (or compliment) her performance have similar characteristics (gender, age, position)? Considering all of these aspects can reveal the pattern of the behavior and the circumstances that dictate its expression.

7. <u>Accept the outcome as truth and develop a plan to address it</u>—Whether you are happy with what your conclusions reflect or not, you are obligated to accept the truth and react to it appropriately. If the outcome indicates that that certain people raise issues no matter what, and that others find Cynthia's behavior to be appropriate and positive, then she must take steps to resolve the situation with those people. Perhaps it will require her approaching them differently than others on the team. Perhaps she needs to speak with them privately and find out why they have a problem with her. Or perhaps she needs to request that they be reassigned to another project. If, however, the analysis reveals a pattern of negative behavior attributable to Cynthia herself, then as much as she might dislike it, she should work out a plan for how to modify her own behavior accordingly. This might include engaging a coach or mentor (who, by the way, would have gone through an exercise similar to this in assessing Cynthia's situation), it might involve working on personal expression and trying to develop better styles, or it might involve looking for another form of occupation where her personality is better suited. The bottom line is to believe in the truth of the outcome and react accordingly even if you wish it has turned out differently.

A Concluding Caveat

I can tell you from personal experience that learning to be objective about your own internal state and the truth underlying your beliefs and motivations is a very daunting task. I have developed my own personal process of reasoning, but only because I've had the benefit of trusted others who worked with me until I could recognize when I was inadvertently stacking the cards in my favor (or avoiding issues I had rather not see). Of course, I often suffered massive bouts of denial and attempts to find any other explanation than my own culpability as I learned to use this process.

The approach above can work, as can other methods of applied introspection, but it is not an easy feat. Humans cling to the personal fictions we create as if our lives depend upon it, which to a certain degree they do! Not in the sense that we will die if we are faced with a truth about ourselves that we do not want to accept, but rather that we believe in our view of life and self so strongly that it is actually disorienting to recognize that our views and motivations may not be what they seem. It takes a great deal of courage to engage in soul searching on this level, especially when it is so much easier to attribute causation to less personal origins, and it is equally difficult to recognize the intent to deceive when the one you seek to deceive is in fact yourself. Nevertheless, do not underestimate the value of applying deductive logic to your own thought processes, as merely being aware that there are unconscious biases at work in your perception will make you a much more critical consumer of information on all fronts.

CHAPTER 5 ════════════

Sociological Truth:
All Truths Are Not Created Equal

I n a proper world, truth should have no borders. Truth should transcend geographical, cultural, national, and societal boundaries. Of course we know that this is not the case. Historically, the most common source of war and dispute has arisen from competing views of truth. Not only do these conflicts exist between countries, but even here within our own culture, we typically find wildly varying perspectives driven by different agendas and interpretation of facts and events. These differences arise largely from the varying belief systems we discussed in the preceding chapter, this time applied to groups rather than a single individual.

It has been common throughout human history for people to gather in social groups based upon a common perspective or set of beliefs. Once a member of such a group, the underlying belief structure is perpetuated through teaching and example and often becomes firmly entrenched as a personal truth that may or may not be founded in factual reality. Furthermore, divergence from the group view is strongly discouraged or even punished from within. Anyone who has seen *West Side Story* or read *Romeo and Juliet* is familiar with the romanticized versions of this type of segregationist approach.

The consensus of the group is always more compelling than dissenting views from individuals outside the group. In fact, competing or contrary views from outside sources will often fuel stronger belief in the established group doctrines. The sometimes stark differences in defining truth are reinforced by the tendency to overestimate between group variability and underestimate within group variability. In other words, we tend to believe that all members of an outside group are the same, and that they are completely different from members of our own group. This *them versus us* style of thinking is the basis for the nucleation of all religions, political parties, and many instances of nationalism. For instance, I have seen numerous examples of members of one political party making judgments about new information based solely upon a stereotypical view of the competing party. They tend to be motivated to embrace whatever view is diametrically opposed to that of the other party, usually without stopping to check the facts or think very hard about the situation in question— if my rivals believe it, then the opposite must be true.

At its best, this type of conceptual fabrication provides the basis for the formation and perpetuation of social groups, where the commonality of belief provides security and a sense of community. The members of the group are nourished by the sense of belonging and the comfort of having one's view validated by others. However, when the belief systems are divorced from a sound foothold in reality and lean toward the extremism, the result is increased incidence of events like terrorism, racial genocide, and war. It is important to emphasize that the individual truth—the individual's belief in the central tenets of a given culture or society—is directly related to the degree to which the group embraces the central beliefs and concepts. The more enthusiastic a given sociological group is about their doctrines and the supposed truths underlying them, the more likely the individuals in that group will embrace and perpetuate that view, even in the presence of conflicting factual information. Furthermore, the individual's identification with the group is strongly influenced by the developmental stage at which they first became exposed to the views. The younger the child is at first exposure, the less likely they will be to question the authenticity of the beliefs and the more firmly entrenched they will become within the community. How then does this type of indoctrination get started and become a fundamental way of thinking?

Impact of the Group on Individual Thinking

Humans have evolved to gravitate toward social groups. We are safest when we co-exist with others in a community. We are better able to find and share resources, raise and teach our young, and protect against invasion. We can build our homes and necessary infrastructure easier working in teams than alone. We have access to more important skills when we live with others than we can ever have on our own (e.g., doctors, engineers, electricians, farmers, etc.). In short, we are stronger when we live in groups. As such, we derive satisfaction from interacting socially with others. Our membership and status in our group takes on a very real importance in our lives. It is not surprising that banishment from the social group has been a severe form of punishment throughout history. Therefore, we seek to maintain membership in our group, and this is most easily accomplished through shared common beliefs and behaviors that serve to cement the social foundation.

A variety of sociological mechanisms impact our thinking in a way that facilitates the sense of belonging within our social niche. The most obvious are social mores—the overtly communicated prescriptions for expected behavior within the group. These would include laws about alcohol and drug use, accepted displays of social intimacy, and expected dress codes. However, there are a number of other social mechanisms that are less obvious, that occur largely beneath our awareness, and whose influence occurs gradually over time. Despite a less obvious linkage to group identification, these social constructs have a profound impact on how we view our group, the people within it, and those who do not belong.

Conformity: Peer pressure is a form of social desirability factor that motivates the individual to adopt the beliefs and behaviors of a relevant social niche in order to be accepted within that group. It gives rise to *conformity*, where going along with an action, even one that may go against the person's inherent beliefs, is required as a socially correct form of behavior. Most of us overestimate our independence from conformity pressures. We tend to believe that we will follow our own personal code of ethics regardless of the situation. However, an impressive amount of evidence suggests this is not the case, especially when the behavior is demanded by a person in authority.

Most people firmly believe that they would never go along with a ruthless dictatorship that shows no mercy towards citizens of their own country. Nonetheless, at least some of the horrific behavior exhibited by Nazi soldiers during WW II has been attributed to obedience to a strong authority figure (in the form of Adolf Hitler), rather than personal beliefs. Those who are impressionable and seek an opportunity for self-promotion can certainly gain by embracing doctrines that they might otherwise consider unacceptable. However, while some of the soldiers who participated in the mass murder of millions of concentration camp prisoners throughout WWII may have done so as a way to better their status and opportunities in society by following orders, others likely used denigration and marginalization of the targeted groups to enhance identification with and acceptance by their own peers, in this case promoting the status of their own culture to the detriment of another. It is an unfortunate fact that one of the strongest facilitators of violent and hate-based behaviors is a strong sense of nationalism and superiority over the oppressed social groups.

It is important to also recognize that some individuals who were compliant in the atrocities of the Nazi regime likely did so due to threats against their own family and selves. In such cases, a significant amount of rationalization is required in order to protect one's self image from the stigma of brutality associated with these acts. Thus, the need to strengthen identification with the beliefs and mission of one's own society has to outweigh sympathy or relevance to the persecuted group. Falsely over-estimating the homogeneity of the targeted group, and simultaneously ignoring overlap of traits with one's own peer group, is the most effective way to increase obedience to authority.

While these sociological factors might account for the behavior of soldiers, what about the general populace that stood by while the Nazi party rose to power? How was it possible for them to conform so readily to such a violent and oppressive government? One of the aspects of conformity that allows it to so easily perpetuate is the absence of a clear cut point for switching to disobedience. The gradual nature of most obedience situations allows the individual to both distance themselves from the action and also to slowly adapt to incremental change over time. If you recall our discussion of Stanley Milgram's work from Chapter 1, you will remember that subjects in the experimental situation were willing to apply what they thought were harmful (even mortal) levels of electric shock to others. They were more willing to do so when the amount of "shock" they applied was increased slowly over time. Individuals who are asked to go straight to harmful levels of punishment typically decline. As such, had the German civilian population known the totality of Hitler's plan at the outset, there would likely have been rebellion within the country before the conquest of Europe got off the ground. Instead, the civilian population experienced a gradual escalation of societal restriction and conquest, with accompanying propaganda by the leadership, which did not draw an obvious line in the sand.

Although the Nazi regime was never shy about voicing dislike of the Jewish people, the direct acts of the holocaust were prefaced by a gradual escalation of anti-Semitism. In 1935, the Nuremburg Laws decreed a separation of Jews from others in the German population, setting up a segregated society and stripping Jews of many of their rights as German citizens. Over the next several years, additional measures were taken to seize Jewish businesses, prevent Jews from ownership, and submit the Jewish people to increasingly restrictive laws. Late in 1938, the *Kristallnacht* event was executed as the first full scale pogrom against the Jewish people, resulting in the burning and looting of numerous Jewish synagogues and businesses, the death of hundreds, and the arrest and incarceration of many thousands more in the newly emerging concentration camps. This process of dehumanization occurred over a four to five year period with gradual acceptance of increasingly levels of violence and discrimination. The process is inherently deceptive as it hides the ultimate purpose of the actions by employing small steps toward the goal. Therefore, people adapted over time to the changing politics and world view until it was too late to take action. The longer you are actively in the mix, the more difficult it is to extricate yourself. This is why it is so rare for people to extricate themselves from cults and exclusionary societies after membership has gone on for a long period of time.

While the events of WWII may seem distant history to some, similar cultural pressures likely underlie modern day terrorist activity. Youngsters in these groups are indoctrinated with a diet of xenophobic hatred, while membership in the inner circle both feeds a sense of purpose and alleviates the void of isolation in a way that is particularly appealing to teenagers and young adults who are looking to establish their place in the world. In addition, as with the Nazi regime, terrorist groups foster a sense of elitism, a perspective that the members are somehow superior to others or chosen for a special mission. The price of membership is conformity with the terrorist doctrine and rejection of all other views. And of course the actions of terrorists only serve to inflame and threaten the target groups, providing an avenue for retribution and reprisal that then serves to further reinforce the apparent validity of the erroneous doctrine. Seldom in the mix is there any actual attempt to explore the truth or validity of any of the underlying tenets of the cultural belief or the required response to it.

A major cause for reflection is that this entire process of conformity goes on largely beneath our awareness. Each of us likely has multiple examples of such influence in our own thinking, but because it slowly becomes a personal truth over time, we do not recognize how we have been impacted by the pressure of our respective social groups.

Labeling and Stereotypes: Humans have a penchant for attaching labels to people and things in their environment. Doing so helps us to form concepts about our world, to easily categorize similar observations and events into a more easily remembered form, and to attach a constellation of relevance to it for future use. Unfortunately, the very act of labeling something can be rife with inaccuracy and therefore may have a negative effect on how we interpret and remember things we have experienced. This often happens because the label might contain more information than the actual observation, some of which is irrelevant and open to misinterpretation. Take this very simple example. Two groups of people were shown one of the following three items:

eyeglasses   dumbbells

When asked to draw the objects they remembered seeing after a period of time had passed, the presence or absence of a label had an effect how they drew the object they were asked to recall:

eyeglasses   dumbbells

Clearly, when a label was present, the label itself was remembered rather than the visual stimulus. When no label was present, the people had little trouble drawing accurate renditions of the objects they had seen.

The act of labeling not only influences how we interpret and remember an event, but also dictates what we attend to when analyzing information. Recall the example from the previous chapter of the subway mugging where participants in the study switched the race of the assailant and the victim in their recall of the scenario. Labeling can lead to stereotypes, or predilections we have about the characteristics of a particular group of people. A stereotype is a cognitive construct, and thus represents a belief system rather than inherent reality. It is also generated about a particular group of people rather than a specific individual, and thus does not take into account individual differences among members of that group. Stereotypes are structured and rather rigid sets of beliefs that ignore information that conflicts with the concept as a whole. Therefore, they dictate the ways in which we perceive members of a group and, because they are based upon ambiguous categories of characteristics not necessarily reflective of the specific individual in question, they obviously can be a profound source of error in judgment and can be used to prosecute a disingenuous agenda that largely goes unnoticed by the average consumer of information.

Most people would agree that stereotypes can be harmful to the groups they describe. Nonetheless, they are prevalent in all cultures and are perpetuated from generation to generation. Why then are stereotypes so common? Some data suggest that stereotypes serve an adaptive function in that they allow us greater ease of communication. A large amount of associated data can be passed on simply by using a descriptive label that is commonly known. For instance, if I say that someone I know is a "raging left-wing democrat," there is inherent in that label a wealth of information associated with that faction of our population (whether it is true about the individual or not). It saves us a lot of time and effort to simply state the label rather than explain the characteristics inherent to the individual in question.

Unfortunately, these types of stereotypes perpetuate, particularly when they involve negative characteristics, because of our habit of behaving towards people in a way that confirms our initial expectations. Let us say that you have the chance to interact with a person labeled as liberal, and you happen to engage them in a conversation about social issues. In the course of that conversation, they may state that they support both the woman's choice in reproductive health, and gun rights protected under the Second Amendment. Your predilection based upon priming by the stereotypical label will be to ignore the contradictory behavior (support of gun rights) and instead focus more strongly on the confirming behavior (pro-choice perspective). You thus spend little or no time talking about the gun rights issue (that might have given you a different view of this person's political perspective) and instead get into an argument over abortion. You thus walk away from the conversation appearing to confirm the stereotype of a left-wing activist. This cherry picking behavior is one of the biggest drawbacks to stereotypical labeling, as it appears to justify the act of labeling the person or group in the first place by providing a false sense of truth in the resulting perspective.

There are several other mechanisms by which stereotypes increase susceptibility to deception. For example, people are more willing to believe the words and actions of a stereotype-consistent individual over someone who does not look the part. For this reason, spokespersons for products and services tend to employ individuals who appear to be knowledgeable and have credentials to speak on behalf of the sponsor, even when they do not. The message from an actor wearing a white lab coat is much more convincing than a person in regular street clothes (as we will discuss in Chapter 10). Furthermore, we tend to believe messages from attractive people over those with less physical appeal based upon a predilection to view beautiful as good. On the flip side, political strategy often seeks to capitalize upon this phenomenon by creating an unappealing stereotype of the opponent using a campaign of negative publicity (e.g., the report that Romney tied his dog to the top of the car or photos of Obama wearing a turban). If the negative stereotype sticks, it makes it easier to discount anything the candidate has to say. This is a much more subtle form of deceptive practice than outright lying, but all the more effective because it makes use of our penchant for using stereotypical information to make judgments.

Prejudice: One of the most unfortunate offshoots of stereotyping is that it frequently leads to prejudice, the unjustified discrimination against a particular group of people based upon their physical characteristics, gender, socioeconomic status, religion, or other belief systems. The mere formation of different groups based upon these types of categories leads to judgments about the value of those groups. In many cases, these judgments are so harsh and restrictive that laws have been passed to address them. However, legal approaches cannot change the mindsets of those that express the prejudice; they can only serve to create the opportunity to explore a different way of thinking and behaving. For example, both national and international pressure helped drive the end of the apartheid era in South Africa, culminating in the democratic election of Nelson Mandela in 1994. While this landmark event resulted in changes in the segregation and citizenship laws, it initially did little or nothing to quell the culture of prejudice against natives and people of color. In 1995, South Africa hosted the "Truth and Reconciliation Commission" that accepted testimony from more than 20,000 people who had been victimized under the apartheid government. In 2003, the commission released its recommendations to the existing government concerning reparation and mechanisms for promoting cultural change. While many aspects of racial discrimination have begun to be addressed as per the recommendations, most notably in government representation, employment opportunities, and participation in national sports, there still remains, even two decades later, a high incidence of racial tension, hate crimes, and underlying prejudice that will take time and effort to overcome.

Interestingly, while the burden of responsibility for prejudice lies with the group who commits the discrimination, there is a growing body of evidence that the mere act of being discriminated against has an impact on the way people view themselves. Taking gender as an example, it is an unfortunate fact that gender inequality still persists in the workplace, either in terms of equal pay for doing the same job, or in terms of the type of position or promotions they can receive in some businesses. However, research has shown that women may be unwitting partners in the discrimination process. Consider the following example: in a research study on quality assessments, both men and women were asked to make judgments about a number of special interest articles across a variety of employment areas. All subjects read the same articles, except half of the articles were supposedly written by men and the other half were labeled as having been written by women. As expected, the male judges rated those articles written by "men" as of greater quality, especially when they were about areas that are traditionally male dominated (engineering, medicine, etc.). Surprisingly, women also followed the same pattern, downgrading the work that was presented with women authors. Thus it is clear that stereotypes can perpetuate harmful and prejudicial behavior both by the groups doing the discrimination, as well as on the unconscious thinking and self-concept of the target individuals themselves. As a result, the inadvertent spread of false and misleading information tends to go unchecked across societal strata.

Little White Lies as Adaptive Social Mediators

Social situations also impact our inherent truthfulness in more adaptive ways. Although we are gregarious creatures by nature, social interaction is not without potential cost. As such, there has evolved a form of deception that affects most of us every day and has become an accepted part of our social fabric–the *little white lie* we use to ward off stressful or unwanted situations. There is a consensus among researchers that most people tell minor untruths in certain social situations on a regular basis. For example, even the most honest person has likely covered for a family member when someone with whom they would rather not interact calls or comes to the door–"I am sorry, he's not here at the moment. Can I take a message?" or any other fib designed to get them to go away. Then there is the proverbial "The check is in the mail" designed to buy time, or calling up the credit card company to say that the bill arrived a week late and would they please waive the late fee. Many people will lie to their parents, spouses, or other loved ones about where they have been or how they are doing to avoid causing worry or creating confrontation. And of course there are the endless falsehoods told in the name of maintaining someone's self-esteem—"That new haircut is cute!" or the much dreaded "No, that sweater does not make you look fat."

The purpose of all of these types of statements is to deceive, and by doing so, to avoid or alleviate a stressful social situation. Far from being condemned by society, these types of behaviors are actually expected, and failure to do so is met with consternation and disquiet. While that hair cut may be the worst one your friend has ever had, the social protocol states that there is no need to confirm what the person already knows and is trying to escape. To tell the truth in such a situation will just end with hurt feelings and a strained friendship. Rather than honesty, your purpose is to bolster the feelings of your friend with false assurances

There is also a common social practice of employing misleading emphasis in order to achieve a greater good. For instance, the case of Bloomberg's campaign against sugary soft drinks discussed in Chapter 1 is deceptive in that it does not address a variety of other factors critical to understanding the relationship between consumptive behaviors and weight-related health issues. However, we can speculate that Bloomberg's intent was not to misuse health statistics in order to ban large drinks outright, but rather to call attention to an important epidemic that requires action. Certainly, there has been much legitimate debate and discussion as a result of the ill-fated attempt to make large drinks illegal, indicating that the scientifically dubious grounds underlying the action may ultimately have a positive outcome.

So, what we have here is a basic fundamental human behavior that reflects the dichotomy of judgment in our culture. On the one hand, we are raised to believe that lying is wrong and we should always tell the truth. Then we find out that there are times when we should in fact distort the truth a bit in the interest of living in an amicable and stress-free environment. Is it any wonder that the line we need to draw between truth and fiction can be so blurred? We are raised with an unspoken guidance that says lying is ok as long as it maintains our way of life. When you elevate that to a societal level, it is a recipe for development of factions and contradicting views. Truth becomes defined more about how you think life should be than the way it actually is, and the end result is a division in cultural perspective in which neither side considers that they might be the ones distorting the truth.

Breaking Out of the Mold

When it comes to judging societal truth, few beliefs are based upon empirical evaluation, despite the strong gut feelings of rightness that goes with our views. Things that make sense from a cultural perspective often turn out to be misconceptions, or are only part of the story masquerading as the whole truth. We gravitate to the things that *feel* right rather than demanding to know what things *are* right–the emotionally satisfying perspective rather than the logic-based one. Partly this is because we do not apply unbiased and rigorous approaches to judgment where societal views are concerned. We believe too strongly in the doctrines of our own group and in our distinction from those who believe differently. We are so enmeshed in our learned perspective that we seldom even see the compelling need to develop and employ the principles of rational judgment in our everyday lives.

Based upon what we have discussed about how societal beliefs are created and maintained, it is clear that identifying and propagating the truth is a challenging endeavor. All of society would benefit from a stronger application of logic and deductive reasoning when it comes to considering the truth underlying cultural beliefs. The simple act of researching the facts underlying any one of the current societal debates in our country could bring very real value to helping us create solutions to the challenges that face us as a nation. Furthermore, gaining some understanding of the adaptive function of social biases and their impact on views of the truth would certainly help us to take better account of the underlying motivators that impact our judgments on a daily basis.

CHAPTER 6 ━━━━━━━

Religious Truth:
Gods and Men and Swords of Right

I will start this chapter with a premise that may at first seem somewhat controversial—all religions, both ancient and modern, are exercises in mythology. I back up this assertion with the following definition of the term. A myth is a:

> ...traditional or legendary story, usually concerning some being or hero or event, with or without a determinable basis of fact or a natural explanation, especially one that is concerned with deities or demigods and explains some practice, rite, or phenomenon of nature (Dictionary.com).

While most people of faith, any faith, will immediately push back on that assertion, consider the case of human history. What we typically think of as myths are the fantastical escapades of characters central to the histories of ancient cultures. The religions of the Greeks and the Romans are now taught in school as mythology. Many of us enjoyed, or at the very least labored through, translations of the Odyssey or the Iliad, and wandered the seas with Jason on the Argo looking for the Golden Fleece. We laughed at the antics and the fickleness of Zeus, Hera, and their plethora of offspring as they consorted with the humans under their dominion. Likewise, many of us have followed the stories of the Norse gods who, under the rule of Odin, wreaked havoc throughout Scandinavia and the halls of Valhalla (and lately on the big screen where Thor amazes us all with his feats of strength and raging good looks). We've studied with fascination the ancient Egyptian gods and their dominion over existence from the sun to the underworld. And we can still read about the many ancient pagan gods of the springs, trees, and mountains who watched over the times of growth and the times of harvest, bringing both justice and retribution to the common man.

Aside from paganism, which still flourishes in some places today, most of us see these ancient religions as myths and allegories of a culture and a time in the distant past, a way that humans used gods of power to explain their world. It is easy to forget that these religions were viewed by their disciples as both truth and immutable law for hundreds if not thousands of years, and their religious leaders held sway over enormous populations of people, dictating their culture, governments, and practices of daily living. These religions were the basis for war against infidels and unbelievers who held different religious views. They influenced the politics of regions. They controlled kings, emperors, and dynasties, serving as the basis for conquest and expansion of territory at every point in human history. They also inspired xenophobia and hatred of those who did not believe, promoting the spread of dominant religions far and wide during conquests, abolishing or driving underground the belief systems of those they conquered.

But of course that was all in the name of now defunct mythologies, laughable tenets that we no longer see as truth and whose core doctrines differ markedly from those in modern times, right? Certainly, no one today would believe that Athena popped out of Zeus' head fully formed, or that an eagle plucked out Prometheus' liver on a daily basis for the audacity of giving man access to fire. Nor would the religions of today be a source of dissension and division, with each claiming to be the true word of an omnipotent deity. Modern gospels would not revolve around stories of miracles and unearthly acts that fly in the face of scientific understanding. Religious groups would not send missionaries out to indoctrinate the infidels of other cultures. Governments would never be expected to bow to one group's god over another, and world leaders would never be puppets to the preaching of religious organizations. And certainly, we would never go to war against another country because they worship a god by a name that differs from ours.

Only that is exactly what we do. The major religions today typically stand in direct opposition to each other. They define creation, life, death, and everything in between from different perspectives that unfortunately give rise to heated and often horrific between peoples. Religion as a basis for war continues today as it has throughout human history, and underneath every conflict is a fundamental disagreement about the nature of truth.

The feud between Christianity and Islam has raged from the time of the Crusades through modern day acts of terrorism. Throughout much of the last millennium, Christian priests and monks subverted the pagan saints and their sacred holidays, giving them new names and meanings as they drove the old religions out. The vendetta of certain sects of Christianity towards Judaism resulted in the death of more than six million people as recently as the middle of last century. Religious differences are the basis of cultural genocide throughout the world even as I am writing these very words. If humans are lucky enough to live another thousand years, I imagine it is possible that the religions of today will have sunk into the twilight as well, only to be replaced by other doctrines designed to explain life and the universe in the fashion of the times. And the disciples of those religions will look back on Christianity, Islam, Buddhism, Judaism, and Hinduism as quaint fables of a bygone era (as well as required reading for hordes of bored youngsters). I know that people of faith today will not agree with me, but I am not aware of a single factual basis that suggests the religions of today will go any differently than those of the past.

That having been said, there is no factual or scientific basis of proof for any religion (not even Scientology, which is based upon science fiction rather than science). Lest you tune me out as being too harsh, think again about what I am saying. There is no factual scientific basis for faith. Faith is, by definition, a tenet that is believed in the *absence* of proof. One cannot point to writings in religious documents, bibles, or other literature as sources of proof. Those are the recorded words of human individuals relating what they observed and their interpretations thereof, dictated by the era and knowledge level that they possessed at the time, not concrete evidence that can be assessed and tested empirically. Religion of any kind is an exercise of the spirit, not the intellect, and the two should not be confused. This does not mean that there are not spiritual truths to which people aspire, but only that these differ quite a bit from truth as we have been defining it so far in this book. It is not possible to apply the principles of deductive logic to any religious tenet, or in fact the existence of God, as there is no empirical basis for judgment. It is not possible to arrive at the truth of one religion over another—that is an individual experience dictated by the mental and emotional needs of the given person, not something that can be checked against a list of facts. Nonetheless, there is a constant flood of examples in our society where religious truths are put forth as the basis for public decision-making, on everything from laws to marriage to classroom curriculum. It is no wonder that such approaches are the source of controversy and public squabbles around whatever issue they touch.

In this chapter, I will of necessity deviate a bit from the

theme of this book so far, in that I will not attempt to prove the validity of any religious principle over another, nor will I approach religious tenets in terms of deceptive practice. Instead, I will examine the impact of perceived religious truths, whatever they may be, on modern life as they cross swords with the world of science, fact, and empirical evidence. What happens when religious beliefs run contrary to government policy? What happens when religious differences cause tension within a given culture, or give rise to discrimination, or to practices that are illegal by secular definition? To begin with, let us consider the fundamental principle that governs the role of religion in the American culture today, and identify the true role of religion in the founding of the country, as well as the meaning and purpose of the First Amendment.

The First Amendment

The First Amendment remains one of the most contested and challenged sections of the Bill of Rights. Arising out of a perceived need to further define the right to civil liberties, the First Amendment actually was created to address the protection of a number of individual expressions of which religion was only one:

> Congress shall make no law respecting an establishment of religion, or prohibiting the free exercise thereof; or abridging the freedom of speech, or of the press; or the right of the people peaceably to assemble, and to petition the Government for a redress of grievances.

There have historically been two interpretations of the meaning and intent of this amendment regarding the interactions of government and religious groups. One perspective holds there is a total separation of church and state in which government cannot interfere in religious expression (cannot make laws inhibiting it) nor can it uphold it (such as providing federal financial support for religious organizations or institutions). Furthermore, the government cannot favor one religion above another. This perspective is typically referred to as the *establishment clause*.

In contrast, the second interpretation holds that, while the government (federal or state) cannot declare an official religion or act in a discriminatory fashion based upon religious beliefs, it can pass laws based upon issues of morality and can extend policies that support religious beliefs, as long as one religion is not given prominence above another. This *accommodationist* interpretation is by far the more moderate and is the prevalent one in terms of modern government policy and the rulings of the US Supreme Court.

It is a myth that our forefathers founded this nation as a Christian country, and any statement to the contrary must therefore be either an act of deception or an act of ignorance. America was founded as a land free from religious persecution of any kind, and as the First Amendment has historically been interpreted, specifically bars the government from establishing an official religion or favoring one religious perspective above another. Many of the earliest pilgrimages of settlers to this continent were by those fleeing religious persecution and, as such, it is easy to understand that our founders sought to create a government free from such tyranny where people would be at liberty to worship (or not as the case may be) in any form they chose. In addition, the break from English rule included turning aside from the influence of the Church of England and religion dictated by the State–*the separation of Church and State*. It is a matter of historical fact that our earliest government did not observe religious holidays with as much rigor as we do today. Congress remained in session through Christmas as a rule until 1857, although it rarely actually met on Christmas day. Early puritans did not even view the celebrating of Christmas as an appropriate religious observance. In fact, the government did not alter its working schedule for any religious holiday until modern times.

The First Amendment clearly states that "Congress shall make no law" that controls religious expression or that forces that expression on another. By reason of the latter, public schools and federal buildings are typically prohibited from displaying religious sayings or requiring prayer or pledges to God. This does not mean that the concept of God and an obligation to a higher ruling power were devoid from the doctrines upon which our country was founded. The first few lines of the Declaration of Independence clearly reference God as an important factor:

> *When in the Course of human events, it becomes necessary for one people to dissolve the political bands which have connected them with another, and to assume among the powers of the earth, the separate and equal station to which the Laws of Nature and of **Nature's God** entitle them, a decent respect to the opinions of mankind requires that they should declare the causes which impel them to the separation.*

> *We hold these truths to be self-evident, that all men are created equal, that they are endowed by their **Creator** with certain unalienable Rights, that among these are Life, Liberty and the pursuit of Happiness.*

Despite the references to God and the Creator, no mention is made of any particular religion. There is no verbiage that establishes our nation as one built on Christianity, and the intent of the First Amendment is clearly to allow freedom of religious worship of all fashions. Therefore, the emerging modern-day mantra that we are a Christian nation does not stand up to evaluation under the principles of objective reasoning. To insist that the principles of Christianity must take precedence in our society flies in the face of the spirit of the doctrines by which our forefathers established this nation, and in fact manifests the very thinking that they sought to avoid in the first place.

It is also an unfortunate state of affairs that our long standing history of religious tolerance has been stretched to the limit in the wake of September 11, 2001. Anti-Muslim sentiment and discrimination have flourished in the decade following that tragedy. While it is true that the acts of terror were conducted by a radical group observing Islamic religious views, the acts themselves defy the teachings of the Koran and are considered unacceptable under the laws of that religion. Nonetheless, as with so many events in history where religion is concerned, the acts of the few have tainted the waters of public opinion for the many. Not only are mosques and Muslim communities the frequent site of protests and discriminatory acts, the President of the United States has been accused of adhering to the Muslim faith with derision and hostility. Despite his public claims of Christianity, and his attendance on numerous occasions at Christian houses of worship, factions within our populace continue to spread vitriolic suspicion around his religious beliefs. This obsession with his religious affiliation is a visible sign of the false understanding of the intent and purpose of the First Amendment that is currently a facet of such a vocal portion of American culture. Even if the truth were that Mr. Obama is a Muslim, the First Amendment guarantees his right to live freely and observe that faith within our society (even as President of the United States!). It is a direct corruption of the principles of this constitutionally protected right to deny a member of any religious faith equal access to expression under the law. Yet the same people who cry out in protest that our founding principles are being subverted are the very ones who are promoting perspectives that violate the intent and meaning of the First Amendment.

Clash of Law and Religion

While the free expression of religion is protected by the First Amendment, it is not an inalienable or concrete right. Government has historically imposed restrictions upon religious freedom in the interests of secular law or in cases of cultural morality. For example, despite the fact that the expression of ALL religions is protected by law in America, the nature of that expression is not completely free. Human sacrifice is illegal whether there is a religious basis for it or not. Polygamy is punishable by law despite it being an acceptable tenet of the Church of Latter Day Saints. The Amish are required to pay income and property taxes despite their desire to be isolated from the secular world. And while the practice of Voodoo is legally permissible, one cannot simply spray chicken blood on a neighbor's door with impunity. In essence, the secular laws of the land supersede certain religious practices.

However, in some cases, religion does have the ability to inexplicably influence the ways in which legal issues are handled. Child molestation is a heinous crime punishable by law, and yet the secular legal system has, until recently, turned aside to allow the Catholic Church to internally handle such indiscretions by priests. Conscientious objectors have historically been exempt from conscription, or have been required to serve in non-combative roles that do not violate their personal or religious beliefs. And religious organizations (specifically churches) are exempt from paying income tax on tithes, donations, and fund raising.

The easiest way to prevent the clash of religion with secular law is to keep religion out of any federal or state-sponsored activities. Certainly, there has been a heated debate about whether reference to God (any god) is acceptable within a public venue, as there is always a risk that one or more religious (or nonreligious) factions may feel offended by the reference. In other words, it is better to avoid any religious reference than to face a law suit from a group with differing beliefs. As such, the words "under God" have been absent from the Pledge of Allegiance recited by school children across the country for several decades now. Although there is a periodic resurgence of debate over reintroducing the Pledge in its original form, the legal decisions continue to come down on the side of disestablishmentarianism. Furthermore, in very recent news, the Air Force has been debating removal of reference to God from the service oath for very similar reasons. They reached a compromise of allowing "under God" to be optional and up to the individual serviceman. While many consider this to be a symptom of dissolving religious freedom within American society, it more likely reflects the burgeoning presence of conflicting religious views. As our nation becomes more and more multicultural, the nature of religious truth becomes more difficult to fathom from a national perspective. And since it is impossible to empirically prove the veracity of one religion over another, the safest legal path may be to avoid the topic all together.

It is clear that the line between religious freedom and the laws of the land is a blurry one at best. It is a constant struggle to recognize the freedom of expression protecting varying faiths and yet adhere to the very real standards of law expected from all US citizens and residents. As such, it is not surprising that the US Supreme Court regularly considers suits that involve the clash of law and religion. Not surprisingly, two of the most emotionally charged of these contests involve women's reproductive rights– abortion and providing health coverage for contraception.

Abortion: The abortion battle has been waging for generations, and the medical procedure itself was largely considered criminal throughout the 19th and much of the 20th centuries. The controversy was supposedly laid to rest with the landmark US Supreme Court decision of Roe vs. Wade in 1973. In this decision, the Court ruled that a woman has a legal right to an abortion until the moment at which the fetus becomes viable. As you might imagine, subsequent argument has ensued ever since regarding the definition of viability. Today, most states employ the trimester rule, with third trimester abortions being considered almost universally illegal with rare exception. The end of the first trimester cut off is fairly common, except in the case of threat to the life of the mother or other medical need.

However, political and religiously inspired factions continue to push for the criminalization of abortion, in some cases even in the event of rape, incest, or threat to the life of the mother. Currently, the Personhood Movement seeks to alter the definition of when a human is classified as a person with individual rights under the law, with the milestone being shifted to the time of fertilization. If successful, this movement will have major impact on a multitude of practices, including some forms of contraception that work by preventing uterine implantation (e.g. intrauterine devices and the "morning after" pill). One can even imagine murder charges being brought up against mothers who miscarry with claims of neglect or reckless endangerment.

But what about when the definition of personhood, as defined by a religious organization, conflicts with the definition imposed by law? The belief that life begins at conception is well established by Catholic doctrine, and hence forms the basis for prohibition of all abortion (and many forms of birth control) and resistance against all laws that would protect such activities. However, secular law is sometimes embraced by religious organizations when there is a clear benefit, such as in the defense put forth in the 2006 wrongful death suit brought by Jeremy Stodghill against Catholic Health Initiatives, a Catholic run hospital in Canon City, Colorado.

In this case, the plaintiff's wife died of a heart attack in the hospital while seven months pregnant with twins. No effort was made to save the lives of the unborn babies by emergency C-section or other means. The hospital defended its failure to attempt rescue of the unborn babies using as defense the principles of the Colorado law that does not consider fetuses to be people. This case achieved public notoriety since it represented such a blatant contradiction with the stance promoted by the Church on such issues, begging further investigation by a panel of high ranking bishops. The Colorado law does not prohibit emergency measures to save fetuses in this type of situation, so it is all the more troubling and untruthful by Church standards to use such a defense in this instance. If you recall, we opened this section with the statement that truth should be independent of cultural beliefs and should not shift to serve the will (or protect the behinds) of any group or organization. This is a perfect example of putting more emphasis on the expediency of a doctrine than on upholding one's religious views.

All divergences from the norm aside, the right to life philosophy may be understandable from a religious perspective, but it still represents a blatant attempt by non-secular groups to subvert the laws by which we abide as a nation, without regard for the beliefs or opinions of those outside their faith. This is in fact the very type of thing our founding fathers sought to avoid. As such, the clash between the ideals of religious truth and secular truth provides a continuous source of tension and discord in our society that cannot be easily resolved by reliance on facts and figures and empirical data.

Contraception and mandated health coverage: One of the loudest and most heated controversies in American society for the past couple of years has been the requirement to provide insurance coverage for contraception as mandated by the 2010 Patient Protection and Affordable Care Act. Although only enacted early in 2012, the act itself was a huge source of controversy and litigation until the US Supreme Court upheld its constitutionality on June 28, 2012. While many parts of the act are now largely in effect, components of the provisions are being contested as separate legal actions, particularly the mandate that requires all health insurance plans to include provision for no cost contraceptive coverage as preventative health procedures for women. Contraception includes not only oral contraception, but also injections, patches, devices, and emergency measures such as the "morning after pill."

From a religious perspective, this is a nightmarish can of worms. Some religions ban artificial birth control procedures outright. Others are generally permissive of birth control as long as it prevents fertilization, rather than working through abortive processes or prevention of implantation. Since the birth control provision covers all forms of female contraception, the opportunity for violation of religious beliefs inspired an immediate outcry from various religious groups.

As a result, an exemption applying to formal church organizations was allowed, but this did not extend to nonprofit or for profit corporations or entities that were affiliated with a religious organization, such as schools, universities, and hospitals, unless the employees of that organizations are primarily members of the sponsoring faith. The exemption was extended only to those schools and universities that self-insure, but not to religiously affiliated organizations that self-insure, or to schools and universities that purchase outside insurance plans. Such exceptions have created inconsistencies and confusion about how to interpret the law in individual cases.

As one would expect, numerous lawsuits, currently numbering greater than forty at the time of this writing, have ensued claiming protection under the First Amendment. Due to the recent enactment of the plan, most of these suits have not yet been resolved and enforcement has been temporarily delayed until the cases have been decided. For example, in late December of 2012, the 7th Circuit Court of Appeals put a temporary hold on enforcing the mandated contraception coverage for Korte & Luitjohan Contractors, a company with Roman Catholic owners who are protesting the law based upon religious grounds. Likewise, the founder of Domino's Pizza received a temporary stay on offering contraceptive coverage for employees while broader questions about the position of the mandate in reference to the

First Amendment right to religious expression are considered. In contrast, a ruling by an Indiana federal judge in January 2013 denied a challenge outright by the University of Notre Dame, citing that the act is still a work in progress and therefore the suit is untimely.

The most public challenge so far to the mandate occurred with the refusal of the Hobby Lobby chain of stores, owned by David Green and family of Oklahoma, to provide contraceptive coverage on religious grounds. U.S. Supreme Court Justice Sonia Sotomayor rejected the company's appeal to block enforcement of the contraception provision, resulting in a potential fine of $1.3 million a day if the owners defied the mandate. However, in June of 2014, the US Supreme Court handed down a 5-4 ruling that upheld the right of the Hobby Lobby corporation to deny contraception coverage if it violates the owner's religious beliefs. Although the court's ruling applied only to "closely held" companies (eg., family owned and operated), this will likely set legal precedent for other pending and emerging challenges to the Act going forward. This is an excellent example of how complicated it can be to employ objective legal judgment when religious and secular truths clash on the public stage.

On legal grounds, the outcome of the clash between faith and rationality on issues such as these is not yet clear. It would seem logical that those institutions that serve secular functions and accept federal funding should be held accountable to secular law without exemption. At the same time, we have constitutionally protected rights to express and practice our religions freely (albeit as long as they do not conflict with secular laws as previously discussed) which should dictate a reasonable resolution to the conflict. Unfortunately, logic and reason are not normally at the forefront of debates based upon such highly charged emotional issues. It is likely that the litmus test of the distinction between religious freedom and civil responsibility around this issue will continue to come down to the judgment of the nine individuals who comprise the highest court in our land, regardless of how many people may disagree with their ultimate decision. History shows us that the interface of secular law and religious beliefs is always fraught with controversy and vitriol, so expect little to be different with this one.

Clash of Science and Religion

The conflict between science and religion has been woven throughout the course of human history, sometimes emerging in unexpected ways. In the 19th century, the field of biology was turned on its head by the uncommon observations of Charles Darwin during his celebrated trip to the Galapagos Islands. Although Darwin's major contribution was proposing the process of natural selection that underlies the evolution of species, his theories had a profound impact on our understanding of psychology and the workings of the human mind as well. Darwin introduced the concept of functionalism—the idea that all processes, including behavior, serve an adaptive purpose. It may appear obvious to us in the present day that behaviors and thought processes function to help us adapt to and survive within our environment, but to a society dominated by the view of determinism,where all acts are determined by and arise from a higher power, his theories were practically heresy in some circles. However, as a result of this landmark change in thinking, we have a better understanding of the human mind and why it works the way it does, and in fact can today speculate in an informed manner about the origins and adaptive purpose of lying in the behavior of our species,

From the legitimacy of fossil records to climate change, the conflict between the tenets of science and religious doctrine continue to this day, creating uncomfortable schisms in popular culture. Keep in mind that this is complicated by the fact that, as previously discussed, scientific truth is predicated upon empirical fact, and religious truth by its very definition is based upon faith rather than facts. Nonetheless, it should be possible to rationally discuss some examples that illustrate such sources of contention and the resulting impact on our successful functioning as a society.

Kids Caught in the Middle

One undeniable fact is that secular public schools teach scientific concepts like evolution and sex education, whereas religious schools tend to avoid these topics in favor of creationism, intelligent design, and the need for sexual abstinence. This has been a long standing source of ire for those religious individuals who are obligated to send their children to public schools, either because they cannot afford the tuition required for a private religious school, or because they do not live in a location where such schools are available. Public prayer is prohibited in most secular schools, the pledge of allegiance is no longer required (largely because of the phrase "under God"), and religion is taught only in optional elective courses. Instead, science predominates. Graduates of public school upbringing are exposed to science courses that instruct about the composition of the earth and the process of its formation. They learn about evolution of species and the ascent of *Homo sapiens* from ape-like ancestors. They are provided with a history of dinosaurs and glaciers and climate change over eons, of meteors and volcanic eruptions, and the mass extinctions that ensued. Furthermore, most secular schools require courses about the human body, sex, and health.

At the root of every one of these lessons is a foundation of fact and scientific discipline, of rigor and objective thought. Carbon dating tells us the earth is a little over 4 billion years old, and astrophysical evidence indicates the universe itself is about 14 billion years. Fossil records clearly provide evidence for evolution of species and for mass extinctions associated with specific geological events. Core samples provide a record of climate change and provide clear evidence of glacier expansion and contraction. And biology has increased our understanding of how our bodies function, of the process of human reproduction and growth, as well as the acts that give rise to procreation.

In contrast, religious schools teach largely from the perspective of their given doctrines. In Christian schools, children are taught principles designed to promote a spiritual understanding of man's place in the world. There is no need for there to be a sound scientific foundation to the teachings. It is acceptable to instruct children that god created Adam and then fashioned Eve from his rib, and that Jesus was born of a virgin. It is considered biblical truth that the origin of the planet is contained within a seven day time frame when God fashioned the heaven and the earth, that the earth has only been in existence for several thousand years, and that mass extinction occurred from a flood imposed by God's wrath at human wickedness. For Jews, Moses parted the Red Sea and led his people out of the desert, and menstruating women are unclean. I do not need to get into more detail or examples here, as all religions have the same basis for their teachings. The events that comprise religious teaching revolve around instructions from a deity, observation of miracles, and the philosophies that grew out of them, not upon empirical fact. Faith is the basis of instruction, not scientific proof or deductive rigor.

None of this would cause an issue if all people of religious persuasion were to educate their children accordingly, while all non-religious individuals pursued a secular approach. The problem arises in that there is not a clear cut line between these approaches in our educational system. It is understandable that people who believe in creationism would not want their children to be taught evolution, whether there is scientific evidence for it or not. Likewise, non-religious parents would be outraged if their children were forced to take religious study courses against their will or be instructed that the earth is only 9000 years old.

Unfortunately, this brings us back to the First Amendment. Our forefathers in their wisdom saw fit to protect religious freedom and at the same time keep religion and government separate. Since tax dollars are gathered and dispersed by the government, the public schools funded by state and federal money are thus secular. This is a fact I do not see any way around. Whether it is fair or not, people who prefer a religious upbringing for their children must of necessity either pay for tuition at private religious schools or practice home schooling. There is no common ground for delineating the line between religious and secular truth when it comes to education.

The Divide Manifested in the Real World

As you might expect, the perspective we are taught as children carries over into our adult world. When it comes to the clash between science and religion, this is a bad mix, particularly when the clash occurs in the public arena. While our constitution protects each individual's right to believe whatever they want, it was not intended for those views to impact our government policies. For example, despite the overwhelming and universally accepted evidence that the earth is several billion years old, Congressman Paul Broun (R-GA) has publicly stated that the earth is only 9000 years old and that his method of governance is dictated by this religious doctrine:

> *God's word is true. I've come to understand that. All that stuff I was taught about evolution, and embryology, and Big Bang Theory. All that is lies straight from the pit of hell... You see there are a lot of scientific data that I've found out as a scientist that actually show this is really a young earth. I don't believe that earth is but about 9000 years old. I believe it was created in 6 days as we know them. That's what the Bible says... it teaches us how to run all of public policy and everything in society.*

> *That's the reason as your Congressman I hold the
> Holy Bible as being the major directions to me of
> how I'll vote in Washington D.C. and I'll continue
> to do that. (Remarks from an address to the 2012
> Sportsman's Banquet in Hartwell, Georgia).*

Let us consider for a moment what this statement actually means. It means that the concerted opinions of thousands of scientists are wrong or, even worse, that they are liars in collusion with evil powers. It means that the dinosaur bones we pull from the earth's crust must have been planted there by some agency to give us a false view of history. It means that archeological records of early human civilizations, of Neanderthals and Cro-Magnons and early *Homo sapiens* are fabrications. It also means that the records we have of early Mesopotamia that date back nearly 12,000 years ago must also be forgeries.

While Mr. Broun is protected by the First Amendment in expressing his religious opinion, that does not allow him to make government policy based upon his religious beliefs in opposition to secular will. As a member of the House Science Committee, he has publicly stated that he will make government law and policy based upon these beliefs. Our Constitution explicitly forbids this type of thing. And it is not just secular versus religious views at play here. He stands to force a particular religious view on to those of different faiths. It is clear that he believes with enormous conviction that he is right in his views, but there is no evidence whatsoever that he is any more correct in those views than those of any other religion. This is exactly what our forefathers set out to prevent with the framing of the Constitution.

The problem with the divide created by the clashes of faith and secular perspectives is that it has a very real negative impact on our ability to rationally assess facts and make decisions on how to address critical issues that are important to all of us. Tempers get inflamed on both sides when statements are made in the public arena that come from a personal religious view that does not represent the secular perspective or that contradicts other religious tenets. Furthermore, when decisions are driven by faith-based beliefs rather than scientific empirical fact, there is no sound basis for rationally resolving the divide.

For example, effective action on climate change is not only held back by the special interest groups that will lose profits by reducing our carbon footprint, but also by religiously-driven philosophies that run contrary to scientific fact. Numerous examples of attempts to supersede the recommendations from international scientific committees in favor of faith-based solutions have become more public over the past couple of years.

Rick Santorum, a 2012 Republican primary presidential candidate, has frequently made statements indicating his willingness to put religion before the secular interest, as in this example from a recent interview on CBS:

> *When you have a worldview that elevates the Earth above man and says that we can't take those resources because we're going to harm the Earth; by things that frankly are just not scientifically proven... this is all an attempt to, you know, to centralize power and to give more power to the government (Face the Nation).*

In 2009, Chairman of the Subcommittee on Environment and the Economy, John Shimkus (R-Ill), advocated following the teachings of the Book of Genesis when it comes to legislating on climate change and regulating greenhouse gas emissions during testimony before the House Energy and Commerce Committee:

> *I do believe in the Bible as the final word of God, and I do believe that God said the Earth would not be destroyed by a flood.*

These are only a few examples in a vastly increasing movement to insert religious views into our government legislation and policy. The relationship between religion and secular society has always been an uneasy one, but the potential for conflict is only exacerbated when the clash enters into politics, government, and legal standards. In this case, the principles of rationality and objective reasoning can do little to close the gulf between the two camps. We must instead rely upon the continued application of the principles of the First Amendment and the spirit upon which our government was founded.

In a democracy, there are always laws and policies that inspire disagreement, sometimes even violently so. However, existence in a civil democratic society means we must either accept the will of the majority or move someplace that better suits our individual principles. After all, our own founding fathers broke from England because of policies with which they did not agree, clearly stating in the Declaration of Independence that"...a decent respect to the opinions of mankind requires that they should declare the causes which impel them to the separation..." Lawful dissent is the cornerstone of our society, and protests and petitions to change the laws with which you do not agree should be encouraged. However, neither willful disregard for the existing law, nor using that same law to force your religious views on those who do not hold them, are protected by the First Amendment, nor were they part of the philosophy upon which our Constitution was formed. Since the process of objective reasoning and judgment cannot be applied to religious beliefs, it is important to keep in mind that the consideration of truth and falsehood based upon religious grounds must remain outside the scales by which all other societal decisions are weighed.

PART 3

Truth, Lies, and Videotape: Deception Run Amok in Mainstream Culture

S o far we have focused upon the nature of truth and deception, and the internal and external forces that govern them both. At the root of our ability to make judgments about truth is knowledge. Knowledge informs us of the facts, of precedent, and of the consequences that go hand in hand with the events we want to judge. And the root of all knowledge is information and experience.

In historical times, reliance on personal experience dominated the way in which we made judgments because we lived in a world much more restricted in terms of the availability of information. Before books and newspapers were widely available, people learned about happenings mostly by word of mouth. Travelers were a major source of news about places and events in distant locales. As such, people had the opportunity to see the facial expressions and body language of the teller, to ask questions, and then to discuss amongst themselves whether the information fit with what they already knew about their world. Trusted sources of advice were those that had been proven right on many an occasion as judged by how things played out in the personal sphere of the audience.

In modern times, we have the good fortune to have access to the largest and most expansive sources of information mankind has ever known—the internet and video media. We have continuous access to news of all types on satellite and cable networks, arising from all manner of perspectives. Any type of information can be found at your finger tips on the internet. We also have access to the experiences and opinions of others in an unprecedented manner through email, blogs, and online chat rooms. As such, we should be more adept than ever at discerning truth from falsehood to gain an informed view of the world.

Unfortunately, the ease of information gathering has had the unexpected and undesirable side effect of largely unplugging the sense of evaluative filtering that is critical to judging truth and identifying deception. We can be bombarded and functionally brainwashed by the constant flow of information, the end result of which is the perpetuation of nonsensical fictions that are embraced with fervor by the masses. We are losing our ability to think critically, to question and investigate and challenge what we hear. Therefore, the following section will explore several major examples of deception that have become so common place in modern culture that we hardly even notice their existence or impact in our lives.

What we have covered so far in this book are a variety of internal and external sources of truth and how they impact our understanding of the world. We have discussed how science and law set standards for judgment, how our own biology and psychology set the stage for deception, and how society often promotes the deceptions we see played out each day. We also discussed the differences between religious truth and scientific truth, and how the intersection of those two perspectives sometimes makes it difficult to make clear judgments of fact and fiction. This section of the book is focused upon highlighting common examples of lying and deception in our society, with an eye toward motivating us to be more accountable for our role in accepting, and even promoting, inaccurate information.

CHAPTER 7 ═══════════

Political Malarkey:
Bad Actors on a Corrupted Stage

A s I mentioned at the start of this book, the appalling examples of disingenuous, and sometimes outright dishonest, political behavior displayed during the run up to the 2012 presidential election served as the inspiration for this book. I wish I could say this was an unprecedented occurrence in an otherwise smoothly functioning government system, but such is simply not the case. The very nature of politics seems to be defined by how well you can undermine the tenets of the opposition and deception is a powerful tool for accomplishing such. And I am sad to say that this trend is not just restricted to those vying for the highest office in the land. The ongoing derisive war of words between political factions has threatened the functioning of government, making it difficult to agree, even on simple fundamental solutions for which there are widespread public support.

This is not news to anyone. Politicians mislead the voting public on a regular basis and scandals erupt as a result. Sometimes those scandals can have very real impact depending upon who, when, and how they emerge, but more often they are simply the news *du jour* before we move on to the next episode. In early 2014, the country wondered whether Governor Chris Christie of New Jersey was sincere in his anger over being lied to by his officials in the eruptive scandal over lane closures on the George Washington Bridge that may have been part of a plan to discredit the Fort Lee mayor. Whether he knew or not will likely be unimportant. Those who oppose him will rally around this latest chance to derail his potential candidacy for the presidency in 2016, those who support him will ignore it.

The bottom line is that lying, especially in politics, exists because it seldom matters to the outcome. The whole culture of politics is based upon it. We actually expect our politicians to deceive and mislead us on the issues. Their job is to do whatever it takes to convince us to vote for them, and we look the other way when what they say contradicts something else they already said. Of course, one ramification of this is that we no longer recognize the truth when we see it in the political arena, and therefore may miss out on opportunities to introduce some game changing paradigms into the mix. But what happens if we actually do start applying logic and deductive reason to the words and actions of our political leaders? Is it possible we could actually bring around a shift in the national conversation that helps us to achieve our goals with more transparency and integrity?

One way we can examine these questions is to look at the types of deception that form the basis of many forms of political behavior, and evaluate how we can accurately assess the veracity of political messaging. The examples of distortion and deception in politics are many and I could write a whole book about just this topic, but nonetheless most political maneuvering shies away from blatant lies that could be too easily discredited. The three most common forms of deceptive politicizing involve omission, exaggeration, or misleading emphasis, all of which serve to distract the listener from noticing any misdirection by keeping the focus around a kernel of truth. In the next section, we will look at some quintessential demonstrations of these forms of deception within recent political behavior and identify the major cues and red flags that let us know when something might be amiss.

Everything but the Context

Omission is one of the most powerful forms of deception because it allows the perpetrator to gain credibility by using the target's own words against them. The beauty of it is that the person in question actually did say those words or commit that act, so any fact checking exercise will clearly identify the accuracy of the supposition. However, as we talked about in the beginning of this book, to take something out of context with the intent to purposefully present a view that distorts the central truth of the event is one of the most insidious forms of deception. When it comes to human communication, context is everything. The very same words can have wildly differing meaning depending upon what else was said in the statement. Politicians have this form of political warfare down to an art form, as it allows them to avoid speaking a *word lie* while still creating a fiction that supports their own agenda. Here are some excellent examples of omission at work.

1) <u>Barack Obama</u>—"Mitt Romney said Let Detroit go bankrupt."
    This statement was one repeatedly used by the Democratic camp during the 2012 Presidential campaign, not only to imply that Romney's philosophy toward business was cold and calculating, but also to highlight the success of the auto company bailout under the Obama administration. For example, during the final Presidential debate on Oct 16, 2012, Obama said:

> *Number one, I want to build manufacturing jobs*
> *in this country again. Now when Governor Romney*

said we should let Detroit go bankrupt, I said we're going to bet on American workers and the American auto industry and its come surging back.

This statement can clearly be interpreted as an effort to contrast the Obama and Romney approaches, with Romney's being largely based upon a lack of faith in the American worker. It implies Romney wanted to give up on the industry and that Obama's plan instead supported auto workers and brought the companies back to prosperity.

The truth here is that Romney did use those exact words, as they comprise the title of an opinion editorial piece he authored for the New York Times on November 18, 2008. However, the article goes on to describe the use of managed bankruptcy proceedings as part of a measured restructuring, such as has been employed by numerous businesses over the past several decades with great success.

The American auto industry is vital to our national interest as an employer and as a hub for manufacturing. A managed bankruptcy may be the only path to the fundamental restructuring the industry needs. It would permit the companies to shed excess labor, pension and real estate costs. The federal government should provide guarantees for post-bankruptcy financing and assure car buyers that their warranties are not at risk.

This is a sound and well accepted business practice and Romney's discussion around employing this approach for the auto industry is cogent and well-articulated. In fact, bankruptcy was also part of the recovery process under Obama. The real difference arises from the proposed source of financial support, with Obama advocating federal funding and Romney emphasizing the need for private sector backing guaranteed by the government.

This is a very good example of a contextomy (discussed in the Introduction) that subverts the meaning of a statement through omission of the full context of the quote. The way to arrive at a correct and factual interpretation of claims and statements such as this is to seek out the original source of the quote. In this case, deductive logic is not even necessary because the flagrant distortion of the meaning is so obvious—a simple application of the ability to evoke a rational interpretation will suffice. Romney did make the statement as alleged, but the way in which it was presented by the Obama camp was clearly designed to mislead the audience and distort the message. Romney never expressed a lack of concern or support for the auto industry, nor did he advocate tossing them over the cliff. As such, this particular political tactic can clearly be classified as a distortion of the facts with intent to deceive.

2) <u>Romney campaign ad</u>—Obama said "If we keep talking about the economy, we're going to lose the election." Nov. 21, 2011 (New Hampshire ad)

The Romney camp was not adverse to spreading contextomies in their political messaging either. This Romney campaign ad earns a gold star for taking a statement out of context and distorting it into a total work of fiction. What Obama actually said during a campaign speech in the run up to the 2008 election against John McCain was:

> *Senator McCain's campaign actually said, and I quote, "If we keep talking about the economy, we're going to lose."*

However, the Romney ad omits the fact that Obama was quoting McCain and instead incorrectly attributes the partial statement to Obama himself. There is little argument that this is a purposeful deception designed to put Obama in a negative light and suggest that his handling of the economic crisis was a major detriment to his re-election. Again, this is a good example where the judgment of veracity need go no further than reviewing the original statement. A quick read of the full text of Obama's comment clearly reveals the level of distortion involved. Unless the people responsible for the ad never listened to the original footage and therefore made a significant error in interpretation, logic dictates that this is a strategic lie committed to promote a false impression of the opposing candidate. Seldom do we see political misinformation stated so categorically, especially when it is so easy to disprove through fact checking.

3) Joe Biden—"We weren't told they wanted more security."

Vice President Biden made this statement during the VP debate on October 11, 2012 in the wake of the tragic attack on the embassy in Benghazi, Libya and the resulting deaths of the US Ambassador and three other Americans, in reference to the unheeded request for additional security for diplomatic facilities in Libya. This issue has been a hotbed of contention since the attacks, with pressure from both sides being applied to uncover the factors that led to the failed intelligence and security lapse for embassy personnel.

As it turns out, both written and verbal requests for additional security for Libyan facilities (that would include Benghazi) were made on several occasions to the State Department by Eric Nordstrom, who was then responsible for regional security in Libya before the attack. While there is no *prima facie* evidence that key members of the White House were aware of these requests, it is the responsibility of the State Department to make such information known to the Secretary of State and subsequently to the Oval Office, and it is highly unlikely that someone at a high level of government was not made aware.

The crux of the matter here lies with the intent and meaning behind Biden's use of the word "we." He appears to refer to the

President, himself, and key White House staff, not the administration as a whole. From that perspective this may not be a word lie, but he certainly omits the fact that it is routine for the Oval Office to be made aware of such information. The White House may not have been informed directly, but key members of the administration were subsequently known to be aware of the request. This is an example where applied deductive reasoning can fairly easily reveal the full nature of an ambiguous statement. In this case, Biden relies upon a very narrow interpretation of the pronoun to make a statement that is technically correct, but still misleading. The evasion is a successful tactic because, in the absence of definitive information about the chain of communication leading up to the attacks, it is impossible to ascertain whether the nature of the statement reflects deception or is simply a case of being poorly informed. This is a perfect example of how statements that are technically true can still result in a false representation of the overall facts. As in a court of law, a simple statement taken out of context may be true but at the same time give rise to a completely different interpretation of events. Only by logically considering the larger context is it possible to ascertain the truth underlying such a statement.

Fall Out: Omission and distortion of context are the most easily debunked of the political deception techniques. The statements made by politicians are available for perusal from a variety of sources with little or no effort. Whenever the red flag of "He said/she said" appears, that is a good indicator that a quick check of the accuracy of the allegation is in order. Nonetheless, only a small fraction of the voting public take this step. I cannot count the times someone has relayed to me some damning evidence supposedly from the lips of one politician or another, and when I ask what the circumstances were around the quote (that is, when, where, and to whom was the statement was made, and under what context), I am rewarded with a blank look. Most of the time, I am told that one or another newsreader or talk show host read the quote to the audience. Was that the full quote? They usually have no idea. So, someone I do not trust to begin with reported something supposedly said by someone else I do not trust....get the picture? Only by taking a look at the actual transcript and considering the full context of the statement can one really ascertain the truth behind any allegation. Considering how easy it is to do this, it is dismaying how infrequently it actually gets done.

Jackass Jargon

The second most common form of misdirection in the world of politics is the art of *exaggeration*. It is easy to be disingenuous when one embellishes the basic facts and figures. The trick here is to make the claims seems plausible by tweaking an aspect here and there while leaving the fundamental basis unchanged. In this way, the central tenet of the story cannot be challenged, thus portraying sincerity, while the less obvious enhancements to the claim foster a diverging view of the facts. An additional benefit of this approach is that it is virtually impossible to prove intent to deceive. Recall my story of the seven foot hammerhead shark that became a fifteen footer with retelling over the course of time? There really was a hammerhead (fact) and we really did need to evacuate the area (fact) and it was big (fact)—it just was not as big as I came to communicate with the passing of time. Did I purposely intend to deceive those to whom I told the tale, or was I guilty only of being overly enthusiastic about the event? How can the average consumer of information possibly tell the difference? Let us look at a couple of such examples of exaggeration in the political arena with an eye for identifying those red flags that indicate when embellishment may at work: numbers, measures, and extreme qualifiers.

1) <u>Michele Bachmann</u>—"The president of the United States will be taking a trip over to India that is expected to cost the taxpayers $200 million a day."

Rep. Bachmann, while not the first to make this particular claim, is credited with discussing it as an indication of Obama's excessive spending during an interview with Anderson Cooper on CNN on November 3, 2010, as well as in subsequent public speeches. She attributes this enormous daily cost to an entourage numbering in the thousands, all lodging at posh five-star hotels, as well as to the high cost of secret service and military protection.

To reasonably evaluate the veracity of this statement, we first need to consider from where the information supporting this claim arose. A little detective work easily reveals that this claim was inspired by a single newspaper article from November 3, 2010 published by the Press Trust of India and attributed to an unidentified Maharashtra Government official who claimed he was privy to the real costs of the visit. The article said:

> The huge amount of around $200 million would be spent on security, stay and other aspects of the Presidential visit," a top official of the Maharashtra Government privy to the arrangements for the high-profile visit said. About 3,000 people including Secret Service agents, U.S. government officials and journalists would accompany the President.

There are no other published sources of this information available, and the figures were flatly denied by White House spokesman. Therefore, this claim constitutes hearsay, which is a convenient way to embellish facts without outright lying. Ms. Bachmann read a news report which she understood to be true. It is not necessarily deception to misconstrue information and then inadvertently pass it along. How can we possibly prove what Ms Bachmann understood about the validity of the report? What proof do we have that the originator of the quote actually understood the true costs of the venture? What other facts could we check to ascertain whether this information about the costing of the trip is correct?

It is important to note that unusually large numbers are likely candidates for exaggeration. It is actually must less common for extreme spending events to occur than one might think, since most expenditure in government needs to be vetted and fall within the budget. Although true cost numbers of current presidential trips are not released for security reasons, a look at past presidential foreign excursions suggests that the $200 million per day figure is probably an order of magnitude off base. Security and transportation for all presidential foreign missions is indeed extremely costly, and the scope of the cost depends upon the region and the nature of the trip. However, even the most expensive trips in recent history seldom go above $10 million per day. Furthermore, the claim of 3000 in the entourage would make this the largest foreign trip in history (excluding reporters and other independent attendees who pay their own way). With only 800 rooms claimed to be reserved, one might also wonder at the high room occupancy required to cram so many people into so few rooms.

In short, while there is no way to prove or disprove these numbers, a modicum of deductive logic suggests the numbers do not likely reflect a reasonable price tag for any otherwise routine foreign visit. It is clear that Bachmann could not have made an attempt to corroborate the claims prior to sharing them publicly, as it took me approximately 10 minutes to find the source of the numbers and verify that there were no other public sources of the information. Obviously, we can accuse her of being irresponsible by sharing uncorroborated figures, but can we identify any specific intent to deceive in her actions? That is a tough ask–the only clear signals we have that this might be a deceptive ploy come from highly exaggerated figures and an apparent failure to consider her source of the information. Nonetheless, a politician does not need to lie directly to do a disservice to the voting public. If the general public does not take it upon themselves to question the numbers, the end result is an unfounded claim that builds negative sentiment in the voting public. That is why exaggeration is such a powerful tool in the political arena.

2) Paul Ryan—"President Barack Obama has doubled the size of government since he took office."

Wisconsin Representative and former Vice Presidential candidate Paul Ryan has been heralded in the DC crowd as the consummate number cruncher, the man with the magic marker that can construct the budget plan we have all been waiting for to deliver us from the burden of the deficit. So when he posted this statement in April of 2012 to a congressional web page dedicated to explaining his budget plan, most people had little reason to doubt his claim. Unfortunately, it also happens to be a gross exaggeration of the truth.

The key red flag here is the claim of *doubling*. The use of quantitative measures is good for expressing relative size differences as long as you understand the definition of the measures you use. Doubling the size of government literally means a 100% increase in employment, which is a large enough change to dominate the employment statistics. To assess this possibility, there are two ways we can interpret Ryan's claim of doubling the size of government—one involves federal outlays (the amount of money the government spends) and the other involves the physical size of government (the number of employees). According to the Congressional Budget Office, the federal outlays between when Obama took office in 2009 and the April 2012 time frame during which this statement was posted showed an increase of about 6%. There is no form of math on the planet that would consider a 6% increase as doubling. In fact, if we use the federal outlays as a percentage of gross domestic product, there is actually a decline in the size of government of about 1.4% between 2009 and 2012.

The second factor, number of government employees, did

undergo more growth during Obama's time in office than the outlays, but still never topped 10%. That puts the Ryan claims about an order of magnitude over the top, a gross exaggeration in any book!

This example demonstrates poor accounting practices and is especially disappointing considering the hype and hope around Ryan's budget plan. Applying the principles of reason and logic, we can easily deduce that interpretation of any claims that involve specific measures should always start with consideration of the numbers themselves. It is fairly common for individuals to exaggerate claims whenever numbers are involved. In this case, even if we consider all federal employees instead of just those involved directly with government, the number in 2009 was approximately 2,790,000. For the workforce to have doubled in size would mean more than 5 million workers on the books by 2012—just over 4% of the total fulltime workforce in the US for that year—but in fact the roster only rose to just over 2.8 million. While we cannot know for certain whether Mr. Ryan made this exaggerated claim with specific intent to deceive, we can say his claims are not supported by the facts and thus create an impression that differs markedly from reality.

3) <u>Howard Dean</u>—"All the really great programs in American history, Social Security, was done without Republicans. Medicare was done without Republican support until the last vote where they realized they had to get on board."

This statement, made to Rachel Maddow on MSNBC on August 25, 2009, was in reference to a query about whether Mr. Dean was concerned that the health care reform bill might be in trouble without bipartisan support. It portrays the use of an *extreme qualifier*—phrases like all, never, and always. They function to lead the audience to believe that there is less variability or controversy around the event in question than actually exists. In real life, few events in government ever truly carn a legitimate use of an extreme qualifier, but their use can be extremely powerful in producing an unfounded bias in perception.

Dean's sentiment perpetuates a longstanding stereotype that Republicans are against legislation that benefits the masses, the poor, the elderly, and that they want to do away with entitlement programs. However, history is not entirely on Dean's side where this statement is concerned. The Social Security Act under President Franklin D Roosevelt was voted into law in 1935 with significant Republican support in both the House and the Senate. Furthermore, the Medicare bill was signed into law by Lyndon B. Johnson 30 years later with nearly a 50-50 split by Republicans (43% of Senate Republicans and 51% of House Republicans voting in support). And while there was early reluctance by some Republicans around the bill, there was a vocal minority who supported it and even worked to increase the scope of the Bill.

What is the consequence of Dean's use of the extreme qualifier in this example? It perpetuates a false interpretation of events that works against solution and change. Certainly, it is not true that all great programs in America were done without Republican support. In fact, there are also examples of great programs that were accomplished with little Democratic support. The majority of work on important national programs is actually accomplished by cooperation across the aisle, even today in one of the most divided Congress in more history. Therefore, the extreme qualifier approach exaggerates the cultural bias between parties, in this case serving to allow the Democratic Party to claim leadership of the progressive legislative acts of the past and reinforce representation of core values of the party's philosophical principles. The functional significance is to foster the societal penchant for overestimating the difference between groups we discussed in Chapter 5. However, when it comes to ascertaining the truth, such a ploy might be useful for solidifying the party base, but it does little to either promote transparent discussion or to accurately inform the voting public on important issues.

Fall Out: Exaggeration is one of the most insidious techniques available for defaming one's political opponent, but at least it is one that is quite easy to verify and debunk. As a public, it should be somewhat insulting for us to have our prospective leaders distort and embellish the facts and figures. We would not accept such behavior from our accountants, our retirement fund investors, or the CEO of our workplace, and yet we do not hold those who aspire to the highest offices in the land to the same level of accountability. Therefore, while exaggeration is by nature a disingenuous approach, the consumer of information must share at least some of the culpability in the success of this tactical maneuver.

Pick a Card, Any Card...

The third major manner in which politicians can be disingenuous without telling an out and out word lie is to employ a slight of hand technique known as *misleading emphasis*. As with any conjuring trick, where you always end up picking the card the magician wanted you to, politicians have elevated the act of misdirection to an art form. The purpose here is to place so much emphasis on one aspect of a story or statement that the listener never notices that there is additional information available that can alter the interpretation of events. This is a very effective form of context management in that the deception is subtle enough to avoid detection and the audience is left with a satisfying sense of having been told the whole truth. Furthermore, it puts the speaker in a highly defensible position since the effects of the emphasis tend to be picked up and propagated more by the downstream communicators than by any obvious act of deception by the speaker themselves; that is, the media and pundits tend to focus only on those aspects of the story that were emphasized, and the full context gets further removed from the picture with the act of retelling through no fault of the person who originated the statement.

Here are some examples that demonstrate misplaced emphasis

and the impact such a tactic can have on the conclusions drawn by the listening public. In each example, note that the statements being made gain credibility by the selective use of highlighting those areas that corroborate the point being made.

1) <u>Nancy Pelosi</u>—"More private-sector jobs were created in the first eight months of 2010 than in the eight years of the Bush administration."

This bold statement was made to Keith Olbermann during an MSNBC interview on October 21, 2010. It is based upon an analysis of employment figures at the start and end of George W. Bush's two terms (an eight year period) which showed a net loss of close to 700,000 private sector jobs, compared to an eight month period in the middle of Obama's first terms during which there was a net growth of just over 800,000 jobs.

The deception here is not in the facts and numbers themselves, but in the selective nature of calculation and reporting of the data. While it is true that there was an increase in job creation during 2010, the decision to not look across all of Obama's first term certainly results in a highly skewed result. In reality, there was a net loss of more than 3,000,000 jobs across his time in office up until that point, as jobs were still bleeding at a high rate during the first several months of the Obama administration. Furthermore, if both government and private sector jobs were included in the analysis, Bush would have outstripped Obama with overall gains of over a million from 2001-2008, compared to less than 600,000 under Obama for 2010.

This is an artful example of distorting the truth by creatively using facts, figures, and statistics. While there is nothing numerically or factually untrue about this statement, it is still misleading because the comparison base is inequitable. You cannot say that you are better than someone else because you had one good period unless you also apply the same selectivity in measurement to the other (i.e., compare high to high and low to low). I remember being floored when I was a student hearing a lecture by a statistician who said "If you do good statistics on these data, there is no difference between groups, but then again, if you do really good statistics, you can find a big effect." Statistics themselves are unbiased but the statistician who employs them might not be! If you recall our discussion about bias, reliability, and rigor of the scientific method, then the negative impact that violating those principles can have on the interpretation should be obvious. Therefore, this is an example of a truthful statement that misleads because it "fiddles the figures" in a biased fashion designed to make one period of time outweigh another without applying balanced analysis across the groups being assessed. While we cannot prove this is a direct lie because we cannot be certain about the underlying motivation (i.e., intent to deceive), the method of analysis employed at the very least represents substandard reporting. More importantly, if the average consumer of information listens to statements such as this without logically considering the broader perspective, including the goals and ambitions of the speakers themselves, it is a simple matter to buy into the misleading claims without ever being aware there is an underlying distortion of facts.

2) <u>Mitt Romney</u>—"I saw a story today that one of the great manufacturers in this state, Jeep, now owned by the Italians, is thinking of moving all production to China."

Romney made this statement during a speech in Defiance, Ohio on October 25, 2012, allegedly after reading a report to this effect. The Chrysler Group issued a denial and clarified that a manufacturing plant would open in China, since imports are prohibited, but that this would not affect US manufacturing jobs. Rather, it would actually expand Jeep's footprint and global revenues allowing for increased investment in US manufacturing.

One could argue that Romney did not purposefully lie with this statement, as he merely repeated a story that suggested a *potential* move that could replace production in the US. However, the Romney campaign went on, even after the Chrysler Group clarified the scenario, to create an ad centered on this false claim.

> *Obama took GM and Chrysler into bankruptcy and sold Chrysler to Italians who are going to build Jeeps in China. Mitt Romney will fight for every American job.*

Notice that now the emphasis has shifted to make it appear that production *will* occur in China, without qualifying that it will be in addition to domestic production. While the wording of this ad does not explicitly state that the plan to build Jeeps in China will eliminate American jobs, the immediate juxtaposition with the statement that Romney will fight for jobs in the US drives the meaning in that direction. And of course Romney's earlier statements already placed emphasis on the potential impact on US production. Furthermore, the large number of Romney supporters who continued to believe that Jeep would be moving American jobs to China reflects the consequences of the failure to employ even vestigial rational ability to statements made during political campaigns. Hence, this is support for my opening statement in this chapter that dishonest politicians seldom reap significant consequences for their actions, especially when voters do not apply their intelligence to the plethora of claims and allegations that fly about during any campaign.

Fall Out: Misplacing the emphasis is a very slick and effective means of influencing public opinion because it appears to present a very factually based, carefully considered interpretation of a publicly acknowledged event. In these examples, using government figures and newspaper headlines that are available for public inspection provides a level of apparent legitimacy, and since the average consumer of information usually fails to follow up on the original source, they are usually willing to accept the suppositions without further question. Add to that the ploy of emphasizing one aspect of the story in order to overshadow others, and you end up with a powerful tool for creating false conclusions. The ramifications go well beyond just impacting your decision of who you will vote for in any given election; they also color our sense of fundamental underlying issues that have widespread global effect, including consumer confidence in the strength of the American economy. Since the stock market rises and falls on the least little hiccup on the financial stage, it is in no one's best interest (except perhaps the myopic politicians themselves) to twist the truth in this manner.

Great Works of Fiction

My assessment of political posturing would not be complete without mentioning that outright lies and fabrications are certainly well represented within the public arena. While it is obviously riskier for political figures to directly lie, there are times when it appears such opportunities are just too attractive for them to resist. Here are two recent examples of unfounded claims that clearly expose the political agendas of their authors.

1) <u>Sen. Harry Reid</u>—"Romney did not pay taxes for 10 years."
Sen. Reid made this inflammatory statement to the Huffington Post on July 31, 2012, and a similar one later to the Senate on August 2, 2012. Sen. Reid claimed that a Bain Capital insider with knowledge of Romney's personal information told him confidentially that Mr. Romney did not pay any taxes for a 10 year period. Reid also cited Romney's reluctance to release his tax returns as proof that he in fact did not pay taxes.

As we know, he has refused to release his tax returns. If a person coming before this body wanted

137

> *to be a Cabinet officer, he couldn't be if he had the same refusal Mitt Romney does about tax returns. So the word is out that he has not paid any taxes for 10 years. Let him prove he has paid taxes, because he has not.*

While the request to provide tax return information from a presidential candidate is a legitimate one, this particular statement borders on the ridiculous and flies straight in the face of Einstein's famous quote "absence of evidence is not evidence of absence." We do not live in a society where we can be accused of anything without proof and are then given the burden of demonstrating our innocence (remember our earlier discussion about slander, libel, and defamation of character). We are not required to prove our innocence in a court of law and neither should we be in the court of public opinion.

Here is an opportunity for us to employ deductive reasoning to ferret out the likely truth, since we do not have access to the documents that would definitively settle the matter. Here is what we do know—while Romney only released his tax returns for 2010 and 2011, he did pay around 14% taxes during those years, largely on investment income. Without access to tax returns from previous years, it is impossible to verify the truth or falsehood of Sen. Reid's claim for earlier tax years. However, according to the Polifact.com assessment of IRS studies on the country's highest income earners, it is extremely rare for individuals to pay no taxes at all. Therefore, it is possible but unlikely that Romney would be among the relatively small number of individuals who paid little or no taxes during the previous years. Reid made his allegation with full disclosure that he heard it from a source he could not disclose, not that he had seen and evaluated definitive evidence of tax evasion. Any claim based upon hearsay is of course suspect to begin with, even without political gains at stake. Furthermore, Reid's claim that Romney did not address his tax responsibilities served a purpose to mobilize public opinion against the candidate, whether it was founded on facts or not. All of these things taken together suggest that Reid's claim was unsupported and not representative of the information we do have available on Mr. Romney's behavior in the recent past.

As before, we cannot definitively prove that Sen. Reid knowingly lied, but he did publicly reveal information from an anonymous source without any corroborating evidence. The failure to fact check the claim in the slightest is at best irresponsible and, at its most nefarious, a deliberate attempt to paint an unfavorable picture of Mr. Romney designed to have a negative impact on his campaign chances. It is reasonable for Americans to demand that there be verifiable proof around such allegations, particularly when they involve an individual whom we are considering for the highest office in the land. However, there is some evidence here that Sen. Reid's personal beliefs about Mr. Romney may have outweighed his execution of reasonable judgment. This is a good example of a situation where, whatever the truth may in fact be, the apparent aim of the statement was to defame the character of a candidate, and therefore it falls well outside of honest behavior. Politics is not a religious organization where one is expected to take on faith the preaching of its leaders. As a democratic state, we should demand more factually grounded actions from our representatives, rather than accepting claims based upon on their gut feelings or personal biases.

4) Sarah Palin—coining the term "Death Panels"

While conservative concern over the possibility that euthanasia might be covered by the Patient Protection and Affordable Care Act (AKA Obamacare) predates her allegation, former Governor Palin is credited with coining the term "death panel." In a posting to her Facebook page on August 7, 2009, Gov. Palin said:

> *The America I know and love is not one in which*
> *my parents or my baby with Down Syndrome will*

> *have to stand in front of Obama's 'death panel' so his bureaucrats can decide, based on a subjective judgment of their 'level of productivity in society,' whether they are worthy of health care. Such a system is downright evil.*

There is nothing in the Obamacare plan that promotes, allows for, or covers euthanasia, although there is insurance coverage for end-of-life counseling for the terminally ill, defined as assistance with health and psychological management of an impending death, not for preparing to instigate that death. It also covers counseling around living wills and do-not-resuscitate orders that are in common use when a person undergoes surgery or any procedure requiring general anesthesia. The fear of government enforced euthanasia was also touted by other conservatives, including unfounded claims that mandatory reviews for seniors every five years would be required to determine if they should end their lives sooner. In addition, comparison of the healthcare plan to atrocities committed under Nazi Germany helped fuel paranoia around the scope of power the government would have under such a scenario.

The rampant spread of the death panel concept is an excellent example of employing psychological tools to promote societal hysteria and misinformation. Almost no one in the general public read the actual health care document, which is fair enough considering it is well over a thousand pages long and difficult to understand for the average person. Therefore, it was easy to make statements about its content and purpose that were not likely to be fact checked by the average American. The situation was ripe for fear mongering and unfounded claims that would tap into societal biases and thus require little proof to be believed. While everyone is entitled to their own interpretations of information, and to express those opinions in public, the line has to be drawn when the concepts being promulgated have no basis at all in fact.

Disseminating misinformation about death panels must therefore be defined as a blatant act of dishonesty with inherent intent to deceive.

As with the other examples cover so far, this type of ploy is very effective in promulgating negative interpretations of an opponent's policies. At the time of this writing, no one is using the phrase "death panel" much anymore, and yet there is a pervasive and extremely strong sense of fear and paranoia from some political groups about the implementation of the Affordable Care Act. Tea Party and other conservatives have now only to make statements such as "Obamacare is going to destroy our economy" and with no supportive evidence at all, many in our society believe this is a true claim.

In Fighting, Delusion, and Self Promotion

Politics are a hotbed of misinformation and distortion across party lines, some of which are quite funny if you can get past the mindset that the statements represent. These bloopers are not always aimed at the other side. Sometimes there is "in fighting" within a party. Sometimes the statements do not serve a party purpose but are designed solely for self-promotion. In both cases, it is the American voter who often gets caught in the cross-fire.

I would like to finish up this chapter with a quick review of some other entertaining comments that have popped out of the mouths of politicians and their spokespeople over the past couple of years. Note that these were chosen for how outlandishly exempt from the truth I found the statements to be, without regard to party lines, so there will not be an equitable political division here. As you peruse these disingenuous examples, see how many red flags you notice that suggest the statement might not be entirely accurate, and consider what logical steps you could employ to ascertain the underlying truth.

Lost in Space

<u>Allen West</u>—"I believe there's about 78 to 81 members of the Democrat Party who are members of the Communist Party. ... It is called the Congressional Progressive Caucus."

This statement was made to a moderator during a town hall meeting in Florida on April 10, 2012. West and his supporters believe that the Congressional Progressive Congress opposes capitalism and the free market, are supporters of Fidel Castro, and that they encourage redistribution of wealth. When queried further on his claim, he stated he was not sure whether they were communists or socialists, and that the label should not matter. Alas, in the real world and in a court of law, the label does matter. In truth, not one of the Congressional Progressive Caucus is a member of the Communist party. That makes Mr. West either a liar spreading inflammatory and libelous material about his colleagues, or just plain wrong and ignorant about his facts.

<u>John Sununu</u> (former New Hampshire Governor)—"President Obama outsourced a major portion of the U.S. space program to the Russians."

This statement was made to CNN on July 16, 2012 as a parry to continued criticisms of Mitt Romney's policy on outsourcing US jobs while he was CEO of Bain Capital. While Obama did close and lock the door on the space shuttle program, the plan for its retirement was initiated by President George W. Bush in 2004. In fact, much public controversy and concern over cessation of the program was expressed in the media throughout the years preceding its ultimate demise, and therefore it was a matter of public note. Since it follows that the intent of the statement was to blame Obama for the termination of the program and the subsequent reliance upon Russian space launches for missions to the international space station, regardless of this publicly available information, this comment must logically be construed as a thinly veiled attempt at politically motivated deception.

Extreme Matters

<u>Governor Scott Walker</u>—"We just had someone last week...near a school kill someone with a bow and arrow."

In a discussion around gun control issues on January 10, 2013, Wisconsin Governor Walker told the press that focusing on the weapon itself when reacting to violent crimes takes attention away from addressing the underlying nature of the individuals who commit these acts. He is most likely correct. However, his argument for such took a decidedly bad turn when he cited a nonexistent event to back up his claims. He was referring to a domestic altercation that took place on January 3, 2013 in which a son allegedly shot an arrow at his father. The arrow struck a car (not the father) and no one was killed. The home in question was 2.5 miles from a school and in fact had nothing to do with a school (by that standard, almost everything that happens is near a school!). This misstatement, and the resultant public ridicule it inspired, resulted in a missed opportunity to make a cogent argument for stronger measures around mental health as prevention to violence.

<u>Rand Paul</u>—"The court struck Clinton down for trying this, and I am afraid that President Obama may have this king complex sort of developing, and we're going to make sure that it doesn't happen."

Kentucky Senator Rand Paul expressed outrage at President Obama's history of using executive orders, especially those around gun control measures, during a Fox News interview with Sean Hannity on January 16, 2013. Paul likened the use of executive orders to an arrogant abuse of power. Interestingly, according to the Federal Archives, Obama has so far in his time in office employed executive privilege about the same as, or slightly less than, any president in recent history. As of the time of Sen Paul's statement, Obama had written 143 executive orders. His predecessor, George W. Bush, invoked executive privilege 290 times, albeit it across two full terms in office, putting Obama slightly ahead in the average order count. George H. Bush wrote 165 executive orders during his one term presidency, whereas Ronald Reagan comes in first with a total of 380 executive orders during his two terms in office. Even Bill Clinton was more prolific, with a total of 363 executive orders across two terms. And Obama's not even the first one to try and address gun control through limiting access to assault-style weapons. Both George H. Bush and Bill Clinton signed executive orders putting limits on the types of weapons that could be imported and/or owned by private citizens. It thus seems that Obama is being less kingly than the standards set by those who came before him.

Ye of Little Faith

Fred Karger—"If a President Romney got a call from the president of the (Mormon Church), he has no choice but to obey. It is obedience over family and country."

Republican Karger of California expressed concern during an interview with the Guardian on October 15, 2011, that Mitt Romney's presidency would be subsumed by his loyalty to the Mormon Church. He made this claim based upon his understanding of the doctrine of obedience to church principles in the Mormon faith (apparently unlike any other religion?), and the belief that such adherence to faith would put the US government in the hands of a religious organization. Here is what the Church of Latter Day Saints actually says on its website:

> *Elected officials who are Latter-day Saints make their own decisions and may not necessarily be in agreement with one another or even with a publicly stated church position. While the church may communicate its views to them, as it may to any other elected official, it recognizes that these officials still must make their own choices based on*

*their best judgment and with consideration of the
constituencies whom they were elected to represent.*

If obedience to the Church of Latter Day Saints is a
fundamental requirement, then the message is frighteningly clear:
Go forth and represent in government as your populace, not your
Church, requires. I am not aware of any other religion that makes
a statement so reflective of the separation of Church and State as
this, so Karger's representation of the facts is way off base.

Mike Huckabee—The signers of the Declaration of Independence
were "brave people, most of whom, by the way, were clergymen."

This is a bit of an old one, made during the Republican debate in
October of 2007, but it so elegantly reflects a point I covered in the
previous chapter that I needed to include it. So many politicians,
especially those of conservative bent, believe and promulgate a
fiction around our founding fathers and the role of religion in the
establishment of this country. A total of fifty-six individuals are
credited with contributing to the writing of the Declaration of
Independence. Only one of those individuals was a clergyman.
By no math known on the planet does 1.7% of the total constitute
most of any group. It may be time for Mr. Huckabee to get some
tutoring in remedial math!

My Own Little World

Obama Campaign website—"During the debates, Mitt Romney
told America how he plans to pay for those tax cuts he wants to
give America's wealthiest tax payers... by killing Big Bird! We've
got to stop this guy."

This posting on the Obama campaign website during the run
up to the 2012 election was inspired by a statement made by Mitt
Romney during the October 3, 2012 Presidential debate. The clear
intent of this ad is to create the impression that Romney wants to

dismantle the Sesame Street franchise while diverting resources to his wealthy cronies. Here is what Mr. Romney actually said during the debate:

> *I like PBS. I love Big Bird. ...But I am not going to keep on spending money on things to borrow money from China to pay for.*

Far from being a death sentence on Big Bird, reducing or eliminating federal support of the Sesame Street franchise would have a minor effects, as only 6-8% of Sesame Street's funding comes from the federal government. Even if federal support for this popular cultural icon were terminated, the prognosis for a long and healthy life for the large yellow avian would be very good. This is an excellent example of misplaced emphasis and exaggeration both at work. Such ploys tend to result in clever sound bites that effectively camouflage the broader message—in this case, that our federal spending needs to be curtailed in order to address our increasing debt obligation to large foreign powers.

Donald Trump—"President Obama has spent over $2 million in legal fees defending lawsuits about his birth certificate... and President Obama's grandmother in Kenya said he was born in Kenya and she was there and witnessed the birth."

Donald Trump emerged throughout the run up to the 2012 presidential election as a provocative voice of dissension for the conservative segments of the country. A highly vocal leader of the *birther* movement, Trump took every opportunity to cast doubt on the birth place of President Obama, as if his credentials would not have been rigorously investigated by government vetting groups prior to his candidacy. This particular allegation from an April 7, 2011 interview to NBC was just one of the many aspersions he cast before the American public. The $2 million number he cites represents the sum total costs of all of the legal expenses the Obama team paid during the campaign. While it is unclear for what the specific fees were charged, it is unbelievable to think that the entire amount went for fees related to the birth certificate issue, especially since all candidates run up hefty legal bills during campaigns.

What we do know is that Obama posted his official certificate of live birth originating in Hawaii on the internet. It has been examined and verified by numerous independent parties. It contains essentially the same information as my own birth certificate, with which I have obtained a social security number, driver's license, marriage license, and passport with no drama and no accusations of falsification. This example of misplaced emphasis serves to focus the public on the issue of legal fees to discredit the documents provided to show proof of birth. To intentionally incite dissension in the absence of evidence, and to continually deny the proof laid before you because it does not serve your own ends, are amongst the most profound forms of dishonesty in politics.

Forgot the Camera was Rolling

Hillary Clinton—"I remember landing under sniper fire. There was supposed to be some kind of a greeting ceremony at the airport, but instead we just ran with our heads down to get into the vehicles to get to our base."

Mrs. Clinton shared this memory of her time as First Lady landing in Bosnia in 1996 in a foreign policy speech in DC on March 17, 2008. The problem is that news footage of the event shows her landing safely and without mishap, and being greeted by a welcoming contingent that included a young girl. Funny thing about memory, it is so often distorted in our minds with retelling over the years, subject to embellishment and grandiosity. To her credit, Mrs. Clinton subsequently retracted the statement and admitted her mistake. Perhaps in this case there was no direct intent to deceive, but the fact remains that her statement was false and a simple check of the news archives could have uncovered the discrepancy even in the absence of her admission.

Debbie Wasserman Schulz—"I didn't say [Oren] said that. That comment was reported by a conservative newspaper. It is not surprising that they would deliberately misquote me."

Ms. Schulz, the Democratic National Committee chair, reportedly repeated a statement that she attributed to the Israeli ambassador during a pre-convention speech. When questioned about it during a Fox News during interview on September 4, 2012, she denied that she made the statement and accused the media of distorting her words. Luckily, in this modern day and age we typically have access to recordings of such events. Here's what Ms. Schulz actually said in that speech:

> *We know, and I've heard no less than Ambassador Michael Oren say this, that what the Republicans are doing is dangerous for Israel.*

There does not appear to be any way to interpret this contradiction as anything other than an attempt to extricate herself from an embarrassing situation by lying about what she said. Politicians (and all public figures for that matter) would do well to remember that every microphone is potentially a live microphone, and virtually every audience member has a cell phone that can record video, preserving what they say for later inspection.

Oops, I Should Have Fact Checked First

Senator Tammy Baldwin—"is fighting for a country where opportunity exists for everyone -- not just the 7,000 millionaires who gamed the system to pay no income taxes on their fortunes."

While this statement made in a campaign e-mail on September 22, 2012 is based upon popularized data from a 2011 Tax Policy

Center report, these data were refuted by several legitimate sources prior to Sen. Baldwin making this statement. The number of people paying little or no federal income taxes for the year in question was actually closer to around 1400, and included people who had business losses, income received in foreign markets, tax-exempt income from municipal bonds, as well as a variety of other legitimate deductions available to all US tax payers. This example again highlights the impact of exaggeration to gain political ground around a controversial issue. In this case, Senator Baldwin may have been justified in her initial citing, but she also should have heeded the follow up reports that more accurately reflected the statistics instead of continuing to promulgate such distorted information.

<u>Governor Rick Perry</u>—"Obama has added $16 trillion to the federal debt."

In a tweet issued on September 21, 2012, Texas Gov. Perry informed the nation that President Obama increased the national debt by... the actual size of the national debt. In truth, the debt increased a little over $5 trillion during Obama's tenure in office. There is no need to dissect this one in depth. While Perry obviously made a false statement, based upon the number of gaffes and misquotes and incorrect statements he made during his run for the Republican nomination, I am going to chalk this one up to just being plain wrong rather than a purposeful attempt to deceive!

And the Big Loser is...

Without a doubt, the world of politics is a rich and prolific wellspring of lies, misinformation, and wildly inaccurate information. Unfortunately, it is us, the average voters, who most pay the price of rampant deception. But you do not need to be a loser in the information game. In this modern day, there is no longer any reason for the average person to take what any politician says on faith when it is possible to apply just a little bit of logic, reason, and objective thinking to any political claim or statement. Numerous websites, like Politifact.com and The Fact Checker (Washington Post), do a fairly good job of conducting the research for you. They present the facts with largely unbiased discussion around the truth or falsehood. If you use these sources as a starting point and then probe a little deeper on your own, you will likely come up with a much more accurate reflection of the truth than you would otherwise receive.

As a result of the amount of purposely neglectful misrepresentation inherent in the process, we should apply the staunchest objective criteria to politicians more than any other public figures in our society. Since that rarely happens, I put the blame for politicians getting away with disingenuous behaviors squarely on the shoulders of the American public. We listen to these people largely without discernment, and few of us bother to check the facts or consider whether there might be some self-serving purpose to the information a politician is presenting. And even when we know they are lying or distorting the truth, we vote for them anyway. Why so few of them would be motivated to walk a more honest line when their wild claims so effectively achieve their goals is not hard to understand. The examples I included in this chapter are at times hilarious, but the undercurrent of corruption and decay that these examples represent should not be overlooked. We get what we are willing to tolerate out of these politicians. If you want the truth, it is up to you to use your intelligence and healthy skepticism to evaluate what you hear and then start demanding more honesty from our public representatives.

CHAPTER 8 ══════════════════

Rhetoric Gone Wild:
Lies in the Media and Popular Culture

W hen I was a kid (back in the dark ages of the 1960's), domestic and world news came in only two flavors: either from print media (newspapers, magazines) or from special slots set aside in your daily television programming for the evening and late night news. Ever since the advent of cable service and the internet with digital news wires, we have had continuous access to news. The advantage is that we now have the capacity to keep abreast of important domestic and global events at the touch of a button. The bad news is that we also get a lot of drivel and pontification on television designed to fill up all the spare space that is not dedicated to emerging disasters, threats, celebrity scandals, sports results, or political rhetoric. Hence the invention of cable news talk shows and discussion panels populated by experts willing to tell you their opinions on just about anything whether you want to know or not.

In fact, I have recently noticed that it is difficult to actually find *real* news in the morning. The closest thing I have found on a national level to a news digest is Headline News that does exactly what the title suggests—provides an endless repeating loop of headlines in the news without particular depth of coverage on any given topic. At least from this format, I can hear about something that might be of interest, and then I do what any discerning consumer who wants to know the actual scoop does—I reach for the internet and read the various news articles available on that topic.

But back to my point—the advent of nonstop news coverage has created a whole new breed of pundit. Gone are the thoughtful measured days of Cronkite and Murrow who gravely provided us the facts with a minimum of bias and bluster about their own opinions. These gentlemen were objective purveyors of news events that were important for any self-respecting American to know. When they spoke to us each night, we had little trouble believing that we were being told the truth. They at least appeared to have our interests at heart and were perhaps not being so mercilessly driven by ratings and other secular interests. Theirs was a noble calling....

Back to present day. Cable news is all about ratings. It is about teams of pundits hawking the political views of their network and their constituency. It is about following the most sensational stories and being the first to drop breaking news into our laps, whether it be the status of the Nicole Smith baby custody battle or the stand your ground law in Florida being used to defend the death of a teen aged boy or the important political news that Mitt Romney once transported the family dog on top of his car during a road trip. And when real news happens, like an attack on a US embassy in Libya or the murder of first graders at an elementary school in Connecticut, the important information is subsumed by a barrage of opinion coming from every panel discussant in the vicinity. Unfortunately, the members of such panels are often working from partial or incorrect information, and may have their own misconceptions about the nature of what they are discussing. The result is a hodge-podge of rumor and rhetoric that is nearly impossible to decipher into a coherent narrative.

Obviously, this is a sore spot for me. I am severely disappointed that an invention with such potential for increasing knowledge and information sharing has been so perverted. And I am frustrated that the careful reporting techniques of the past have largely given way to the goal of capturing the lion's share of the market without capturing the viewer's intellect as well. But on the bright side, the nature of today's media and mode of disseminating information has given me plenty of material for this chapter, as along with the increased access to information comes the opportunity for distortion, misinformation, and occasionally outright lying!

So let us apply the principles of rational judgment to examine some well-known personalities who capitalize upon the inherent trust that we, the public, place upon those in the spotlight, and see how well they measure up to our standards.

Pundits in the Porridge

The unfortunate reality we need to accept is that news networks are no longer unbiased and dedicated to factual presentation of information. Our national news providers are now known for their political leanings and it shows in the type of reporting they do, the types of stories they cover, and the slant they put on discussions of those stories. Of the three major cable networks, Fox News without a doubt falls on the conservative side of the mix, MSNBC leans significantly liberal, and CNN hugs closer to the middle with a definite leftward tilt. One of the things I find the most amusing is that each network maligns the others for their biased reporting while being blind to their own. For example, Fox News consistently and often (I mean *ad nauseum*!) refers to the others as "mainstream media." Hello?! Does not their viewing audience comprise about 50% of the market share? I would think that makes them fairly mainstream. But then again, they also use the term "liberal media" which I guess means everyone but them. To this I typically shout at the TV "Who cares which way you lean? You're all supposed to tell us the NEWS, not your opinions!!"

Alas, my pleas for unbiased reporting go unanswered, although I must admit that every network has some folks who are better at providing factual information than others. Of course, they are much less interesting to read about and do not really fit with the spirit of this book, so I will devote this section to highlighting those pundits who have made the most incorrect and/or outrageous claims over the recent past and yet remain incredibly popular within their own base. In other words, I have chosen those personas who receive more than the occasional "Four Pinocchios" or "Pants on Fire" or other ratings of lies and misinformation by fact checking organizations. For consistency of comparison, I will specifically highlight here some gems of falsehood identified by Poltifact.com, not because they are necessarily superior to any other fact checking agency, but because they regularly include pundits in their analyses more than some of the others. They also list quotes covering the breadth of ratings from true to false, and do not promote an overtly obvious political leaning in how they deal with their subjects.

Rachel Maddow

Ms. Maddow is a well-known liberal personality on MSNBC and host of the Rachel Maddow Show. I was disappointed to place her in this list as I had always found her to speak reasonably, to cover subjects thoughtfully, and to convey confidence in her statements. She makes the list, not so much because she says outrageous unsubstantiated things or engages in media trolling, but because her own fact checking comes up short in areas where she has routinely criticized others. In a review of fifteen recent statements she made during 2012, she scored "false" or "mostly false" 47% of the time. Ms. Maddow may likely be unimpressed with this statistic, as she herself attacked Politifact for several examples of alleged inaccuracies in their reporting. Ironically, her criticism of Politifact for a "mostly false" rating about an anti-abortion group's claim that the White House screens unborn babies as part of their security process only serves to focus the spotlight on herself:

- *Mostly? You can get something 'wildly' wrong and still only be mostly wrong about it? What does it take to get a False rating at a Politifact?" (May 10, 2012, The Rachel Maddow Show).*

Fair enough I say, but let us take a look at what it took for the fact checking organization to grant Ms. Maddow a false rating for her own statements. Here are some recent quotes she made that could have done with a second look before she released them.

- *Despite what you may have heard about Wisconsin's finances, Wisconsin is on track to have a budget surplus this year.(Feb 17, 2011, Rachel Maddow Show)*

The independent Legislative Fiscal Bureau report she cited did predict a surplus in the general fund of about $121 million, but the memo went on to describe outstanding commitments to Medicaid and other obligations that had yet to be paid, thereby putting the state at a projected deficit of about $137 million. Good journalistic reporting requires reading the entire document.

- *Fox News said the New Black Panther Party decided the election for Barack Obama.(Dec 15, 2010, David Letterman Show)*

Fox News did talk extensively about the dismissal of a civil action against several members of the New Black Panther party for alleged voter intimidation tactics during the 2008 election. They discussed it in terms of legal, racial, and media coverage issues. They did not mention the potential impact on the election or any other political function. Unfortunately for Ms. Maddow, this statement was not just misleading, it also put the spotlight on her some of the same sensationalist behavior she was decrying.

- *I of course think that we are much more true than Fox is true. The problem that I think is reasonable to assert about Fox and its coverage is that they make up stories out of whole cloth and then make a big deal out of them.*

Apparently no one on MSNBC would do something like that! Oops, it seems that they did....

- *President Bush never did one interview with the New York Times during his entire presidency. (Oct 22, 2009, Rachel Maddow Show)*

This is an easy one to fact check, and no need to rely on Politifact.com. The fact checking organization alleges three, and I found at least two in a simple web search of the *Times* archives before I got tired of digging.

- *Gov. Sarah Palin got precisely zero support for her call for Alaska's Democratic Senator Mark Begich to resign because Ted Stevens' corruption conviction was overturned.(Apr 6, 2009, Rachel Maddow Show)*

Wrong on two counts—it was not Palin's idea (she just supported it) and it was backed by the state Republican chairman and a number of conservative organizations (e.g., ConservativeHQ. com). While it might not have been wildly supported, some is still a far cry away from "precisely zero."

Ms. Maddow in general strives to provide a rational discussion about important issues in America, and she should be applauded for such. She certainly brooks little from those media pundits who aim more to incite their audience than to promote intelligent discourse. However, to be admired for exceptional journalism means more than just being critical of the approaches of those in the other camp, it also means being meticulous in your own investigation.

To ascertain truth using the principles of deductive reasoning, we must consider whether the examples above are the result of unconscious personal bias in the interpretation of public events, or a purposeful intent to deceive. What is the motivation for the misinformation and distortion? Is she lying or simply making unconscious and overly enthusiastic embellishments to the fact? It is impossible to tell from the data we have in hand, so we need to weigh the possibilities and probabilities associated with the outcome: precedence, prevalence, and pay off. There are certainly aspects of exaggeration at play here that could arise from enthusiasm more so than intent to deceive. On the other hand, she makes no pretense about her negative opinion of competitors in the conservative media, setting a foundation for negative bias. The most damning evidence is that she apparently believes that her reporting and that of her network is more accurate than that of Fox, a claim clearly contradicted here by the facts and information readily available to her. Although not conclusive, the evidence does suggest that she has more to gain from exaggerating and distorting her statements than she gets from telling the straight up truth.

Glenn Beck

Mr. Beck is a popular conservative news pundit who hosts a syndicated talk-radio show (The Glenn Beck Program), and also the Glenn Beck show on TheBlazeTV (formerly on HLN and Fox News). His broadcasts are notable for having among the highest ratings in the industry. He is also well known for promoting controversial, conspiratorial, and often incendiary topics and for defending conservative American values.

One of the mainstays of provocative journalism is to tell the hard truths, as well as to point out the inconsistencies and eccentricities of our public leaders and the laws under which we live. But for such an approach to be productive and useful to us as a nation, the hard truths must be just that—truths, not yarns or stories or fabrications being spun in the interest of controlling the narrative. Unfortunately, Mr. Beck seems to have a bit of work yet to do in terms of maintaining the high standard of truth. Of twenty-nine quotes that were fact checked by Politifact, 52% came in as false or mostly false. Here are some examples of where he seems to have strayed quite far off the path of truthfulness.

- *Forty-three people! I think Nancy Reagan may have been the one who had the most people on the staff. She had three. Three! The first lady's office needs 43 people? For what? These people are out of control.(Feb 25, 2011, The Glenn Beck Program)*

This comment was made in reference to the size of the First Lady's personal staff, comparing Michelle Obama with the historical precedent set by Nancy Reagan. A simple search of the archives revealed that Mr. Beck is incorrect in his understanding of First Lady staffing. Mrs. Obama has approximately twenty-five staff, virtually identical to that of Laura Bush. Mrs. Reagan had on average about fifteen during her husband's presidency, not three. The increase in staff over the recent past is due to the expansion of the First Lady's role and thus the need for increased coordination around those activities. While Mr. Beck is certainly free to argue whether the First Lady needs an office at all, let alone how many people should staff it, it would be prudent for him to actually get the numbers straight.

- *The government is trying to now close the Lincoln Memorial for any kind of large gatherings. (June 28, 2010, The Glenn Beck Program)*

Glenn Beck alarmed the listeners of his talk-radio show when he warned them that the upcoming rally he was hosting at the Memorial might be the last that the government allows. Aside from some possible disruption caused by renovations that occurred throughout 2012, there were no changes to the public accessibility of the site for rallies, speeches, or other First Amendment activities. In fact, no reported examples of significant impact in visitor access have been reported. Perhaps the government was just trying to discourage gatherings of Beck fans…

- *In the health care bill, we're now offering insurance for dogs. (Nov 12, 2009, The Glenn Beck Program)*

Likely designed to rally the opponents of the Affordable Care Act, this wild claim refers to the fact that a small percentage of the scholarships and funding outlaid in the bill for public health research include monies that would go to veterinarians. However, unlike Beck's claim, the veterinarians in question would be working on ways to address swine flu, mad cow disease, and other animal diseases that are potentially harmful to human health. This one gets a prize for completely fabricating an outlandish interpretation of the provisions of the Act!

- *John Holdren, director of the White House Office of Science and Technology Policy, has proposed forcing abortions and putting sterilants in the drinking water to control population.(July 22, 2009, The Glenn Beck Show)*

John Holdren co-authored a book in 1977 (*Ecoscience: Population, Resources, Environment*) that included a discussion of a wide range of aggressive and controversial approaches to controlling population growth. These approaches were not advocated by the authors, and in fact there was much debate in the chapter around the moral and technological problems associated with such approaches. If inclusion of a topic in a discussion means that the individual automatically supports that topic, then Mr. Beck is guilty of any number of liberal attitudes and questionable activities himself.

The commonality among all of Mr. Beck's statements shown here is that they are wildly inaccurate and gross distortions of the concepts in question. They are designed to achieve maximum impact and controversy within the audience in a way that the truth never could. For three of these statements, there is not even a shred of evidence to back up the claims, suggesting either that Mr. Beck did not research the information at all, or that he purposely chose to provide misinformation in an attempt to influence public opinion and inspire an emotional response in his audience. The best standard of judgment we can bring to play here is weighing what can be gained by not being truthful. When an individual takes it upon themselves to spout numbers in support of their theories, the onus of checking the veracity of those numbers sits squarely with them. By the principles of deductive logic, the nature of these statements suggest intent because they involve claims that are clearly able to incite the public, thereby providing a window into the underlying motivation. If it is fair game to take a piece of information out of context and then distort it for public consumption, imagine what we could do with virtually anything Glenn Beck himself opines on his shows.

Ed Schultz

Ed Schultz, the down-to-earth and enthusiastic host of the Ed Show on MSNBC, has only been fact checked by Politifact.com five times recently. Astoundingly, 80% of his statements were rated mostly false or worse (and the remaining instance earned a half true rating). Now to be fair, that might simply be because he tends not to say controversial things that grab the public's attention, so maybe he comes to the notice of the fact checking organizations only when it is a whopper. Nonetheless, some of his incorrect statements provide an opportunity for us to exercise our informed judgment about truth.

- Wisconsin employees who earn *$30,000, $40,000, $50,000 a year might have 20 percent of their income just disappear overnight.(Feb 15, 2011, The Ed Show)*

In 2011, Wisconsin Governor Scott Walker proposed an increase in the amount state workers would need to contribute for their health and pension benefits. While Walker's spokespeople claimed the increases would amount to about 8%, Ed Schultz aggressively claimed that it would be substantially more—hitting closer to 20%. Apparently, when asked for the numbers upon which this calculation was derived, the MSNBC office was not too forthcoming. But, to cut Mr. Schultz a bit of slack, the numbers put forward by various experts were also less than definitive, ranging from 6-13%, depending upon overall income and other factors. That is still a marked jump in deductions from take home pay, but Schultz's claim clearly crosses over into the realm of exaggeration. As we discussed in the previous chapter, exaggeration is a very effective way of evoking an emotive response from the audience while building upon a core of actual evidence.

- President Obama's decision to remove General Stanley McChrystal from head of the US troops in Afghanistan was an example of his need *to fix yet another problem he inherited from the Bush administration.(June 22, 2012, The Ed Show)*

Mr. Schultz expressed outrage over disparaging comments made by General McChrystal concerning high ranking senior officials in the Obama administration. While Schultz's belief that McChrystal shoud be dismissed is opinion and therefore we cannot fault him on it, he is wrong to blame the Bush administration. McChrystal was certainly noteworthy in the military throughout George W. Bush's tenure in office, but Obama himself appointed McChrystal to the post of US commander in Afghanistan in 2009. This is an example of the misplaced emphasis approach we discussed in the last chapter. Hard as it might be for some to accept, not everything that goes wrong during the Obama administration can be blamed on George W. Bush.

- *Louisiana Sen. Mary Landrieu received almost $1.8 million from BP over the last decade.(May 5, 2010, The Ed Show)*

Ed Schultz has made several public claims that Senator Landrieu received this exorbitant sum of money from British Petroleum, certainly an amount about which to be concerned. However, it turns out that this statement is a complete fabrication. Senator Landrieu received less than $30,000 from BP during 2000-2010. It is easy to check using websites like Opensecrets.org (used by Politifact) or Federal Election Commission disclosure data search page (my source in this instance). Furthermore, the amount of contribution that Schultz claims went to Sen. Landrieu equals about 38% of the total contributions made by the BP Corporation. That is a bit much to go to only one woman, especially for a company with as many global interests as BP. This is a perfect example of numbers that raise a red flag by their exaggerated magnitude, and therefore a situation that definitely called for fact checking.

- *Ninety-eight percent of the American people will not see their taxes go up due to the House health care bill.* (Nov 20, 2009, The Ed Show)

There has been a lot of talk and rhetoric around this issue, and I do not want to belabor the point too much. What I do want to say is that if Ed Schultz makes this type of statement as pure truth, he knows more than the rest of us. There is no way to accurately calculate how many people will experience a tax increase, as we do not know how many people will elect to go without the mandated health insurance and thus be hit with the penalty tax. We also do not know what individual health care providers will do as they restructure to comply with the implementation of the Affordable Care Act. If Mr. Schultz has hard numbers on that, I would like to borrow his crystal ball.

Schultz's statements on whole represent an eclectic mix of exaggeration, ignorance of facts, and wishful thinking. Since the function of pundits is supposed to be providing the public with reliable information, it does us little good to have it subverted by emotionality and personal bias. In the worst case scenario, several of these comments had the possible impact of defaming the person about whom they were made, a consequence often overlooked or ignored and which could have incalculable impact on careers and livelihood. At the very least, the implications of the sentiments reflect irresponsible journalism. Any claim with hard numbers is easy to assess via the principles of objective reasoning. If actual numbers exist, they are typically easy to find and fact check. On the other hand, if the claims involve figures that even the government cannot provide empirical data to back up (like 98% of Americans will not see their taxes go up), then you have an obvious red flag. In the final analysis, the emotional manner in which these particular statements were delivered, and the lack of data to support the claims, suggests these comments belong in the category of purposeful fiction.

Rush Limbaugh

Rush Limbaugh may be one of the most controversial talk-radio hosts in the history of the genre (I say might be because I am not aware of any objective scale by which to weigh up my claim). What I do know is that there is no middle ground where Mr. Limbaugh is concerned—you either love him or hate him. He is a self-professed ultra-right-wing conservative hosting the most popular show in America (*The Rush Limbaugh Show*) with a regular listening audience of over 15 million. He is no holds barred when it comes to voicing his opinions, and he does so at notable volume.

That of course does not mean he is accurate. Of the fifteen comments evaluated on Politifact.com, 80% of them were rated as mostly false or worse. To add salt to the wound, not a single comment was rated as true. While one could easily write an entire book on the many and varied emanations from the lips of Mr. Limbaugh, here are a few of the most notable ones captured by the fact checking organization in recent years.

- Sotomayor *ruled against the white firefighter...just on the basis that she thought women and minorities should be given a preference because of their skin color and because of the history of discrimination in the past. The law was totally disregarded.(May 26, 2009, The Rush Limbaugh Show)*

A reverse discrimination suit (Ricci vs. DeStefano) was brought against the New Haven, Connecticut Civil Service Board because of issues with performance on a promotion exam. Very few minorities passed the test, so the Board decided not to certify the results out of concern for potentially violating the anti-disparate impact requirements of Title VII of the 1964 Civil Rights Act. In Limbaugh's opinion, the agreement of the Second Circuit court panel of judges (which included Sotomayor) with a lower court ruling constituted a disregard of the law. In fact, they upheld the lower court interpretation of the civil rights law, allowing the city of New Haven to throw out test results based upon racially disparate results. Limbaugh's claim that Sotomayor made the ruling on the basis of the history of discrimination proved the Court actually regarded the law, as that is the very point of the Civil Rights Act. You cannot disregard the thing that supplies the very basis for your ruling.

- People *can't go fishing anymore because of Obama. (Mar 9, 2010, The Rush Limbaugh Show)*

To cut Mr. Limbaugh a bit of slack, he was not the first to foist this rhetoric into the public domain. However, he did manage to take it to a ridiculous extreme. Arising originally from a comment made on Media Matters (a media watchdog website) and an opinion spread throughout the conservative bloggersphere, the premise that recreational and/or commercial fishing were on their way out was an incorrect interpretation of the interim reports by the Interagency Ocean Policy Task Force. The output eventually led to Executive Order 13547 --Stewardship of the Ocean, Our Coasts, and the Great Lakes, signed by President Obama on July 19, 2010. Nowhere in the order does it suggest that fishing will be banned. Among the numerous specific definitions of Sec 2 Policy (a) is the following:

(vi) respect and preserve our Nation's maritime heritage, including our social, cultural, recreational, and historical values

Far from banning a beloved pastime of our rich cultural heritage, the Stewardship order seeks to preserve and protect bodies of water for continued enjoyment by the current and future generations. Talk about a fish story!

- *You can't read a speech by George Washington ... without hearing him reference God, the Almighty." (Apr 8, 2009, The Rush Limbaugh Show)*

Rush Limbaugh addressed what he saw as the concerted attempt to dilute the role of Christianity in America by claiming that our first president himself endorsed the evocation of God in public life. According to historians, Washington was known for making reference to a deity in some of his public speeches, but this only seldom involved the word God. According to author John C. Fitzpatrick (*Writings of George Washington*), he was substantially more likely to use the word "providence." In addition, the common myth that Washington is responsible for adding the words "so help me God" to the Constitutional oath is belied by the fact that the first attribution of such did not appear until the mid-1800's. However, according to historical record, he did say in his first inaugural address that America was a nation "under the special agency of providence." Obviously, one can argue that "providence" and "god" are interchangeable and that it is mincing words to accuse Mr. Limbaugh of speaking falsely on this point. But it is also safe to say that he exaggerates what historians claim Washington's religious views in public to be. Historical record provides us with numerous examples of public speeches where Washington did not make reference to a deity in any manner.

- *"...it is President Obama who wants to mandate circumcision. ... and that means if we need to save our penises from anybody, it's Obama." (Aug 25, 2009, The Rush Limbaugh Show)*

I am pleased to end this section with one of the most ridiculous claims I have heard, even from so prolific a source as Mr. Limbaugh. Limbaugh alarmed his listening audience with the news that an upcoming Center for Disease Control and Prevention (CDC) report might result in obligatory circumcision for all men and boys in this country. In fact, broad ranging epidemiological research by the CDC found that:

Male circumcision reduces the risk that a man will acquire HIV from an infected female partner, and also lowers the risk of other STDs, penile cancer, and infant urinary tract infection. In female partners, it reduces the risk of cervical cancer, genital ulceration, bacterial vaginosis, trichomoniasis, and HPV. (CDC website—http://www.cdc. gov/hiv/malecircumcision/)

From this, Limbaugh leapt to the conclusion that circumcision would now be mandated without a shred of evidence or logic. Anyone who hears such nonsense and believes it without doing a bit of checking deserves the alarm they experience. There is no link between Obama and the White House with this CDC report. The CDC is not suggesting that circumcision be mandated, they are instead recommending that it might have health benefits, particularly around reducing the spread of HIV/AIDS (thus perhaps it should be covered as preventative care by health insurance- my thought, not the CDC's). With the same sentiment with which I admonished Ed Schultz's feelings toward Bush, Rush Limbaugh cannot levy blame and accusation on Barack Obama for every event (or nonevent) in our country, especially when there is no evidence other than his opinion to back it up.

The case of Rush Limbaugh introduces a notable challenge for application of deductive logic to understanding the veracity of media reports in general. Many media pundits are openly biased in their approach to information sharing. As we mentioned in the Introduction to this book, stating one's opinion, even if it is false, does not necessarily constitute lying. Half of the statements listed here qualify as exaggeration or the end result of ignorance. It is clear that Mr. Limbaugh does not have sufficient grasp of the law or history to be able to make an accurate assessment of facts. If that was the extent of his misinformation, we could rate him as uninformed rather than deceptive by the principles of rational judgment. However, the other two comments represent complete fabrications, and reason suggests that their purpose was to incite and inflame the listening audience. Not only does that kind of behavior put his product outside of respectable journalism, it also places him in the category of entertainer rather than thought leader. Since he is considered one of the major voices for modern conservatism and many people look to him for guidance in politics and current events, his failure to provide factual and truthful information to the public is unconscionable.

Other Assorted Nonsense

Before I close out this chapter, there are a few other comments of notable mention that I thought were worth sharing as opportunities for applying your own deductive investigative skills. These are excellent examples of the popular penchant for skewing information, preying on psychological and cultural biases, and just plain making stuff up!

<u>Kimberly Guilfoyle</u>—*If you log into the government's Cash for Clunkers Web site (cars.gov) from your home computer, the government can "seize all of your personal and private information, and track your computer activity." (July 31, 2009, The Glenn Beck Show)*

This was based upon a DOT security statement regarding the Cash For Clinkers program described on cars.gov that applied specifically to car dealerships, not individuals, and was subsequently revised on the website. This is the actual original security statement.

> *This application provides access to the DOT CARS system. When logged on to the CARS system, your computer is considered a federal computer system and it is property of the United States Government. Any or all uses of this system and all files on this*

system may be intercepted, monitored, recorded, copied, audited, inspected, and disclosed to authorized CARS, DOT, and law enforcement personnel, as well as authorized officials of other agencies, both domestic and foreign.

The language here is quite Hitlerian and even a bit frightening, particularly if it applied to individual consumers. But it did not. And the Guilfoyle/Beck duo exaggerated the threat to the individual, categorically stating that using the website would give the government ownership of "everything in your home." While it is admirable to point out potential danger to consumers, fabricating government conspiracies where none exist does more harm than good. Countless individuals who might have benefited from the Cash for Clunkers program might have declined out of an unfounded fear that their privacy might be invaded. In this case, an action that should have protected consumers may have actually caused real harm.

Bill Maher—*Do you know that we have pipes carrying natural gas in this country that are made of wood? I am not joking. (Sept14, 2010, CNN Larry King Live)*

Bill Maher is known for his wit, but in this case it is too bad he was not joking. In the beginning of the natural gas industry, rather than iron or steel pipes, a small number of pipes were made of coated wood—a very small number. Most have been decommissioned and replaced with modern materials (currently plastic). Occasionally, obsolete wooden lines are dug up to make room for expanded lines, but most remain buried where the original lines once ran. It is possible that an extremely small number of wooden pipes are still in existence somewhere, but it is truly a minute number. Maher's statement is technically true, but fails to pass the standards of objective reasoning because it misleads the audience into believing that there is an issue that does not actually exist. After all, there still might be examples of wooden teeth in existence, but I do not think dentists have to worry about them much anymore.

Victoria Jackson—*A clause hidden in the Obamacare bill, which is now law, gives Obama the right to form a private army. (July 15, 2011, WorldNetDaily)*

Ms. Jackson, a well-known comedian and Tea Party supporter, likewise was not joking when she made this comment. She came to this conclusion based upon her interpretation of the meaning of a clause within the Affordable Care Act that gives the President power to create and staff the Ready Reserve Corps, under the auspices of the U.S. Department of Health and Human Services. This emergency response team would be populated by medical staff for the purposes of responding to health and public safety emergencies, such as hurricanes, earthquakes, or outbreaks of infectious disease. These individuals are not trained by military, nor do they carry weapons (except against microorganisms). As such, if Obama wants to form an army of doctors and nurses to invade disaster zones with medicines and hi-tech equipment, I say all the more power to him. History would likely have been quite different if Hitler had attempted to invade Poland with tourniquets and defibrillator machines instead of guns and tanks.

Mary Matalin—*There is climate change, but for the last decade the climate has been cooling. There is the science. There is the data on that. (Oct 22, 2009, CNN News)*

Political commentator Mary Matalin asserted that, contrary to scientific opinion, the earth has actually been cooling for the past decade. According to NASA, since the year 2000, there has been a continuation of a long-term warming trend, including nine of the warmest years since the temperatures were first recorded in 1880. Overall, the temperature in the last decade was 1.4°F warmer than at the end of the 19th century. While many could argue about the significance of the temperature rise, the data clearly show the earth is warming. Perhaps Ms. Matalin was looking at the temperature graph upside down?

Footnote: This by no means comprises an exhaustive list of all of the incorrect or disingenuous comments made by pundits on a national level. Everyone makes misstatements or exaggerated claims at some point in time. However, most pundits do not make claims that are so wildly inaccurate that they get brought to the attention of fact checking organizations on a routine basis. As I stated at the outset, I went specifically with comments researched by Politifact.com in order to maintain consistency in the way the analyses were applied to the statements. Furthermore, I did additional investigation of my own on these ratings to verify their accuracy as much as possible. Note that despite all of my efforts, I might be off the mark on some of these as well, because our accuracy is only as good as the data we use to make judgments. Nonetheless, the point I am trying to get across from all of this is that many inaccuracies can be avoided just by doing a bit of digging into the background information. And if your intent is actually to deceive, you had better know what the facts say in case someone decides to challenge your assertions in public.

Solving the "Pundit Puzzle Box"

Not one of the examples discussed in this chapter pass the rigor of applied rational thought, and many clearly represent careless journalism (of course, that is why I picked them as examples). Many display blatant signs of bias, exaggeration, and embellishment, and certainly most could easily be debunked with a few minutes of careful fact checking. Most reputable newspapers and some other news sources (e.g., National Public Radio) regularly print or air retractions of incorrect or false information when it is brought to their attention, but seldom is that the case with television personalities. And yet these pundits remain popular, they continue to influence the public, and few are ever called to task for the disservice they do to the spirit of journalism. How it is that such widespread deception and misinformation is permitted, sometimes even condoned, by the consuming public?

The problem with the inaccuracies and lies perpetuated by pundits is that we do not live in a rational society where truth and honesty are effectively evaluated. People listen to these public personalities and simply believe what they say. Few people stop to question whether something they hear makes sense. They tend not to fact check any objective sources or look for the actual data from which the claims are made. They simply swallow it hook, line, and sinker and then perpetuate the myth by sharing it with all of their friends. A friend of mine recently told me "Bill O'Reilly has never been wrong once in fifteen years." I find it hard to believe that anyone, even the most rigorous journalist, could escape making a blunder or two across such a period of time. O'Reilly might be a good pundit, but to state that he has never once been wrong certainly raises the red flag of doubt.

One of the biggest forces driving this lack of rationalism is the cultural phenomenon of group perception discussed in Chapter 5, specifically the overestimation of between group variability and underestimation of within group variability that gives rise to "them vs. us" cognitions. Conservatives believe pundits like Glenn Beck and Rush Limbaugh tell the truth because they see them as "us"—a part of the social fabric of ideals that makes up the conservative culture and therefore there is no need to check their facts. Because they agree with them about the basic principles and approach to society, they tend to believe that everything they say is well founded, especially when it is said about "them" (the liberals).

The same factors are at play with the liberal side of the coin. Liberal viewers tend to consider Rachel Maddow and Ed Schultz to be the spokespeople of their culture, playing watchdog on the issues and problems they think are important in our society today. In fact, the audience watches these pundits as a source of information about what the other side is doing and saying. Because the liberal viewer already expects the conservatives to behave in a certain way, they are not particularly motivated to go out and fact check any of the apparently confirming information that comes to them from members of their own team.

The other major factors at play are the perceived authority of the pundits themselves, the confidence with which they speak, and the supporting panel of experts they typically have on hand to back up their views. Our favorite news anchors are enthusiastic, they speak well, they speak aggressively, and sometimes they shout until we cannot help but get the message they are sending. And whether we like it or not, the claims of unbiased reporting which several major news networks postulate that they live by are only thinly veiled secular pep rallies. It is very common for both the show host and other panel members to beat up on the sole "outsider" representing the opposition view on many of these discussion panel shows, and then claim to have shared the breadth of ideologies about the topic in question.

So if we want to actually know the truth, we will need to completely revamp the way our media work. The problem is that the entertainment value goes right out the door along with the ratings. It is never going to happen in our society the way things currently stand, where reality shows (filled with little reality) top the popularity charts and dashing personalities argue with each other 24/7 for our amusement. As it stands now, if you want the truth, you have to dig. If you hear someone say something that catches your interest, the onus is on you to look it up and see if it is true. The pundits are not going to do it for you. They have no motivation and no incentive to change tactics in how they report the news. TV news personalities will not change their behavior unless there is a negative effect on ratings.

This country has a real problem if the public cannot trust that the information that they are given is factual and correct. So maybe the responsibility needs to rest with the producers and the programmers who should be demanding more accuracy from their pundits and newscasters. What would happen if news celebrities were made to publicly declare and retract their mistakes, distortions, and falsehoods on the air? How long would their careers last if it became that obvious how much disingenuous behavior was really out there? If that is what you would prefer, then tell them. Accountability can only be driven by ratings and if you keep tuning in, or never send an email or tweet or text or any other form of comment describing your outrage about untruthful reporting, there is little point in employing rationality and logic in the first place.

CHAPTER 9 =========

Days of Our Lies:
The Dark Side of Popular Culture

T he world around us is often not as it appears. As we have seen so far, the average person is constantly faced with the difficulty of sorting fact from fiction across virtually every aspect of life. But there are also certain facets of society where we, the consuming public, actually expect lies and deception to hold sway. For example, in the glamorous and exotic world of Hollywood, we never bat an eye when celebrities lie about their weight, with whom they are sleeping, or how much they cheated on their taxes. We may excitedly follow the scandals that arise from the truth leaking out into the public domain, but we are largely forgiving of their little foibles. Furthermore, a large portion of our population eagerly purchases the tabloids that expound upon the scandals, usually with a fair amount of embellishment and outright lying. We admire actors because they weave a fiction that captures our imagination (note that all acting is a form of deception). Likewise, not one of us is offended by the sleight of hand and misdirection that comprise the magician's trade; rather we jeer and want our money back if we are not completely fooled by the act.

But not all of popular culture receives as much tolerance when it comes to deception. For other types of celebrities and stars, honesty and sincerity are demanded without exception and vocal condemnation akin to public hanging results when the exalted ones fall from grace. Among those held to this higher standard are individuals with exceptional physical skills, whose prowess in the world of sport elevates them to role model status for millions of young aspiring athletes. When these folks come up short in integrity, the ripple effects through society are profound. Fans and admirers alike lose confidence, it sullies the game, and there can be enormous financial impact for the perpetrator and the sponsor alike.

In other cases, duplicity can have widespread impact on the public purse and mindset through the purposeful presentation of false or misleading information. For example, authors and artists who fake their work take inappropriate advantage of a very real financial investment on the part of the consumer (and the publisher). In other instances, the deceit might be restricted to a much smaller segment of the population, but with much more devastating impact, as in the case of con artists who portray a false identity for financial and social gain.

In all of these cases, perhaps the most damaging yet downplayed effect is the sense of betrayal left in the wake of the scandal. We are left believing the world is a poorer place, bereft of the usual enthusiasm and sense of enjoyment associated with common social activities. In this chapter we will examine some highly publicized examples of dishonesty in popular culture with an eye to considering both the means by which the duplicitous acts were played out, as well as the consequences for those within the sphere of deception.

Wide, Wide World of Sports Scams

Everyone is familiar with the prevalence of attempts at under the wire cheating that go on in sports at virtually every level.

From the not so accidental shoulder charge in rugby to supposedly unintended pass interference in gridiron football, players everywhere profess the purity of their intentions to the clamoring crowd. Much to their dismay, the philosophy of "you get away with what the referee cannot see" has taken quite a turn in recent times with the advent of television replays, but that still does not stop many athletes from putting on an innocent expression and shaking their heads with disbelief when the referee blows a whistle or shows them a red card or flag. While such behaviors are demonstrations of deception and misdirection, on the whole these acts are tolerated as a normal part of the game.

But there is a level of deceit that goes way beyond the adrenalin-driven moments of denial on the field of play, particularly in professional sports where salary, sponsorships, and team revenues are so dependent upon the outcome of competition. Let us take a look at some examples where dishonesty raises universal objection within the court of public opinion, not only because of cheating (a disingenuous behavior in its own right), but also because of the lies that are told to shield the duplicity from the public eye.

Doping and Duping

Allegations of doping are extremely common in high level athletes of all sports. The pressure to win is enormous and the differences between competitors might only be a matter of milliseconds. It is easy to understand the motivation for "juicing" and other types of performance enhancement to obtain any edge possible, which is why virtually every sport bans the use such substances and requires drug testing of competitors. A small percentage of competitors are always on the lookout for ways to beat the testing system or use products or procedures that have not yet been banned. And anyone who physically dominates in a sport is often subject to doping allegations, whether they test clean or not, creating a vast quagmire of suspicion and mistrust. It is no wonder that identifying dishonesty in doping allegations is so difficult, but luckily not everyone gets away with it in the end. Lies tend to come to light and the ramifications can be profound, and in some cases, the mere rumor of deceit is enough to ruin careers.

Roger Clemens is a professional baseball pitcher whose career spanned 24 seasons with four different teams. He is considered one of the top one hundred all-time great ball players and won the Cy Young award seven times. Unfortunately, his career will always be marred by controversy stemming from allegations of performance enhancing drug use (anabolic steroids and human growth hormone). Clemens had been named by another player and by a trainer as having used illegal performance enhancers and was thus brought before a Congressional committee in 2008 to testify in response. He publicly stated that he had never used these or any other illegal substances. Whereas the evidence around his actual drug use was tenuous, the committee, because of inconsistencies in his testimony, recommended that the Justice Department investigate whether he provided false testimony to Congress. In 2010, a federal grand jury indicted Clemens on charges of obstruction of Congress, making false statements, and perjury. In 2012, after a mistrial and a subsequent second trial, Clemens was found not guilty on all counts. Clemens did not emerge scot free, however. While vindicated of the charges of lying to Congress, he has been denied induction into the Baseball Hall of Fame as recently as 2013. In addition, he has been dropped from association with certain charitable activities, and his name has been removed from a Sports Medicine Institute in Houston. Despite being cleared of the charges, there will likely always be controversy around the doping allegations and his honesty because of the investigation of potential perjury.

In a very similar story, *Barry Bonds*, one of the greatest baseball home run hitters of all time, became enmeshed in controversy around a widespread doping scandal with the Bay Area Laboratory Cooperative (BALCO) near the end of his career.

Bonds' trainer was being investigated for distributing anabolic steroids to a number of athletes through BALCO and Bonds was called to testify before a federal grand jury. The subsequent investigation of Bonds himself did not center around drug use, but rather the truthfulness of statements he made to the grand jury about the BALCO scandal. In this case, Bonds was found guilty of obstruction and perjury (2011 conviction) and sentenced to 30 days of jail time to be served in his home. As with the Clemens' case, Bonds was also denied entry into the Baseball Hall of Fame in 2013. Although Bonds denies ever knowingly using performance enhancing drugs, mandatory testing was not in place for much of his career and thus there is no evidence to confirm or refute the charges. Since he was charged with perjury, his denials around the drug use are more difficult to accept and thus questions about his use of these substances as contributors to his home run record will likely always remain a part of the conversation.

Doping allegations are by no means restricted to members of team sports. One of the most disappointing doping scandals of recent times belongs to former Olympian and international track sensation, *Marion Jones*. The five time medal winner from the 2000 Olympic Games in Sydney Australia was also caught up in the net of the controversial BALCO scandal. Jones gave testimony during the BALCO investigation, denying ever taking performance enhancing substances, despite testimony by a BALCO member that he had repeatedly given her a number of different illegal performance enhancing substances. In 2007, Jones came clean to the public and the courts, admitting a history of doping and making false statements during her testimony during the BALCO investigation. Partly because of her voluntary admission, Jones was not sentenced to jail time for the doping but was penalized for lying to a grand jury in an unrelated incident. She accepted a mandatory two year suspension from competition in track and field (precipitating her retirement) and was stripped of all medals and awards from 2000 onwards. The loss of sponsorship and international standing, as well as the erosion of public trust in her honesty, has left Ms. Jones in financial difficulty as well as public disgrace.

That brings us to one of the longest running and most publicly debated doping scandals in all of sporting history. *Lance Armstrong*, international cycling legend and seven time Tour de France winner, was accused of doping throughout much of his illustrious career. He repeatedly denied all charges, he passed repeated drug tests, and he fought back (sometimes quickly and harshly) against those who accused him of wrong-doing, including teammates and other supporters. However, despite his emphatic denials against performance enhancing drug use, his extensive history of lying was finally brought to public view. Over the course of several years, the US Anti-Doping Agency conducted a comprehensive investigation around alleged doping behavior for Armstrong and other members of the US Postal cycling team, culminating in a report released on October 10, 2010. This report unequivocally revealed the duplicity behind the actions of Armstrong and his teammates:

> *Today, we are sending the 'Reasoned Decision' in the Lance Armstrong case and supporting information to the Union Cycliste International (UCI), the World Anti-Doping Agency (WADA), and the World Triathlon Corporation (WTC). The evidence shows beyond any doubt that the US Postal Service Pro Cycling Team ran the most sophisticated, professionalized and successful doping program that sport has ever seen.*

The report goes on to discuss details of the investigation, the compelling evidence, and the role played by Armstrong in the doping conspiracy. In 2012, the USADA banned Armstrong from competition for life and stripped him of all titles and medals from

1998 onward. The Union Cycliste Internationale (the international governance body for cycling) accepted the findings and Armstrong announced that he would not appeal the decision in the interest of foregoing any further exhausting and lengthy effort. In January of 2013, Armstrong finally admitted to having doped during his career during a televised interview with Oprah Winfrey, leaving whatever remnants of fan base he still had feeling both bereft and betrayed. After more than a decade of denial and lying, of vilifying his teammates and accusers, and of damaging the reputation of the sport, it was a little late for his admission to carry much weight with the public. He has subsequently been removed from association with Livestrong, the cancer charity he founded, has been stripped of his cycling titles, and has been banned from sport indefinitely. Inexplicably, he eluded jail time or any other corporal punishment outside of public condemnation. While he might have avoided some of the worst consequences of duplicitous behavior, the impact on the sport and the enjoyment of fans going forward will likely be profound.

Hedging with Shortcuts

While cheating is not new or even unusual in the realm of sporting competitions, some individuals take it to a whole new level with creative interpretation of the rules. For example, while most of us believe that a race is run from start to finish, some competitors try to put the emphasis on start and finish without regard for what goes on in between! Take the example of *Rosie Ruiz* who appeared to have won the 1980 Boston Marathon in record time. Her enjoyment of the title was short-lived however, as compelling evidence was amassed that indicated she did not run the entire race. Firstly, her race time was scorching, taking 25 minutes off of her qualifying time and also breaking the event's record. Secondly, she was not sweating, fatigued, or in any way exhibiting the normal signs of physical stress brought about by such a grueling event.

Furthermore, her apparent level of fitness (muscle development, body mass, heart rate) was substantially below that exhibited by the other top women contenders. Then there were the issues that she did not know her race stats (something all top runners can recite for each race), she did not notice or recall things along the race path that should have been obvious, she did not appear in the race videos or on check point rosters, and no one remembers seeing her for large sections of the race (especially the actual first and second place runners) — all these gave rise to suspicion about whether she ran the race at all. The final damning evidence came from two witnesses who observed Ruiz entering the race from the crowd about a half mile from the finish. As a result, Boston Marathon officials have subsequently instituted a more rigorous surveillance system that monitors the arrival of competitors at the race checkpoints to prevent attempts to skip out of sections of the course in the future.

In a somewhat similar act of blatant disregard for the nature of the rules of engagement, jockey *Sylvester Carmouche* took his horse, Landing Officer, to a twenty-four horse-length win at Delta Downs in Louisiana in 1990 in the midst of extremely heavy fog. The magnitude of the lead was especially exciting considering that Landing Officer was a 23-1 long shot in the race. However, the race was protested on the basis of a number of incriminating pieces of evidence. First, none of the other jockeys saw or heard Carmouche pass them during the race, and most of the video coverage of the race shows only eight horses on the field instead of the nine that started. Second, the horse was not breathing hard or sweating after the race, and neither the horse nor his leg wraps were covered with mud and turf like the other entries. Race officials speculated that Carmouche directed his horse into the infield shortly after the start and then picked an opportune time to re-emerge at the head of the pack for the finish. While Landing Officer's win was nullified, Carmouche continues to profess his innocence and chalks the huge lead up to the surprising fleetness of his mount.

The truth unfortunately will always be held secret by the thick Louisiana fog on that day but the odds are long that the horse chose that one race of its career to display unprecedented speed.

Literary Pros and Cons

The lure of fame and fortune in the public limelight does not elude the world of literary scholarship. Although life is usually a little more private for authors than other types of artists, there is ample opportunity to increase social status and make a whole lot of money if you are good enough at the craft (and if you have an excellent agent and marketing plan!). And of course nothing captures the public imagination more than tales of hardship, horror, retribution, and triumph over impossible odds. Therefore, it is no wonder that biographical and autobiographical works that tell the tale of personal tragedy and growth can easily become best sellers, leading to guest appearances on celebrated talk and news shows (and perhaps even a movie deal down the road). But sometimes those inspiring biographical works are actually spectacular creations of fiction.

In 2003, screenwriter *James Frey* made his nonfiction debut and the best sellers list with his autobiographical hit, *A Million Little Pieces*. This compelling memoir followed Mr. Frey's experiences through the hazy and painful veil of crime, addiction, and imprisonment as he struggled to gain control of his life. His sales were given a boost after a gripping interview with Oprah Winfrey who had selected the work for her book club, and its selection as "favorite book of the year" by Amazon.

Unfortunately, Mr. Frey's book, while based upon his real struggle with substance abuse, was rife with fabrication, exaggeration, and embellishment. Many facts were distorted, and some were outright false or overblown. In hindsight, the publishers might have been suspicious since he had originally tried to market the work as a novel. When skepticism began to surface, Frey initially claimed that he only changed details that might reveal the identity and invade privacy of certain persons, and other minor details that enhanced the literary effect. However, when pressed hard by Oprah Winfrey during a follow up television interview, Frey finally admitted to making up some of the key details and events in the book, including his alleged jail time (which was five hours of detainment at the police station rather than eighty-seven days of imprisonment) and violent encounters with the police.

It is unknown why his publishers made no effort to fact check the events in the book, or why he thought that the fabrication would go unnoticed. Perhaps it is just another example of passivity and acceptance on the part of the public that it took time before the work was questioned. Following the public admission of deceit, Frey was subsequently dropped by his publisher, lost contracts for further book deals, and was required in a legal settlement to offer refunds to any readers who felt defrauded by the false nature of the content. Undaunted by the public humiliation and retribution, Mr. Frey went on to publish *Bright Shiny Morning* in 2008, a successful fiction novel, with a different publisher. Apparently, his notoriety and success at fooling the public with his "nonfiction" work convinced some people he could spin a good story!

While James Frey may have done a fairly sloppy job of hiding the fiction in his autobiography, *Margaret Seltzer* turned it up a notch in terms of covering her tracks for *Love and Consequences: A Memoir of Hope and Survival*, a highly acclaimed 2008 nonfiction memoir, written under the pseudonym Margaret B. Jones. *Love and Consequences* told the tale of a mixed race woman (white and Native American) who grew up as a foster child among black gang-bangers in South-Central Los Angeles. She ran drugs, carried a gun, got caught up in gang violence, and finally survived the struggle to emerge from chaos to graduate from college with a degree in ethics studies. Ironic that the major was ethics, since she fabricated the entire story! Furthermore, she extended the ruse to radio interviews where she spoke with an African- American dialect and used vernacular to give the impression of someone straight out of the heart of gang territory. In reality, Ms. Seltzer was white, middle-class, lived with her parents in Sherman Oaks California, and was well educated at private school.

Unlike James Frey, Ms. Seltzer had prepared a dossier to support her ruse, including letters and photographs. She got people to pose as her foster siblings. She had respected references to back up her story. She signed a contract in which she promised the work was factually correct. She was represented by a literary agent with whom the publisher had previously worked. Everything seemed legitimate, and thus the publisher never did background checks or contacted the child services department to corroborate her story of being fostered at different locations. Alas, Ms. Seltzer's crowning achievement was her ability to weave elaborate fiction in such a profound way that no one thought to question it. If it were not for Ms. Seltzer's real life sister contacting a newspaper about the fabricated story, and Seltzer's subsequent confession, no one may ever have known what a good liar she was. No one thought to check, and as a result, the public got sold a dummy. The book was apparently a really good read, but the publisher pulled the remaining copies from the shelves in the wake of the scandal. Maybe they should re-market it as fiction.

Then there are the instances where truth vs. fiction are much more difficult to tell apart. Take the story of *Kathy O'Beirne*, whose 2006 best-selling memoir, *Don't Ever Tell*, chronicles the story of a childhood filled with rape, abuse, and involuntary institutionalization in Ireland. She was shuttled from one Catholic children's home to another, gave birth to a child of rape at the age of 14, and was ultimately imprisoned in a Magdalene laundry, a type of Catholic institution where promiscuous women were made to work at sewing and cleaning in penance for their sins.

Doubt was subsequently cast upon the legitimacy of O'Beirne's story by several of her siblings who claimed that large portions of the book were fabricated and that Kathy's history of psychiatric illness made her delusional about her past. The inconsistencies in her recollection of events and claims she made in the memoir were reviewed in another work, *Kathy's Real Story*, by author Hermann Kelly in 2007, who came to the conclusion that the memoir was a fraud. However, other siblings corroborate Kathy's story and allege that they were also victims of abuse and rape while growing up. At this point, there seem to be points for and against the veracity of the story from both sides and the actual truth is hard to discern. What this demonstrates most is that lying, fabrication, and deception for personal gain have become so common in our culture that we have no difficulty believing someone might make up such horrific stories of abuse in order to sell copies of a book. New literary scandals come to light every year, so it is not a stretch of the imagination, no matter how cynical, to entertain the possibility that she made most of it up for monetary gain. At the same time, events like she describes are also commonplace enough to be plausible. If so, then allegations of fraud are just throwing salt in the wounds of a damaged woman who had the courage to stand up and share her story. Since it is not clear whether the allegations of fraud are supported or not, this book is still available in print and no action has been taken against Ms. O'Bierne.

The three examples of documented or alleged literary fraud described here raise a serious concern about the need for fact checking and assurance by publishing houses to insure that what they are marketing is real. But how can we as a consuming public even begin to tell fact from fiction when ethical standards of conduct are so easy to cast aside? Surely we have the right to demand that a label of nonfiction be associated with an actual and true story, not one where embellishment changes the nature of the tale, or where purposeful fabrication is used to dupe unsuspecting readers. While it is certainly possible for the consumer to apply the principles of deductive reasoning to examples of this type, it does appear to be an undue burden to expect the reader to carry out such due diligence every time they pick up a nonfiction work. And while it might be fair to ask publishers to extend more rigorous evaluation to the works they promulgate in print, the advent of self-publishing opens the gates for material of any level of truth or falsehood to flood the market.

Wolves in Celebrity Clothing

Whereas cheating and lying in competitive fields like the media, sports, and literature are commonplace, there are those who work on a level miles above this in terms of duplicity. Perhaps the most intriguing and shocking examples of lying in popular culture come from those individuals who create an entirely fictitious identity and use it to infiltrate social circles otherwise outside their reach. No, I am not talking about identity thieves who steal your personal financial information, drain your bank account, and use your credit card to make enormous and untraceable purchases. I am talking about people who successfully convince others, often whole groups of people, that they are someone other than who they are, usually a someone with a higher social standing and reputation than their own.

For example, consider the case of *David Hampton*, aka David Poitier, the supposed exiled son of screen actor Sidney Poitier. Hampton, actually the son of a lawyer in Buffalo, NY, thought up the son of Poitier ruse while trying to get into a popular nightclub in New York City. Hampton used this false persona to con various celebrities and NY social elite from 1981-1983 until he was caught and prosecuted for fraud and made to pay retribution to his victims. He was also banned from New York City, and his failure to comply resulted in a short stint in prison. The tale of his exploits inspired the popular play, *Six Degrees of Separation*. Undaunted by the exposure of his ruse, Hampton went on to exploit numerous other victims with a string of aliases until his death of AIDS-related complications in 2003.

Claiming fame as a little known or neglected relative of the rich and famous is a tried and true method for successful scam artists, especially if one can claim kinship with the blue-blood rich of the American socialite scene. The more respected the family name, the easier it is to fool people into believing you might be from a lesser known branch of the family tree. And few families trace back as far into the dawning of the American social elite than Rockefeller. The family has been around for centuries and consists of various offshoots spread around the country (and the globe). So when *Christophe Rocancourt*, a French born confidence trickster, claimed to be a member of a Paris-based branch of this illustrious family, no one raised an eyebrow. His success at scamming and conning dozens of celebrities and unsuspecting wealthy socialites is legendary and the subject of public note, including a television interview on NBC's *Dateline* and an autobiography in which he talked about the victims whom he defrauded. He fostered friendships and investment relations with well-respected film stars and directors, and he had standing relationships with two Playboy models, one who he married and with whom he had a son, as well as with a former Miss France pageant winner, with whom he had a daughter. He was caught and prosecuted multiple times, ordered to repay millions in restitution, served time in prison, and has subsequently been banned from the country of Switzerland until 2016. To this day, he remains unrepentant and likely to perpetuate further cons if circumstances allow and the gullible potential victim with a soft spot for French flamboyancy crosses his path.

Similarly, *Christian Gerhartsreiter*, aka Clark Rockefeller, and subject of the Mark Seal's incredibly riveting book *The Man In The Rockefeller Suit*, made use of alleged ties to the Rockefeller family to conduct one of the longest running cons of all time. German-born, he traveled to the United States as a teenager under false pretenses, posing as a foreign exchange student. He subsequently attended college in Milwaukee where he met his first wife, whom he married in order to obtain a green card (reportedly leaving her the day after the wedding!). For a number of years, he created and abandoned a string of false identities, including one while he lived with a west coast family where two members went missing. In a strange recent twist, the remains of the missing individuals were discovered years later in the backyard of the home where he lived and Gerhartsreiter has recently been convicted of their murders. After his stint on the west coast, he moved east and fabricated credentials as a film producer. He also held high profile positions with financial firms on Wall Street. Ironically, at one of these firms, it was discovered that the social security number he had provided actually belonged to serial killer David Berkowitz! Despite the appalling breadth of duplicity in his actions and the trail of suspicion he left behind, he was not fired or prosecuted.

It is around that time that the persona under which he was living disappeared from the New York scene and he reappeared as Clark Rockefeller with fabricated ties to the Rockefeller family. He became well known in social scenes as an eccentric and affable bachelor with interest in art and philanthropy and who was working with international agencies to solve debt in third world countries. Through his affiliation with a socially elite house of worship, he met and later married Sandra Boss, a highly successful financial attorney with whom he had a daughter. They lived an affluent lifestyle for twelve years until Boss filed for divorce on the grounds of emotional abuse. As she got ready to exit the marriage, she hired a private investigator only to discover that his claims of partnership in a start-up company and other stories about his activities were entirely unfounded. Not surprisingly, the divorce was granted and Gerhartsreiter was awarded only limited visitation rights to his daughter. In 2008, Gerhartsreiter abducted the child during a supervised visitation in London and fled until he was apprehended by authorities a short time later while living under a yet another false name and identity in Baltimore, Maryland. It was then that the web of lies really began to unravel. The FBI search for Gerhartsreiter for the west coast murders had been nationwide, and his photo was widely publicized. As a result, in depth investigation started to reveal identity after identity and the scope of deceit (and the success he had with perpetuating it) became fully known.

You might wonder how such an elaborate ruse could be kept up for so long. How is it possible that the man's own wife never questioned a completely fabricated background, or the fact that she never met or interacted with any of his work colleagues or friends go on without suspicion? How could a noteworthy financial consultant like Boss never question the lack of evidence for his supposed net worth, or the fact that they seemed to live solely off of her income? We are clearly observing here the profound effects of labeling and association upon perception discussed earlier in this book. In other words, we see what we expect to see. Gerhartsreiter chose identities where eccentricity and flamboyant social inconsistencies were par for the course. Weirdness in his behavior could easily be explained away with thoughts like "Well, he's a film producer and that's Hollywood for you!" or "He's a Rockefeller, of course he's eccentric." Since he crafted himself with the trappings of the socially elite (clothing, places he ate dinner, and even a purebred dog), he easily fit the mold of the estranged son of noble lineage. No one questioned his credentials because he was introduced to new contacts by people they trusted. In essence, his label impacted how those around him perceived him, and once invested in the association, it became harder to see anything odd about his behavior. As the old saying goes, in for a penny, in for a pound.

A Question of Consequences

This chapter has discussed numerous examples of deception and dishonesty, from cheating in professional sports, to misconduct in literature, to fraudulent identities by confidence tricksters. What are the common themes that motivate dishonest behavior across these various examples? Obviously, they all succeed to some degree because they have the ability to perpetrate the ruse for at least a period of time, with impunity. For the most part, they have the experience of success before the truth catches up with them, and that is a compelling motivator. And although punishment when they are caught involves loss of titles, loss of monetary rewards, and sometimes jail time, the perception of reward is significant enough to compel these individuals to risk exposure and the subsequent consequences thereof. In essence, the benefits are legion and they harbor the belief that they can get away with it indefinitely.

The duped are also, unfortunately, complicit in the process. These behaviors typically continue because the public is either accepting or immune from the emotional impact. They condone it through inaction or with penalties far below the benefits the perpetrators reap if they are not caught. When victims find out that they have been duped, they shake their heads and rub their hands in agitation, uttering "tsk, tsk" platitudes. So what makes the general public so gullible that they swallow the lies, cons, and scams so easily? What quells the outrage when we find out we have been fed a dummy? Part of the answer relates to the difficulty of achieving any kind of recompense. What do we as a public expect will address the disappointment we feel when beloved sports figures turn out to be cheats or dopers? Stripping them of their titles does little to erase our national embarrassment or the tarnish on the game. What mitigates our disappointment when we find the exciting tale we have just read is actually a pack of lies? Getting our money back cannot begin to make up for the sense of betrayal that arises from the scandal. As for con artists, recouping some of your money might be nice, but that does not make up for the shock of discovering you could be drawn into such a web of deceit and actually live within it in ignorance.

The other part of the equation sits with our expectations—our passivity in expecting a different standard of behavior and an overestimation of our own ability to see through frauds. These types of scandals happen so often that we now come to expect dishonest behavior, and in expecting it, inadvertently condone it through inaction. There is nothing rare about an athlete who dopes and lies about it these days. It is certainly not unheard of for an author to distort the facts to increase sales. And while con artists of the caliber discussed in this chapter are a fairly rare occurrence, we tend to blame the victims when we hear of the crimes, incorrectly assuming we would be savvier than the poor individuals they took in. The bottom line is that we all need to be smarter about the natures of those around us, to question credentials, and to demand a higher standard of behavior from those we revere if we want to see any shift in the level of morality and honesty displayed by celebrity figures in the future.

CHAPTER 10

Selling the Dummy:
Lies and Gimmicks in Advertising

F alse advertising has been around about as long as the concepts of trading and selling. From the days of snake oil salesmen to modern day subliminal marketing techniques, sellers have always tried to fool unsuspecting consumers into believing that miracle cures, youth, and beauty are available in a bottle. While the majority of advertisers make well informed and legitimate claims, some do walk a fine line between painting a picture that is appealing to the consumer and one that is a complete fabrication. The latter breed has learned many tricks of the trade to try and tip the balance in their favor. For example, TV ads for weight loss programs that show people who have dropped half their previous body weight usually have small print that appears somewhere on the screen saying "results not typical." This covers them for legal liability under false advertising laws, but we all know that most people do not read (or even notice) the fine print. The end result is the duplicitous claim of a weight loss program that appears to promise miraculous results but is really one that will disappoint many people who sign up for it.

In earlier times, sellers were fairly free to hawk their goods without legal reprisal regardless of what incorrect or unfounded claims they made about the product. Sometimes this was the result of ignorance, as when tobacco was marketed as a treatment for asthma before modern science established its role in producing respiratory problems. In other cases, marketing was technically accurate but important information about the product was undisclosed, as with ads from the turn of the last century inviting people to refresh themselves with a glass of Coca Cola without alerting the consumer to the fact that the sense of invigoration came from cocaine extract contained in the beverage. In modern times, government agencies attempt to intervene and protect the consumer from the unfounded claims of unscrupulous advertisers.

Impact of Litigation and Consumer Protection

There have historically been many attempts to legally regulate false statements in advertising, particularly at the state and local level. However, success in receiving redress under false advertising laws has often been hindered by the lack of factual evidence, as well as inconsistency in how deceptive practices have been defined from State to State. In addition, many defendants seek to avoid prosecution by invoking the First Amendment's protection of free speech. Therefore, it was an auspicious day for the vulnerable consumer when the Lanham Act was passed by Congress in 1946. This Act defined trademark infringement and false advertising practices and set the criteria for the federal standard of judgment for infraction across a wide range of advertising media. False advertising culpability is deemed to have been incurred if:

1. *The defendant made a false or misleading statement of fact in a commercial advertisement about a product;*

2. *The statement either deceived or had the capacity to deceive a substantial segment of potential consumers;*

3. *The deception is material, in that it is likely to influence the consumer's purchasing decision;*

4. *The product is in interstate commerce; and*

5. *The plaintiff has been or is likely to be injured as a result of the statement.*

(from Reichman & Cannady (2002) Franshise Law Journal, 21: 187-197)

As a result of the Lanham Act's ratification, there was a significant change in the way advertisers marketed their products. For example, many of us may remember from our childhoods that products like laundry detergents were often advertised as being better than specific other brands. Those head to head ads have disappeared, largely because of the absence of any empirical evidence to back up the claim and the possibility that the competitor might be harmed unfairly. Legal standards under the Consumer Protection Act also mean that advertisers can no longer omit important information about the product, particularly if it might involve potential adverse health effects. In modern times, the Federal Trade Commission (FTC) takes action against businesses that are accused of false or misleading advertising practices, providing a federal level venue for consumer complaints. In addition, all States have some form of anti-deception laws providing recourse for the consumer.

Yet despite increasing penalties and punishments arising from legal suits and consumer complaints, trickery and unfounded claims in advertising continue to be a part of our daily lives. Therefore, it behooves the consumer to develop a strategy for evaluating information contained within commercial advertising in order to make valid judgments about the products and their willingness to invest their money and health in purchasing them.

Luckily, an objective and rational process of judgment is a perfect approach for making sound intelligent decisions around consumer goods.

Prescription Drugs

Pharmaceutical development companies are among the most heavily regulated of all businesses in the world. Considering the fact that their products have the potential to place the health of the public at risk, it makes sense that their processes and claims would be highly scrutinized. In the US, pharmaceutical companies are monitored by the Food and Drug Administration (FDA), which provides review and approval for all steps of the drug development and manufacturing process, including final market approval. Any drug that is not deemed safe, taking into account the tradeoff of benefits to risks, is not approved for use. The problem is that even the extensive late stage clinical trials required to ascertain the safety and effectiveness of a drug employ only a fraction of the potential people who might be prescribed the drug once it is available on the market. Thus, it is not possible to detect or predict every possible adverse effect that might occur once the product is in the public domain.

To address the potential for unaddressed harm, the FDA continues to monitor the effectiveness and safety of all drugs once they are on the market. Sometimes, drugs turn out to have unforeseen adverse side effects and these are either withdrawn from the market, or the label is adjusted to warn consumers of the potential risks. While companies are held accountable for the safety and effectiveness of their drugs, even after FDA approval, the act of discovering an adverse event after the fact is not considered false advertising. Based upon my long experience with the pharmaceutical business, I am pleased to say that most companies make every effort possible to uncover and address potential risks before the drug goes on the market. Rather, false advertising becomes an issue when a manufacturer knowingly misleads potential consumers by omitting important safety information from the label, minimizes the risks of taking the drug when advertising it to health care professionals or the public, or makes unsupported claims about the effectiveness of the product. Furthermore, companies are not permitted to advertise or promote "off label" use of a drug. The FDA approves a product only for the indication(s) for which it was developed and tested. Despite the ability of physicians to prescribe a drug for other unapproved uses, any encouragement of such by the manufacturer is treated as coercive and false positioning. Under modern law, companies that mislead consumers or pitch unapproved indications to care givers are usually dealt with in a decisive and often very public matter. Here are some examples of recent false advertising claims that were investigated and addressed by regulatory agencies around prescription drug products.

- Drug manufacturers frequently make use of relevant celebrities to help market their products. Such was the case for *Kaletra*, a high profile and first of its kind drug combination developed to block the replication of the HIV virus that provides a fairly well tolerated treatment option for AIDS. In 2009, Abbott Laboratories, who manufactures the drug, was investigated by the FDA regarding a promotional DVD where basketball legend, Magic Johnson, gave personal testimony about the effectiveness of the drug. Unfortunately, the claims suggested that the drug is actually more effective than it is and these were viewed as misrepresentations of the treatment, as well as promoting off label use. The FDA served Abbott Labs with a warning letter (contrary to what you might think, FDA warning letters are taken very, very seriously by drug manufacturers) requiring that they cease using the promotional video, and requiring them to create a plan of action to address how they would correct the message to the relevant audiences.

- Do you remember the TV commercial with Brooke Shields looking out at the camera with her thick and sultry eyelashes, touting the benefits of thicker lashes through *Latisse*? Latisse is an eye drop solution applied to the base of the upper lashes marketed by Allergan for conditions of thin or sparse eye lashes. In this case, there was no deception about the effectiveness of the drug. It works. It really works. It works so well that it can cause hair to grow other places where the solution might touch, not just on lashes. It also causes eye pigment to irreversibly darken, and can promote susceptibility to bacterial infections with a risk of blindness. None of these potential side effects were mentioned in the original ads for the product, until the FDA cited Allergan with a warning letter in 2009 requiring them to alter the content of the ads to include information about side effects and risk. Allergan's website for Latisse now includes a list of potential side effects and a link to the FDA website for reporting adverse events.

- Celebrities are not the only coveted spokespeople for drug advertising—high profile medical professionals are worth their weight in gold for endorsements on relevant products. For example, Pfizer made excellent use of Dr. Robert Jarvik, the inventor of the artificial heart, for a series of ads for the cholesterol lowering drug, *Lipitor*. Until it went off patent in 2011, Lipitor was one of the world's highest grossing drugs and it remains a highly effective agent for lowering cholesterol. The problem the FDA had with the ads was not the claims of effectiveness or hiding side effect issues, but rather that Dr. Jarvik was not licensed to practice medicine. While a medical license would not have been necessary for him to speak on behalf of the drug, the FDA determined that the ads misled consumers about the spokesperson's credentials, implying more medical knowledge behind the statements than perhaps was warranted. That is why many advertisements that show actors portraying doctors include a disclaimer that says "not a real doctor." Perhaps the best known example was when Robert Young, the actor from the 1970's TV series *Marcus Welby*, hawked aspirin to the public in a TV ad with the famous statement "I am not a doctor, but I play one on TV." To millions of Americans, his stint as Marcus Welby gave him enough status to convince them to buy the product over other competitors despite a lack of credentials.

- Unfortunately, at other times the marketing angle is to hide serious adverse side effects that pose a danger to the general public. Such instances are the most serious form of false advertising to the FDA and meet with the gravest repercussions. Such was the case with *Avandia*, a drug marketed by GlaxoSmithKline for treatment of type 2 diabetes. Stemming from a 2007 independent clinical study report showing a substantially increased risk of heart attack and resulting death, the FDA launched an investigation into whether GSK withheld important safety data about heart related side effects. The FDA issued an alert notice to health care professionals and the general public, warning that there might be hitherto unreported risks of using the drug, and set up a "Avandia-Rosiglitazone Medicines Access Program" to which medical practitioners must enroll if they plan to prescribe the drug. In addition, the label and prescribing information required changes to reflect the information about risk. While the drug is still available on the market, GSK was required to pay $3 billion in fines for fraud damages around this and two other drugs for which it marketed the products for unapproved use. To date, this is the largest penalty assigned by the FDA to any drug manufacturer.

As an average consumer likely without a medical background, how is it possible for you to apply your personal standards of rational judgment to commercial advertising with any chance of ascertaining the truth? It is much more difficult to identify whether claims are exaggerated or negative side effects have been reported when you do not have access to the research and clinical study reports. In this case, you have to rely upon the rigor and knowledge of agencies like the FDA.

Luckily, the FDA is making it easier than ever for prescribing medical professionals to stay informed on relevant information with the launch of the "Bad Drug Program." This initiative of the FDA's Division of Drug Marketing, Advertising, and Communications provides enhanced guidance of promotional practices, and guidelines for recognizing and reporting for false or misleading claims. In addition, a partner program for the general public, the "FDA Online Guide for Consumers," provides a resource assessing prescription drug advertisements to avoid the types of infringements we have discussed here. If you have a concern about the safety or effectiveness of a drug that you have seen in an advertisement, check out this online resource. It will provide you with the information you need from medical professionals who have the appropriate credentials in order to evaluate commercial information in an honest and straight forward manner.

Health and Wellness Aids

In addition to prescription health products, there is an enormous market in health and wellness aids, supplements, and over the counter agents that unfortunately are not monitored to the same degree by the FDA or other consumer watchdog agencies.

Therefore, it is easier for these manufacturers to market these so-called nutraceuticals with false or unrealistic claims. Many of these involve enormous potential for profit for the company, and provide little or no benefit to the consumer. While manufacturers are required to possess substantiated scientific evidence for the claims of health benefits for dietary supplements, they are not required to submit the evidence to the FDA prior to marketing the product. Furthermore, label information for these products is unregulated, except for a requirement that it state the product has not been reviewed by the FDA.

Such a lack of oversight for products that are consumed daily by millions of American seems counterintuitive, especially when the regulations for prescription products, meat, produce, and other consumables are so rigorous and exhaustive. According to an October 10, 2012 report from the Office of the Inspector General for the U.S. Department of Health and Human Services, a study of 127 dietary supplements on the market revealed:

> *...substantiation documents for the sampled supplements were inconsistent with FDA guidance on competent and reliable scientific evidence. FDA could not readily determine whether manufacturers had submitted the required notification for their claims. Seven percent of the supplements lacked the required disclaimer, and 20 percent included prohibited disease claims on their labels. These results raise questions about the extent to which structure/function claims are truthful and not misleading. (Report (OEI-01-11-00210), Dietary Supplements: Structure/Function Claims Fail To Meet Federal Requirements)*

As a result, the FDA has been urged to tighten regulation around advertising claims for dietary supplements and over the counter remedies, and to increase surveillance practices around such advertising claims. Until the FDA decides on a plan of action, it is up to the consumer to recognize false and unrealistic claims around health and wellness products. Let us take a look at some of the more popular products currently on the market and determine how well their claims stack up to rigorous empirical evaluation.

- I remember when the delicious and nutritious *Acai berry* first hit the market, Not only was the juice of this berry tasty to drink, but the high content of anti-oxidants was being marketed as an effective means of promoting weight loss and as a prevention for colon cancer. Who would not want to slim their waist and ward off cancer with a glass a day?

  The truth is that Acai berries are very high in anti-oxidants and that there is a scientific link between anti-oxidants and the clearance of cellular free radicals that have a role in aging, metabolism, and immune function. There is no reason to think that Acai berry juice is unhealthy, and in fact it likely supplies important dietary nutrients. However, there is absolutely no scientific evidence that this berry is superior to any other anti-oxidant rich fruit (e.g., cranberry, raspberry, blueberry), nor is there any support for the ability of this fruit to prevent aging, cancer, or weight gain. Central Coast Nutraceuticals, a Phoenix based manufacturing company, was slapped with a $1.5 million fine for false advertising early in 2012,including false statements and phony endorsements by celebrities, including Oprah Winfrey. The consensus is that this berry, while certainly good for your general health, unfortunately will not turn you into a younger, slimmer, healthier version of yourself all on its own.

- We would all like to eat whatever we want and still lose weight. That is why I sat straight up from my slouched position on the couch when I saw a TV ad for **Sensa**, a saffron based supplement that one can sprinkle on their food and watch the pounds melt away. I was especially impressed by the delighted expression on the face of the police officer while he ate a donut, apparently guilt free, after sprinkling on a bit of Sensa. Before you prepare to munch your way through all of your favorite foods with impunity, be prepared—it doesn't work! There is some anecdotal evidence that saffron curbs appetite, but there is no scientific basis for any claims that Sensa allows a person to eat whatever they like and still lose weight. Furthermore, claims that a clinical study, peer reviewed by the Endocrine Society, showed substantial weight loss in the Sensa treated group appears to be a fabrication. Therefore, it is not surprising that Intelligent Beauty, Inc., the makers of Sensa, agreed to pay over $9 million in a class action suit around false claims of the supplement's efficacy in promoting weight loss. Sorry folks, no magic cure for over eating here.

- It is an empirical fact that chronic stress increases the secretion of cortisol (the "stress hormone") from the adrenal gland, and that excess cortisol promotes fat deposition in order to promote survival during environmental challenges. Therefore, the claims that **Relacore**, a presumptive cortisol blocking supplement, can trim away belly fat seem intuitively logical. Unfortunately, none of the ingredients in Relacore (a combination of vitamins and herbal extracts) have been clinically proven to reduce cortisol levels. Furthermore, there are no scientific data showing enhanced loss of fat (around the belly or anywhere) for people taking this product. That is actually not surprising, since the only situation in which reducing excess cortisol would have an effect on ability to deposit belly fat is under situations where cortisol is chronically elevated. Most of us, even those of us who feel harried and stressed out, usually do not have excessive cortisol levels. This is a case where the concept is intriguing, but if the product worked at all, it would only do so for a small number of people who are living in extraordinarily stressful circumstances (like active combat or illness). As a result, the New Jersey Supreme Court ruled in favor of a class action law suit against the makers of Relacore for promoting false claims about the efficacy of the product. Unfortunately for many wishful Americans, there is still no better approach to reducing belly fat than reducing caloric intake and increasing exercise.

- Body weight is not the only thing we wish we could change simply by taking a pill. Millions of American men are influenced by ads for male enhancement products every day. While some prescription products (e.g., Viagra, Cialis, Levitra) do effectively treat erectile dysfunction, they do not alter penile size or performance. Therefore, it should raise suspicion when advertisements for *Extenze*, a natural herbal supplement for male enhancement, claim to have succeeded where the commercial drug manufacturers had failed. Despite the huge grins on the faces of "Bob" and his wife in the ads, the supplement has no empirically documented effect on penis size leading to a multitude of civil suits against the manufacturer, Biotab Neutraceuticals. In addition to various State settlements, a class action suit claiming false advertising has been preliminarily approved. I am afraid Bob is not smiling so much anymore!

When it comes to judging the truth underlying advertising for health and wellness aids, finding accurate scientific evidence to back up the claims is even more difficult than for prescription products. Manufacturers are not regulated to the same degree as pharmaceuticals, and there is little oversight for the claims they make to the general public until consumers actually lodge a complaint. The application of the principles of logic and reason is also a bit impeded by two important psychological variables in the consumer: 1) the claims seem to make intuitive sense, and 2) we would really, really like them to be true. In the first instance, the apparently reasonable nature of the claims fails to raise a red flag for many of us, and we do not bother to do any further investigation to check out the facts. In the second instance, our desire to possess an easy and effective solution to a physical or health problem (particularly one that does not involve seeing a doctor) promotes inherent personal bias against looking for contradictory facts.

The answer, however, remains the same. The wary consumer should approach all advertising claims in this genre with healthy skepticism. Having spent much of my career in the pharmaceutical industry, I can tell you that researchers have looked for a quick fix to issues like obesity for decades. You can bet that if enhancing mood or blocking cortisol resulted in weight loss without the need for diet or exercise, companies would already have discovered, developed, and packaged it and would be reaping in the revenue. The bottom line advice to any consumer in this area is "If it seems too good to be true, IT IS!"

If you are interested in finding out whether an advertised product actually works, do a web search using key words like "scam" and "false advertising." Do not rely upon the manufacturer's sites—they are the ones putting out the false information in the first place and will likely have no documented scientific evidence to support their claims (even if they say they do). Use medical sites like WebMD where the pros and cons of the products are discussed by medical professionals who have not been paid to endorse the product. These postings will often discuss whether there is any scientific evidence to back up claims of clinically proven effects, and will save you time, money, and the possibility of risky side effects by spending a few moments digging on the web.

Exercise Gimmicks

Similar to the case with miracle diet products, Americans are also always on the lookout for easy ways to get fit and toned without having to put out any effort. That makes us prime targets for buying any number of exercise gimmicks that claim to do everything from shortening a workout to six min to the promise of giving us "six pack abs" while we sleep. As much as I would really like to be able to slim my waist and tone my posterior while I am writing these words, the sad truth is that no such thing exists. Muscles only get toned with use, and fat only burns away with caloric expenditure. So why do some exercise gimmicks suck us in despite our intuitive knowledge that it cannot possibly work? The lure is in the apparent sincerity of the advertising and the manufacturer's ability to convince us that the impossible is actually plausible.

- One of the biggest fitness crazes of the past few years has been the concept of shoes that tone your muscles while you walk, resulting in "buns of steel" with relatively little effort. Companies like *Sketchers* and *Reebok* made millions with this marketing ploy, and retail businesses had trouble keeping the shoes in stock. Kim Kardashian, spokesperson for Sketchers, assured the public that weight loss would result from simply wearing the shoes. Reebok backed up the effectiveness of the Easytone shoe with statistics purportedly arrived at by scientific study that would provide enhanced muscle firming of up to "28% in the gluteus maximus, 11% in the hamstrings, and 11% in the calves." Who could possibly resist? Unfortunately for the exercise phobic, these shoes provide no particular muscle toning benefit over any other shoe (except perhaps that people tended to be more enthusiastic when they thought that the shoes were firming their bottoms and thus walked a bit more). Not surprisingly, the FTC smacked both companies with heavy fines for false advertising ($25 million for Reebok, $50 million for Sketchers) providing for refunds to customers who had been bamboozled by the advertising hype.

- Imagine the luxury of a gadget that effectively trims and tones your waist while helping you lose weight, all while you sit on your couch or even while you sleep! It is no wonder a number of such devices are available on the market today. However, as I said earlier in reference to pills that help you lose weight without diet and exercise, the lure of easy returns is waylaid by the fact that the device simply does not work that way. Since 2002, the FTC has ruled that the claims of weight loss and toning benefits that meet or exceed those obtained through physical training are unwarranted, therefore charging the companies with false advertising. And the US is not alone in taking action. Advertisements for Emerald Ocean's **Slendertone** electronic abdominal toning device have been cited in numerous countries, including a ruling of breach of the Trade Practices by the Australian Competition and Consumer Commission for claiming the device had the same benefits as extensive exercise. Sorry folks, looks like vigorous abdominal exercise remains the only effective means of getting those six pack abs.

- Ok, so maybe we cannot firm up our tummies while we sleep, but surely there is a way to do it more effectively than endless and rather repetitious series of sit ups and crunches every day. Enter the enticing world of abdominal machines for home use. Bigger and more expensive versions of these devices are seen in virtually every gym in the country, so it seems reasonable that we could buy something for home use that would allow us to tuck and tone without the embarrassment of sweating in public. And so there are, and in most cases, these devices work. By that I mean that if you do enough repetitions over a long enough period of time, you will definitely see improvement in muscle tone. However, these devices are relatively expensive and offer little benefit over sit ups and other exercises you can do on your living room floor, and certainly do not reduce the amount of time and effort required to get the effects. In the case of **Ab Circle Pro**, a swiveling device that costs about $250, the FTC recently ruled that the manufacturer's claims of "3 minutes = equivalent of 100 sit ups and results in 10 pounds lost in two weeks" were unfounded and misleading and required the company to refund roughly $25 million to dissatisfied consumers.

- One more device deserves notable mention in the exercise and fitness gimmick category. The **Velform sauna belt** is one of many devices that claim to sweat off extra fat, relax muscles, and remove toxins from specific body parts. There is no doubt that use of this device on the waist, hips, back, or buttocks regions will in fact work like a miniature sauna causing sweating and fluid loss, as well as applying heat that can be soothing to sore muscles. However, there is no scientific evidence that this approach will induce true weight loss in the absence of caloric restriction and exercise, as any fluid lost during the application is quickly replenished when the person drinks. In addition, improper use of the device can lead to burns and skin reactions. It is not surprising that both the FTC and the UK's Adverting Standards Authority cited the manufacturer for false advertising claims in 2005, requiring them to rework their advertising campaign.

The commonality among all of these gimmicks is that they provide results in record time with no effort. In terms of applying logic and reason to this area, first consider with skepticism any claim that weight loss and fitness are easy to achieve. The very nature of human biology (and that of any other animal for that matter) is that work and effort build muscle, exercise expends calories, and reducing calories compared to physical need burns fat stores and results in weight loss. No matter how much you might want to believe otherwise, that is nature's formula and our very evolution depended upon it. But if you want to consider a claim that is too good to be true just in case a breakthrough miracle actually has occurred, simply go to the internet and type in the name of the product along with "scam" or "false advertising." Any pending or decided FTC or Consumer Protection actions will be easy to find. If it still looks like a clear path, consider whether you could accomplish the promised outcome as effectively with standard exercises or items lying around your house before you pay hundreds of dollars for the latest exercise fad.

Technology

Whereas many readers might have scoffed at the gullibility of consumers to the fads and gimmicks described above, more of us are caught every day with technology scams and hype that are harder to spot without expert assistance. While quality information sources like Consumer Reports can certainly help us make appropriate judgments before we buy large ticket items, not every potential technological deception gets picked up by such sources. Many times, information about the scam or deceptive practice does not come to light until many customers are already invested in the product. The following are some recent examples of technology products or services that were less than upfront in their advertising practices.

- One of the biggest and most exciting technology advances in smartphone function was the introduction of *Siri*, iPhone's personal assistant based upon revolutionary voice recognition and response software. Millions of consumers lined up for the launch in an attempt to be among the first to obtain this technological marvel. Unfortunately, the bugs had not all been worked before it hit the public, and Siri frequently misunderstood voice commands or provided incorrect responses. It certainly did not work with the ease and efficiency depicted in various TV ads about the product. As a result, at least two class action law suits have been filed in the US alone during 2012 for false and misleading advertising about the capabilities of the personal assistant software. Apple claims that it was transparent about the stage of development of the technology, and that, in essence, the first wave of consumers were part of a large beta test to further development. However, consumers claim that the ads clearly hyped a functionality that the software could not deliver. While the suits have not yet been decided, it is clear the controversy is not around whether the product had been perfected for public use, but rather whether consumers had a right to expect a higher level of performance, based upon advertisements, than the product was able to deliver.

- In contrast, the clear cut nature of false claims made by auto makers Kia and Hyundai around the economy and mileage ratings of several of their automobiles stimulated a class action lawsuit that could approach $125 million in cash and credits to affected customers. The Environmental Protection Agency (EPA) confirmed that, after independent testing and audit, the mileage ratings listed on the window stickers of at least 1.1 million cars reflected an inflated value. And it is not the first time such exaggerated claims by these companies have been prosecuted. In 2002, Hyundai got nailed for overstating the horse power capabilities of some models. Luckily, in both cases, skeptical customers were able to mobilize the resources of the EPA in a way that shed light on the deceptive marketing and resulted in an aggressive response by the government watchdog agencies.

• Some companies do not try to increase sales through false statements about their products, but rather attempt to increase market share by generating a reputation built upon a false image. *Samsung Electronics* advertises its organization as striving to be "one of the world's most ethical companies." However, in 2012, the New York based China Labor Watch group published child labor allegations around underage workers and working hours that exceeded the legal limits in at least six Samsung factories. These reports have been picked up by three workers' rights groups in France who have filed lawsuits alleging false advertising about the company's public claims of employing ethical work standards. This example is notable as it seeks to prosecute the company's failure to abide by child labor laws indirectly by targeting false claims of ethical behavior.

In all of these examples, the average consumer would have little recourse to judge in advance that the products in question were misrepresented. Only after a time on the market do these situations typically come to light. Therefore, it is difficult to apply the principles of your personal process of rational judgment to such instances before you make the decision to buy. You do, however, have the opportunity to evaluate the truth and accuracy of claims and allegations that subsequently result by being knowledgeable regarding the sources of information you use. Organizations like the EPA, various government watch dog groups, and publications like Consumer Reports typically have a reputation for providing straight forward critiques for you to judge. They tend to be unbiased and use scientific approaches to providing data and conclusions about a product or situation. If you cannot catch the deception prior to the fact, at the very least you can apply sound, logical evaluation to assess the extent of the problem once it comes to your awareness.

Subliminal Advertising

While not technically false advertisement by definition, I believe that subliminal advertising deserves a mention in this chapter due to its obvious goal of falsely influencing the consumer. The concept of subliminal advertising first reached the public awareness in the 1950's when James Vicary, a well-known marketing consultant, published reports on the effects of presenting product information in a manner that cannot typically be consciously detected on the subsequent mood and behavior of the unwary subject. Vicary reportedly flashed phrases about soft drinks or snacks to audiences at movie theaters and monitored how many subsequently went out and bought the products. Many examples of using similar techniques to embed words or images in larger advertisements ensued, raising a certain level of anxiety in the general public who feared the effects of "mind control."

After reading about this advertising gimmick during my freshman year of college, my roommates and I used to spend long hours poring over the ads in popular magazines, looking for examples of subliminal messages in everything from ice cubes to clouds to the folds in an evening gown. I have no idea if any of the supposed examples we found were actually purposeful attempts at subliminal messaging, but we now know that Vicary's movie theater study results were in fact fabricated. It is unclear how much effect, if any, subliminal messaging actually has on behavior, but numerous laws have been created against its use to protect the consumer anyway. Nowadays we instead see more blatant, but still tricky, advertising approaches like product placement. Take for instance the popular reality show, American Idol, sponsored by Coca Cola. It is not just for the benefit of the thirsty judges that there is a big red cup with Coke written on it in plain view of the camera, but also to entice the viewing audience to pour a glass for themselves. Whether this gimmick works or not, advertisers pay big money to have their products visible in television shows, movies, and other publicized events so that their brand is on your mind next time you make a purchase. It is worth a moment of reflection before you buy something to make certain you actually want it, and are not just the rube at the center of an advertising gimmick.

The Good, the Bad, and the Gullible

We all know in our hearts that the underwear we buy from Victoria's Secret is not going to suddenly change us into the lithe and sexy women who model the garments in the ads. We might not want to admit it, but we know that no amount of hair conditioner is going to morph us into Jennifer Lopez, nor will foundation make-up make us look like Andy McDowell even if it does cover up our wrinkles and lines. Yet we continue to be duped and scammed by unsubstantiated product claims to the tune of millions of dollars every year.

There are obviously good and accurate advertisements out there that can alert us to products with potential benefit, but it can be difficult to see through the hype and deceptive advertising in order to weed out the quacks and the counterfeits. This is a perfect opportunity for you to deploy the process of deductive reasoning you have been developing, and submit any potential purchase to a few well designed and probing questions:

1. What is the source of the endorsement? How credible is it?

2. Does the product have any endorsements from unbiased expert consumer review organizations?

3. What evidence exists to support the claims and is it scientifically or medically proven?

4. Are there any complaints or allegations of scams and false advertising out there? Is there litigation pending?

The internet, consumer review magazines, and consumer alert agencies (FTC, EPA, etc.) are all useful resources for evaluating the truthfulness of a variety of product advertisements. It is usually pretty easy to catch a potential problem by doing a simple search. For instance, while I was writing this chapter, I did a great deal of research on the internet looking for examples of false advertising that have been reported across the different categories. I actually intended to review four examples in the technology section, including one with an interesting twist where the manufacturer actually sued the celebrity spokesperson for misrepresenting the product publicly. I wrote the section using my research material and was really pleased at how it balanced out the points I was trying to illustrate. However, when I went to do a final fact-checking exercise on the section, I discovered that none of my information about the story came from credible sources. When I subsequently cast a wider net and looked at litigation involving the parties concerned, it turns out that I had been misled about what happened by stories that originated in gossip columns and got picked up by newswires. Imagine how embarrassing it would be to spend an entire book touting the value of rationally determining the truth only to be tripped up by failing to follow my own advice!

The best defense you, the consumer, can have against scams and product fraud is your own healthy skepticism and the willingness to spend just a little time checking out the available information before you make that purchase. Be careful to evaluate the credentials and possible motivations of those who give endorsements. Look for corroborating evidence from unbiased product review organizations. And certainly, check to be sure that there are no existent complaints about the products or litigation for false advertising before you make your decision. Following these few simple steps will save you a lot of grief in the long run. And remember the most important axiom—if it seems too good to be true, then it likely is! The gullible consumer just provides fodder for unethical and misleading practices, so do your best to keep them from achieving their goals by using rational and empirical assessment practices before you shell out your hard earned cash.

CHAPTER 11

Through the Dark Glass: The Role of the Internet in Perpetuating Deception

M any of us can hardly remember life without the internet. As a scientist and an academic, I began using this amazing electronic resource from its inception as a powerful, quick, and effective means of researching information. Gone were the days of hours and hours spent in quiet musty old libraries pouring through journals and books and news archives for relevant items. Not to mention the fun of being able to look up anything, even the most esoteric and bizarre queries, and being able to find sites with reams of facts available right at your fingertips. If I wanted to know something, you could pretty much guarantee that someone else had posted information about it for all to see.

Alas, as with many great inventions, the power of the internet comes with a dark side. Unlike information obtained from peer reviewed journals, carefully edited newspapers, or respected periodicals that have a reputation to uphold, information on the internet can be populated by anyone from anywhere, whether they know what they are talking about or not. Even one of the greatest online resources currently available—Wikipedia—which harnesses the collective brain power of subject matter experts across the world, cannot guarantee the accuracy of everything posted to their site. The best they can do is post warnings that information on the site has not been verified or is in question. In contrast, most other sites, from blogs to personal websites to company and commercial portals, are not monitored for accuracy. In essence, anything might be out there and anything probably is!

As curious creatures and insatiable consumers of information, humans have now become inseparable from the internet and its lure of quick replies to our most pressing questions. As I have mentioned repeatedly throughout this book, I depend upon the internet multiple times every day to gain information, fact check something I have heard, or to try to prove my husband wrong about one assertion or another. Therefore, it is all the more critical that we understand how to filter the information that is so readily accessible, and consider what we read with rigorous standards allowing us to fulfill our need for information while avoiding the pitfalls of the inaccuracies that abound throughout this medium. What better approach to apply to such a conundrum than the principles of deductive logic?

Know Your Source

As with any other source of information, understanding the potential biases and the agenda of information websites is a critical first step to judging the veracity of its contents. Whether intentional or not, postings by political and special interest groups are prime candidates for imbalanced or distorted reporting. The very purpose of these sites is to share information that supports the inherent views of the constituency, so it is not surprising that information that contradicts their views will be omitted.

Furthermore, as we learned in Chapter Four, our own inherent psychology renders us capable of subtle distortions in information that can change the nature of our expression without us ever being aware. We tend to interpret things in ways that perpetuate our pre-existing beliefs, we emphasize certain aspects of information over others, and we tend to ignore things that do not support our views. These factors certainly have an impact upon the nature and content of information on any special interest website, even when there is no overt intent to distort or deceive.

Take for example a political site supporting a liberal candidate for office. Let us say that this hypothetical candidate has a history of voting as a moderate on many issues, but that the current political climate favors more liberalism. It is not uncommon for the candidate's website to list and emphasize past decisions and achievements around liberal issues, and to downplay or totally omit those past actions that were more right-leaning. It is not that the content of the website is untrue—a bit of fact checking can verify whether it is or not—but the impression given about the candidate's views and philosophy may be misrepresented by cherry picking the information, and by the ways in which facts are presented overall.

Similarly, websites for special interest groups that are lobbying for or against particular legislation that could affect its constituency are typically slanted toward reporting information that either supports their position or undermines their opponents. Take for example the National Rifle Association that is currently very visible in the ongoing debate around reforming gun control regulations. Logging in to the NRA site, the first thing that you notice is a rolodex of high profile headlines reflecting news stories about private citizens who were punished for defending themselves or their homes and families with legally owned firearms, as well as celebrity endorsements for gun rights and calls for action to push back on impending gun control proposals. There are no headlines about innocent people that were shot by individuals who had not undergone background checks. There are no statements from celebrities who advocate for stricter gun control. There is no discussion about potential ways to tighten gun regulations to close loopholes that can be exploited by criminal elements while still protecting the Second Amendment rights of private citizens. And you would not expect there to be because this is a special interest website supporting their particular interests.

There is nothing inherently wrong with such postings. They serve an important purpose for communicating with the constituents of the group who created the website. The problem arises only when people mistakenly consider these to be unbiased and balanced sources of information. It is ok to use these sites for information gathering, but be certain to exercise a few simple rules to aid your judgment before you come to a final conclusion.

First, verify that the site reports actual facts and is not one of the many spoof or satirical sites that are designed for entertainment purposes only. For example, *The Onion* is an incredibly well done satirical publication that at first glance closely resembles a legitimate news source. If you were to run across an article without knowing it originated with *The Onion*, it might be easy to be fooled that you are reading something real.

Second, consider the source of the content and what stake the creators of the particular website have in the game. There are a variety of websites, ranging from unbiased news reporting through encyclopedic knowledge archives through academic peer-reviewed materials, to choose from in researching any particular statement or event. Snopes.com is particularly useful as they were created to debunk untruthful information circulating on the web and other forms of media. Be aware of sites that look official but are not. Virtually anyone can post a website very easily these days and make it look extremely official, but that does not change the fact that the source may be unvetted and the credentials might not be sound. When perusing unsubstantiated websites, search for the pieces of information that the website creators left out and construct a bigger picture of your own for making judgments. The more information you have about a thing, even contradictory information, the more likely it will be that you can come to an accurate conclusion of the facts.

Lastly, do some searching for contradictory opinions and weigh the evidence from both sides. Ask yourself which sources of information are the most rational, and which are supported by factual evidence as opposed to circumstantial or exculpatory evidence. Ask yourself whether any reasonable person coming across the information without any prior history would consider it plausible. And of course the hardest thing to do is try to highlight your own areas of bias and consider whether you believe it because the facts are sound and compelling, or simply because it fits in with your *a priori* view of the world. Considering rationally both the nature of the information and your reasons for judging it will likely deliver a more informed view of the hodge podge electronic soup that comprises the internet.

In the next section, we will examine some highly provocative sources of information currently existent on the internet or through related emails circulating across social networks. These examples cover the gambit from conspiracy theories to special interest interpretations of political activities and current events. For each example, I will demonstrate the process employed in investigating, evaluating, judging, and in many cases ultimately debunking the information by using the rigorous and deductive principles that we have been discussing throughout this book.

Key Conspiracies of our Era

<u>The Unthinkable Day</u>—On September 11, 2001, the country and the world looked on in horror as the hatred-inspired plan of anti-American terrorists to crash commercial airliners into key financial and government locations in New York and Washington DC unfolded before our eyes. There is no doubt that the events of

that day changed our lives forever, impacting everything from our security processes to exercises of civil liberty to the very basis of our national mindset. It is also not surprising that any number of conspiracy theories about the attacks grew up like weeds in the aftermath, as the human mind is more open to considering the inexplicable when the unthinkable happens before our very eyes.

Shortly after the tragedy on 9/11, disturbing conspiracy theories began circulating across the internet (e.g., Patriotsaints. com, Whatreallyhappened.com) and were spread more publically by speaking personalities such as Michael Rupert (seminars and testimonies easily accessible on YouTube). While many questions remain unanswered about how such a tragic event could happen on our own soil, perhaps the most insidious of the alternative explanations involves collusion by the Bush government with the terrorist faction, ranging from accusations that Bush helped plan the event to the less damning, but no less horrific, assertion that the Bush government knew about the planned attacks and let them happen in order to garner national support for what would otherwise have been very unpopular foreign policies. Some propose that bombs set before the collision of airliners into the Twin Towers were responsible for bringing them down. Others claim that the US government fired a missile at the Pentagon rather than believe the devastation resulted from a crashed plane. Still others point to the suspicious coincidence that military war games were in progress on that date resulting in loss of air coverage for large portions of the US at the time of the attacks and therefore leaving the terrorists free access to their targets. One major theory even claims that the attacks were designed to provide the final impetus for an invasion that would promote a decade long plan to establish an oil pipeline through Afghanistan.

The individuals and groups who create and publicize these theories usually do so with enormous conviction. They speak with obvious belief in what they say. They provide apparently compelling evidence for their claims and are adept at weaving a theme of collusion that seems to make sense while preying upon the ever increasing paranoia of a society reeling in shock. But how well do their claims hold up to inspection? What actual evidence supports any of these contentions? What facts and information go against the theory and how reputable are the sources on each side? And finally, what are the larger ramifications if any one of these conspiracy theories is actually true?

Any number of potential scenarios can be constructed to indicate that the Bush government could have benefited by the national response to a tragedy of this proportion. It is certain that public support for action against Afghanistan and the Taliban government for harboring Bin Laden and his followers was enormously high in the wake of the attacks. And even though the public outcry against invading Iraq, and questions about the legitimacy of the claims around weapons of mass destruction, made for a much more polarized national debate, it is extremely likely that the impact of being attacked on our own soil caused many Americans to view the actions against Iraq more favorably. It is also clear that Americans would never have embraced the many changes to our civil liberties (The Patriot Act, increased security screenings, decreased personal privacy protections, etc.) if the attacks on 9/11 had not happened.

On a basic level, these arguments have a certain internal consistency that satisfies the psyches of those who have experienced a highly emotive and traumatic event because they help assign blame in a more concrete fashion. As strange as it may seem, it can be more comforting to a person to believe that a horrific event transpired because their government was in on it than it is to believe that the government was an ineffective deterrent and that protection from such events cannot be expected in the future. And it is particularly powerful if you happen to be a person who disagrees with the philosophies and the platform of the government in question. Remembering back to our earlier discussion of attribution theory, it is easy for a person to interpret circumstantial evidence in a damning way if it reflects what they believe to be dispositional characteristics of the person (or government) about which they already have a negative view.

The elegance behind accusations of collusion between the Bush government and the Al Qaeda terrorists lies with the fact that there is no evidence to refute it. While a lack of evidence does not prove anything, it certainly does help perpetuate conspiracy theories. It means that it becomes more difficult to evaluate facts and instead we must focus on evaluating the plausibility of scenarios. For example, there is no evidence to refute a potential decade long plan to invade Afghanistan in order to establish an oil pipeline, this is true. We cannot refute the accusation based upon facts available to the average American, but we can consider what it means and whether it is plausible. If there was a plan ten years or more in the making that only culminated with the a terrorist act on US soil, just to provide justification for action against Afghanistan nationals, that would mean that the plans existed across the terms of at least three presidents. The governments of both George H. Bush and Bill Clinton would have been part of the planning along with that of George W. Bush. This would necessitate cooperation from both conservative and liberal governments. Considering the fact that we have been enjoying some of the most politically polarized government factions in recent memory, this seems highly unlikely.

Let us also consider what such a scenario would mean about the personal nature of these three presidents and their respective governments. When the proponents of these conspiracy theories pin the acts on our government, they are saying that we elect and appoint the type of people who condone mass murder in order to further secular interests. Whether you like a given president or not, I would think it gives pause to consider the ramifications of such an accusation. It also means that hundreds of government workers who may have come in contact with information supporting such hcinous plans were somehow compelled to remain silent, a feat that seems veritably impossible for the Capitol Hill with which we are all familiar. Nonetheless, we have no evidence that these individuals are not the types to perpetuate violence and terror for their own ends. Luckily, we live in a society where lack of evidence does not hold up well in a court of law.

What about some of the more substantive claims involving physical evidence that we can consider, like explosives to bring down the towers or the missile strike on the Pentagon? In this case, the lack of evidence actually goes the other way. There is no evidence that bombs exploded after the World Trade Center attack. Many structural engineering experts have testified that the impact of ignited jet fuel combined with the structural damage from the crashes would be sufficient to cause the collapse. Photographs taken during the disaster show bowing of the perimeter columns just prior to the collapse, thus supporting the theory that extraordinary heat caused the compromise of the structural integrity. Hundreds of firefighters who were well trained in all types of incendiary events corroborated the nature of the fire and subsequent collapse. Despite months of investigation and involvement of many hundreds of rescue and restoration workers, not one verifiable claim of evidence supporting an explosion not tied to internal combustible materials has ever been filed. The proposition that the towers fell due to structural and combustion-related damage as a result of the crash of airliners into the towers remains the only valid and evidence-based explanation for the collapse of the World Trade Center towers.

As for the Pentagon, the biggest piece of evidence refuting the conspiracy claims of a missile strike is the testimony of numerous witnesses who saw the plane crash. Not to mention the reports from the FAA and American Airline representatives corroborating the loss of Flight 77 and all passengers and crew onboard, as well as the families of the victims, some of whom received phone calls from passengers onboard. Some have claimed that not enough damage was seen in the wake of the accident to be accounted for by a plane crash, but these have been refuted by numerous photographs showing the extensive damage to the installation, extending as far in as the third ring of the building. Furthermore, numerous photographs exist from the period immediately after the crash, taken by private citizens as well as media, showing clear evidence of portions of the fuselage and other plane-related debris. And perhaps one of the most compelling things to consider is that the attack was made upon our military nerve center, with thousands of military personnel and civilian employees, not one of which ever provided testimony supporting a missile strike on the installation. While conspiracy theorists can argue that gag orders or employment codes or even threats of bodily harm kept those people from coming forward, that makes little sense in a world where leaks to the press are commonplace.

Despite our deep seated paranoia and shock as a nation in the wake of 9/11, the simplest and most accurate explanations of events on that day indicate that a carefully planned and executed terrorist attack was perpetuated using highjacked commercial airliners as weapons of mass destruction. While our government may be guilty of not keeping enough vigilance on our borders, of not detecting the significance of the entry of the terrorists into the country, and of not heeding or picking up on warning flags in advance of the attacks, there is certainly no evidence to support a role for collusion on the part of one or more US presidents in the planning. In this case, the standards of reason and logic drive us to reject the conspiracy scenarios. It is much more likely that theories of this type arise from unfounded, provocative, and inflammatory reactions to a fear-priming traumatic event that threatens our personal sense of security in a manner that requires emotional resolution regardless of the facts.

The Darkest Day in Connecticut History—On December 14, 2012, a lone gunman entered the Sandy Hook Elementary School in Newtown, CT and massacred 5 adults and 20 young children. The murders were perpetrated by Adam Lanza, a reportedly disturbed 20 year old who started the killing spree by shooting and killing his mother in their home and then stealing her registered firearms to use in the attack. Lanza fired repeatedly on members of the staff and several classrooms before he reportedly shot himself as the police arrived to apprehend him.

The news of the killings shook the nation, and it is not surprising that initial news reports were inconsistent and fraught with errors as the story unfolded. As information slowly became available, some previous reports needed to be rescinded or altered to accommodate the emerging evidence. At the time of this writing, the full police investigative report still has not been released, but enough information has been made available to understand the basic facts in the case. One would think that the events on that date were tragic enough without concocting conspiracy theories to complicate the mix, but that has not stopped the spread of misinformation and rumors of cover-ups from winding throughout the internet. Among the most nefarious of these conspiracy theories is the tenet that the entire tragedy was orchestrated by the Obama government to provide an emotive platform from which to garner support for implementation of stricter gun control regulations.

Within days of the tragedy, a two videos ("The Sandy Hook Shooting Fully Exposed" and "Sandy Hook Fully Exposed Part 2") were posted to YouTube. These videos question information provided to the media about the shooting, and go so far as to consider that the shootings may not have occurred at all. Rather, believers of this conspiracy theory (known as Sandy Hook "truthers") propose that the entire event might have been staged by Homeland Security and FEMA. They propose that no adults or children actually died, and the families who allegedly lost children in the massacre may have been paid actors. One would certainly have thought that the parents and loved ones of those killed in this tragic event had enough to cope with without also having to face accusations that their grief is not real.

What kind of evidence can fan the fire of paranoia in those who embrace this particular conspiracy theory? There are a vast number of allegedly suspicious activities surrounding the event, many of which were easily refuted by subsequent news reports as the details became available and the full picture started to unfold. Others have persisted because they are more subjective and harder to explain. I have chosen three such circumstantial pieces of evidence to discuss here to see how well the theories hold up to the process of deductive reasoning.

One source of contradictory information arose early on about the firearms used in the shootings. Early reports alleged that there were four handguns found in the school. Later reports countered that there were two handguns and an AR-style semi-automatic rifle (Bushmaster .223), with the latter being responsible for all of the deaths. While it is easy to chock up the initial discrepancy to the confusion that typically surrounds such a fast unfolding event, conspiracy claims were subsequently fueled by video footage showing law enforcement agents removing a long gun from the trunk of Lanza's car. This was taken as proof that the Bushmaster .223 could not have been used in the killings, since Lanza never returned to the car once he entered the school and started shooting. The Connecticut State Police website later listed the long gun in the trunk as an Izhmash Canta-12 12-gauge shotgun. The problem arose from the fact that the Izhmash shotgun does not look like a standard shotgun, but instead closely resembles the configuration of AR style rifles like the Bushmaster. I watched the video dozens of times trying to ascertain the model of gun in the trunk and was confounded by the visual appearance of the weapon and the fact that it appeared to be bolt action rather than the more usual pump action used in typical shotguns. I did, however, see what appeared to be a red shotgun cartridge ejected from the gun rather than a bullet as one would find with a rifle. I confirmed the Izhmash shotgun uses a bolt action configuration by watching several videos online depicting the action and function of that specific weapon. It is easily plausible that the gun in the trunk was indeed an Izhmash shotgun. Applying logical deduction here, the available evidence and information supports the contention that the weapon in the trunk was a shotgun, not an AR-style rifle. Therefore, it is completely plausible that the Bushmaster rifle was indeed found in the school. While I cannot definitively rule out the possibility that the police are lying about the weapons found in the school, there is no evidence to support their complicity in a cover up about the types of weapons used.

A second major source of fuel for the Sandy Hook truther movement involves the accusation that the event did not actually happen, but instead was staged to incite public support for gun control measures. The evidence they supply for this assertion is that aerial videos of the events taken throughout the day do not show the expected amount of activity associated with mass shooting events and there were no signs of students being evacuated from the school. This is another case of absence of evidence is not evidence of absence. While it is true that only one or two ambulances were seen in the school parking lot on some videos, it is not clear that there should have been more present at the time when the video was taken. There were no shooting survivors, so there was not an urgent need to transport injured individuals from the scene. The bodies of the victims were not removed from the school for quite some time while identifications, forensic activities, and crime investigation reports were compiled. Thus, there was also no need to transport the bodies from the site until much later. The lack of children in the aerial footage could easily have resulted from the timing of the news coverage. The school was in lockdown for a period after the initial shootings, and there is no way to prove that the absence of children in the footage in question demonstrates anything other than the fact that children were not leaving the school at that moment. It is also possible that all of the children had been evacuated by the time that footage was acquired. There is no way from the available evidence to refute these particular accusations, but that does not make them true. It would seem to me a difficult thing to keep the media from noticing the absence of children through the long vigil around the event and that reporters would have been quite vocal about it at some point throughout the day.

Thirdly, suspicions arose over the legitimacy of family members and bystanders who spoke to the media during the event, including Gene Rosen, whose home was located in close proximity to the school and who allegedly provided some care and shelter for several children who had been traumatized by the event. Rumors circulated that Gene Rosen was actually a crisis actor hired to provide a story line supporting the alleged shootings. Supporting evidence quickly surfaced that Mr. Rosen was a member of the Screen Actors Guild, which he is—Gene Rosen of New Jersey, a man who has never resided in Connecticut. Gene Rosen of Newtown is a retired psychologist and a longtime resident of the area. Similarly, some of the parents who were interviewed after the event were accused of being actors hired to play the role of grieving parents, with virtually no evidence to support the claim other than a vague similarity in appearance to actors who live in other parts of the country. Simple record checking indicates that the families of victims in question do indeed exist, they live in proximity to the school, and funerals for the children and loved ones they lost have been held with public attendance and documentation in public record.

The claim that twenty-six people were *not* murdered during a shooting rampage is impossible to support. By using a rigorous process of deductive thinking, it is clear that the facts support the official story of a lone gunman working on his own, while the conspiracy theories are based upon the need to connect many tenuous circumstantial and unlikely dots that require an untenable amount of cooperation amongst the agents to pull off. While one can take a cover up fairly far by hiding or withholding information from the public, it is difficult to perpetuate a hoax on this scale when it involves complicity by so many in the community who personally knew the victims. Hundreds of community members, law enforcement officers, hospital staff, and reporters were all on hand to observe what transpired, with not one stepping forward to offer testimony to refute the official statements as they eventually unfolded. It is inconceivable that so many participants, including young children who were enrolled in the school, could keep such a secret under wraps from the probing of our typically aggressive media agents. What is clear is that unfounded allegations of this type are designed to sow doubt and suspicion in order to drive an agenda based upon fostering fear. As such, there are always those who are willing to work from sketchy and circumstantial (and often fabricated) evidence to embrace outrageous theories that support the belief that the government is "out to get us." What the conspiracy theorists do not consider is the toll such accusations take on the very real family and friends and community of the victims. The benefits associated with creating a following of believers far outweigh any sense of common decency or respect that should be afforded those affected by the tragedy.

The Homeland Security Exercise Gone Awry—There is a startling amount of similarity between the claims of a hoax in the Sandy Hook School tragedy and the horrific attack on Rep. Gabby Giffords (Dem., Arizona) and eighteen others in a supermarket parking lot near Tucson, Arizona in January of 2011. A lone gunman, Jared Loughner, shot Gifford in the head at close range with a .9mm semi-automatic handgun before opening fire on the crowd, killing six people and wounding twelve others. Evidence was found during the investigation indicating that Loughner had constructed an elaborate plan to assassinate Giffords. After first being deemed incompetent to stand trial during several hearings, he was finally brought to court, convicted, and sentenced to life in prison in November of 2012.

Despite the consistent testimony of surviving victims,

numerous eyewitnesses, and Giffords herself, a conspiracy theory that claims the events on that date did not unfold as communicated by the media spread like wildfire throughout internet channels. Conspiracy advocates claimed that Loughner was actually a government agent hired to lead a Homeland Security exercise on that day. They also claimed that there were no real victims—the alleged casualties were portrayed by actors hired to fulfill the roles. To what end? As before, to add weight to the government's growing agenda to complete a gun grab exercise on the American public. Let us take a look at the key pieces of evidence put forth in support of this theory and evaluate how well it lines up with the known facts as well as the logical interpretation of events.

Much of the basis for the conspiracy theory around the Arizona shooting seems to have arisen from information posted to Wellaware1.com, an alleged investigative site dedicated to analyzing and sharing controversial information about current events. The first piece of evidence offered to back up the claim of a hoax involved the leak of a Homeland Security Exercise plan from the Pottawattamie County Iowa Emergency Management Agency. In this document, they lay out plans for performing a staged exercise to recreate the emergency events surrounding a school shooting in order to test readiness to meet such a crisis. The plan details various exercises and activities to be performed by actors in order to create scenarios that are life-like and useful training opportunities for staff. The author of the Wellaware1.com posting states that this document provides substantive proof that the Giffords shooting was a hoax. It is not clear how he comes to that conclusion. The exercise reflects an activity planned for March 26, 2011 in Iowa. The Giffords shooting occurred on January 8, 2011 in Arizona. It is a stretch to claim that an exercise plan for a preparedness drill around a school shooting in one state is proof that the same holds true for a shooting outside a shopping area in another state, especially one that predates the published plan by two months. Furthermore, preparedness drills are run all of the time by numerous agencies, including utility companies and infrastructure agencies, although we seldom hear anything about them. It is somewhat irrational to assume that the Arizona shooting is a hoax just because drills do occur to prepare for just that kind of event.

Secondly, the Wellaware1.com posting alleges to provide compelling photographic evidence that the victims and bystanders at the event were actors hired to play a role during the exercise. This evidence is largely based upon seeing less blood visible on the clothing and bodies of individuals than one would expect from a shooting. In one photograph used to defend this point, the individual is wearing a red shirt, making it virtually impossible to determine from the distance in the picture whether blood is present or not. Other evidence is allegedly supplied by comparisons of the individuals in the photos from the event with stock photos of various actors. A surprisingly large number of people present on the day do in fact look similar to some professional actors, including Rep. Gifford herself. However, no more conclusive evidence of the identity of these individuals is provided, so it is difficult to confirm or refute the claim based upon facts. Let us apply some of the principles of reason and logic we have been discussing to this scenario and see how well it stands up.

For the theory that Gabby Giffords and others were actors staging an exercise to be truth, we need to accept the premise that Giffords' acting extended to her entry into government office. This means she needed to play a part that not only fooled her staff and fellow members of the US Congress, but she needed to fool the voting public as well. One would think it a fairly risky venture to undertake fraud of this magnitude for the simple purpose of pretending that a shooting event had occurred. It also means that the medical and emergency staff, law enforcement officials, bystanders, and media reporters were collusive in perpetuating the event, and that not one of them decided to leak conflicting information to the press in the aftermath, despite the serious ramifications of the event that have occurred across the nation as a result. The hospital personnel and surgeons interviewed after Giffords' surgery would need to be either in on the scam or actors as well. It also means that Rep. Giffords' husband, astronaut Mark Kelly, was a part of the cover up, pretending to support her during her lengthy convalescence. Rep. Giffords' testimony to Congressional committee about the events would thus be classified as perjury and is punishable by law. And of course the public trial and incarceration of Jared Loughner would also need to be part of the ruse, requiring a serious waste of tax payer money and would require the corruption of additional judicial and law enforcement staff in order to accomplish.

These activities would take an awful lot of time (years worth in fact) and resources invested, not to mention an Herculean ability to keep the gag on hundreds of participants, for the sole purpose of perpetuating a ruse that might allow the government more leverage to implement stronger gun control regulations. Logic says that if the government has the kind of scope and clout necessary to pull off a scenario of this kind, they would not need any help getting their way on gun control issues in the first place. In the absence of hard facts and evidence to support this conspiracy theory, we are left with reliance on logic and rationally-considered thought, both of which support the simple contention that Jared Loughner tried to assassinate Rep. Gabby Giffords and killed and injured a lot of other people in the process.

The consequences of such conspiracy theories are overlooked and often insidious. This particular theory has gained so much traction that people have begun showing up at the homes of survivors and victim's families demanding to "know the truth." While First Amendment rights protect the publication of such information whether it is valid or not, it is important to recognize the impact that spreading falsehoods of this kind has on those individuals who were involved. Imagine being the parents of the young girl who was killed by Loughner on that day coming face to face with someone who claims your child never died and may not even have existed. The mental and emotional ramifications are dire, and as such, demand the very best in rational and deductive thought that we, the consumers and purveyors of information, have to apply in making judgments about events.

The US Invasion by the Muslim Brotherhood—President Barack Hussein Obama may be the focus of more conspiracy theories than virtually any other president before him. Perhaps it arises from the exotic nature of his name, or because he is a person of color and mixed heritage. Whatever the reason, there have been an unprecedented number of attacks upon his background and his integrity since he was elected to office, ranging from questions about his sexual orientation to his political philosophy to the country of his birth. Perhaps the one that represents the state of paranoia in our country in the post-September 11 world best is the claim that Obama is a secret Muslim whose religious agenda threatens to topple the government as we know it.

It is likely that the claims of a link to the Muslim religion were fed by misinformation circulated by the "birther" movement—a persistent activist group that purports Obama was not born in the US and thus is not legally eligible to hold the office of President. Since his election to office in 2008, rumors have circulated that his birth certificate was forged and that the announcement of his birth in a Honolulu Hawaii newspaper was the result of a wired message sent in to the paper by his mother from Indonesia. I, myself, have been the frequent recipient of an internet hoax that claims Obama received aid as a foreign student under the name Barry Soetoro (his father's surname) while enrolled at Occidental College, a hoax that has been discredited multiple times since its inception in 2009.

With family linkage to a Muslim ancestry, an exotic Middle Eastern sounding name, and accusations that he was born abroad, it is no wonder that the ground was fertile for theories to develop about his religious beliefs. Despite his repeated assurances that he adheres to the Christian faith, these rumors have multiplied with every circulation around the internet. To understand this conspiracy theory, it is important to get a feel for the extent of anti-Muslim propaganda and fear mongering present in our modern culture. Here are some of the main points upon which these assertions have been founded.

In one video entitled "Obama admits he is a Muslim" making its way around the internet, various pieces of information and statements made by President Obama have been used to establish his ties with the Islamic religion. The claim that he admits to being a Muslim ("I know because I am one of them" in reference to kinship with people with Muslim backgrounds) comes from this statement (given with full context):

> *Many Americans have Muslims in their families,*
> *or have lived in a Muslim majority country. I*
> *know because I am one of them. My father came*
> *from a Kenyan family that includes generations of*
> *Muslims. As a boy, I spent several years living in*
> *Indonesia...I have known Islam on three continents*
> *before coming to the region where it was first*
> *revealed. That experience guides my conviction..*
> *(recording cuts out).*

This statement does not indicate that Obama is a Muslim but rather that he belongs to a group of individuals whose personal experiences interacting with people of the Islamic faith have given them an understanding of and respect for people of that faith. One would think that an understanding of the mindset of individuals in the Islamic world would be an asset in terms of managing foreign policy for a US president. The video goes on to revile the President because he is able to recite the Islamic call to prayer in Arabic. Just this morning I saw on the news that President Obama presided over a Whitehouse Passover Seder, but I have not heard any alarm being raised that he might be a secret Jew. In contrast, Obama is able to quote teachings from the Koran and this is taken as defining evidence that he is a Muslim. Apparently, the fact that he is able to quote various Christian bible verses as well does not add credibility to his claims of being a Christian. All of these pieces of shaky evidence do not add up to provide proof of membership in the Islamic religion. Rather, they indicate that Barack Obama has a very well educated view of religious doctrine across faiths and that he has had the benefit of firsthand experience of different cultures. These should be positive attributes in a president, not a source of fear and suspicion.

Further proof of our President's secret religious leanings has been touted across the internet in reference to his supposed unwillingness to wear jewelry during the Muslim holy month of Ramadan, based upon photos taken during that period that indicate he was not wearing his wedding ring or watch. Spokesman from the White House supposedly attributed the absence of these items to a need for their repair, a fact that the conspiracy theorists found unsatisfying. While I cannot corroborate the jewelry repair claim, I was able to search photo archives for other images and videos of speeches and press conferences taken during the month of Ramadan and found several examples where the president was wearing either his ring or his watch or both during the period of the Muslim holy month. Therefore, he is either not a secret Muslim or is one who does not rigorously follow the doctrines of the faith.

Lastly, conspiracy theorists have claimed that President Obama is not a Christian because he does not buy his children Christmas presents. Even on face value, using gift giving practices as proof of a particular religious belief is tenuous at best. There are probably many Christians in this country who might consider giving of secular gifts to be outside the teachings of Christian scripture, and thus it is a practice they do not readily support. Likewise, many non-Christians buy Christmas gifts as well. Nonetheless, this claim can easily be refuted, as there is ample evidence that the President purchases Christmas gifts for his family on a regular basis. In fact, the media ruined the Christmas surprise for the Obama girls in December of 2011 when they followed the President around BestBuy and published the list of what he had purchased four days before Christmas!

In conclusion, the proposition that President Obama is a secret Muslim because he understands and respects the Islamic faith, he has been seen not wearing jewelry during Ramadan, and inaccurate claims that he does not exchange Christmas gifts with his family, is laughably hollow. What is more, even if President Obama were a Muslim, it would not be cause to call for his impeachment. Our country was founded upon the principle of freedom from religious persecution, and all faiths, including Islam, are protected by our Constitution and our legal system. However, it is not unheard of for one's religion to cause political and public tension in our country. Certainly, the election of John F. Kennedy, whose Catholicism was feared by many to open the governing of our country up to the whims of the Pope and the Vatican, resulted in rumor and innuendo throughout much of his tenure in office. Considering the tragic events of September 11, 2001, and the resulting War on Terror, it is perhaps not surprising that some factions of our population would feed off rumors of secret alliances with the Muslim Brotherhood and efforts to undermine the largely Christian majority in America. Nonetheless, the evidence to support either President Obama as adhering to the Islamic faith, or the infiltration of our government by agents of the Muslim Brotherhood, have not been proven as anything other than fabrications of conspiracy theorists.

It is worth pointing out here that we do exist in a country where free speech is protected by our Constitution. Therefore, rumors such as these will continue to be used for fear mongering and spreading racial hatred for as long as the principles upon which our country was founded continue to exist. The sad thing is that most people who buy in to such outrageous theories do not stop to consider how much they disrespect both the man and the office of the Presidency. Ironically, these very same people profess a strong love of country and Constitution, apparently never even realizing how much they undermine the fabric of our society with their hate-based behavior.

The Consumer's Role in the Conspiracy

In order for conspiracy theories to flourish and spread, there must be complicity by the audience with the theories that are presented. In the examples described here, that audience is YOU—the American public who surf the web or who peruse and pass on the multitude of emails that circulate on a daily basis through the information highway. Every time you read one of these missives and pass it on to friends, family, and acquaintances without first checking the facts in a rigorous and unbiased fashion, you are assisting in the circulation of propaganda and misinformation. Every time you receive one of these circulations and do not question or push back on the person from whom you received it, you are passively accepting complicity in the conspiracy agenda.

I receive alerts and warnings and propaganda email from friends and acquaintances on a regular basis. I try to make it my common practice to check out the validity of the claims whenever I can and to set the sender straight if there is nothing to back up the story. For example, several months ago I received a link to some internet postings warning that changes to the tax code were going to result in a significant capital gains tax burden for all Americans who sell their homes (all part of Obama's anti-American plot). Since my husband and I had our home for sale at the time, I thought this might be highly relevant to our situation. It was especially worrisome, since the postings claimed there would be an additional 5% tax on the total of the house sale regardless of profit margin. After reading the posting, I went straight to the

IRS website and read about the changes to the tax code. As it turns out, there is a small capital gains tax increase, but only on homes with a profit of more than $500,000 and where the money is not invested in the purchase of another home. Most Americans would not be affected by this change in tax code, since most (including myself) were not likely to make a profit that substantial and most would be looking to invest in another home. My response to the sender was to thank them for bringing the issue to our attention and then I explained the actual nature of the changes and how the internet postings had omitted certain key pieces of information, thus making it appear like the changes would affect all Americans. In other words, I took the opportunity to quietly refute the information in an appreciative manner.

At the very least, when faced with questionable or unsubstantiated inflammatory postings, I choose not to pass the information on to anyone else. Sometimes I do not have the time or energy to debunk the waves of misinformation that come my way, but by simply not perpetuating that information further, I can at least break part of the cycle of fear-mongering and spare someone else the initial alarm associated with conspiracy theories of this type. Ultimately, the choice is yours. The internet cannot be a source of propagation for falsehoods and distorted information if you do not play a part in spreading the unsupported claims.

CHAPTER 12

Red, Black, and Blue:
The Culture War in Action

E arlier in this book, we discussed the social processes that shape and mold our understanding of the world and our ability to ascertain truth within a societal context. Humans have a penchant for believing that we are more independent from biased social pressures than we actually are. The impact of these cultural (and often unconscious) mechanisms results in polarized behavior across many functional strata of our country, and often takes precedence over fact-finding, information seeking, or other rationally-based forms of behavior.

The subtle impact of societal beliefs on our thinking is demonstrated by many of the examples we have covered so far in this book. On an individual level, the structure and beliefs of the group to which we belong (or aspire) certainly color the way we judge and react to information in our personal lives. However, these same pressures are clearly at work in a larger sense on a cultural level, giving rise to starkly contrasting ways of judging fact from fiction. The collective biases of multiple individuals can give rise to cultural movements that gain sufficient momentum to erupt on a national level, giving rise to debate, derision, and conflict between warring factions of the general populace. When the effects of societal bias and conditioning are played out on such a level, it is often difficult for individuals to apply rational forms of judgment about truth, and instead we are swept along by emotional messaging that does not reflect the sumtotal of factors underlying the situation.

In this chapter, we will examine two such debates currently raging within the American population with an eye to determining how the stark contrasts in belief systems are created and maintained, and how rationally evaluating data can uncover the true picture, whether it supports our cultural preconceptions or not.

American Exceptionalism

We heard a lot about American exceptionalism in the years running up to the 2012 elections in the US. Candidates accused their competitors of not believing in this ideal with an aim to riling up the outrage of the electorate. But what exactly is the concept of American exceptionalism and what is the evidence that it reflects a true construct within our society?

American exceptionalism is a deep seated societal belief that our country is culturally and morally distinct and superior from others, and that it is our sacred duty to foster liberty and democratic practices across the globe. When the phrase was first coined during the turn of the last century, the exceptionalism concept was meant to reflect that America rose from revolution to create a society based upon the concept of equality with a government and socioeconomic system largely devoid of the same class distinctions seen in other industrialized countries of the time. Since then, the populist view has come to regard exceptionalism as denoting a moral superiority and justification for super power status. The phrase was first popularized by the American Communist Party in the 1930's as a denigrating treatise on the American economic crisis. Today, it has become a rallying cry for conservatives to celebrate a belief in America's greatness and its unique role on the world stage. Furthermore, the concept has been recently used to support a belief that America should be separate from the laws of the rest of the world out of fear of the influence of outside agents. For example, the US senate recently voted against the United Nations Disability Treaty, despite the fact that it was modeled on our own law and had already been signed by 126 other countries. The failure to ratify arose, not from disagreement with the contents of the treaty and the need to assist disabled persons, but rather out of resistance to allowing any outside influence on our internal policies.

So by today's standards, what evidence demonstrates that we are superior culturally, morally, or technologically? I have identified four different concepts that are relevant contributors to cultural and national exceptionalism, ranging from quality of life, health, and education to military supremacy. In the following section, we will consider the available evidence to deduce whether America has earned the right to consider ourselves superior across these domains.

1) Quality of Life Indices: An exceptional nation should be one in which the citizens thrive in an environment of opportunity and security. The economy should be strong and self-sufficient while promoting a thriving exchange of import and export of goods on the global market. Workers should be paid appropriately for their effort and have access to affordable housing options. They should be able to live in communities free from violence and crime. Certainly, an exceptional nation should be one with a standard of living that others emulate.

The following table summarizes statistics on several key indicators of quality of life in the US compared to the world at large.

Factor	Source	Year	US Value	World Rank
Gross Domestic Product	World Bank	2011	$15T	1
Consumer Price Index	Numbeo	2012	83.06	33
Exports (total in USD)	WTO	2012	$1.5T	4
Imports (total is USD)	World Factbook	2011	$2.2T	1
Child Poverty Rate (developing nations)	UNICEF	2012	23.10%	2
Total Crime Incidence (% pop)	NationMaster	2012	21.1%	15
Imprisonment rate (% pop)	NationMaster	2012	0.74%	1

On financial indicators, the US still ranks among the best in the world, despite the recent recession and subjective sense of economic discomfort. We are ranked # 1 in GDP, coming in at over twice that of # 2 ranked China ($7.3T) and # 3 ranked Japan ($5.8T), and accounting for just over 20% of the world's total GDP. Purchasing power in the US is still moderately strong, with the Consumer Price Index ranked 33rd in the world, meaning a cost of living less expensive than Australia, New Zealand, and most of Western Europe. We are fourth in the world in total exports, but come in first in the world for imports at $2.2 trillion, more than all of the European Union combined. However, despite these encouraging statistics, the US ranks second in the world in the rate of childhood poverty (only Romania has a higher incidence).

While our crime rate is reasonably high, it is still less than many other westernized cultures (e.g. Australia, New Zealand, France, Canada). However, we imprison more of our population than any other country in the world.

Applying the fundamentals of deductive logic, these data indicate that there is some basis for exceptionalism when it comes to financial prosperity. We are certainly still the biggest economic superpower at this time in history, and have much influence on the state of the global economy. But when it comes to other important quality of life factors, we start to fall behind our westernized counterparts. Our children do not benefit from the national economic success of the country to the same degree as seen in other nations. It is troubling that a country of such wealth and opportunity has nearly the highest rate of childhood poverty in the world. And our crime rate, coupled with the startling rate of imprisonment, is not supportive of a well-adjusted and prospering society. Our sense of exceptionalism in terms of quality of life is therefore largely based upon financial prosperity as a whole, rather than the impact of that wealth on our general populace. This is likely an important distinction to recognize in a country where many indicators warn of a shrinking middle class and thus a redefinition of our cultural constituency.

2) <u>Indices of Health and Well Being</u>: We have heard a lot in the news over the past several years about healthcare in our country. On the one hand, we tend to view our standard of care and access to healthcare as exceptional in the world. On the other hand, we are concerned about the rising costs of quality healthcare and of government policies that will change the way we administer this important social service. Much of the opposition to the Affordable Care Act (aka Obamacare) arises from a belief that our healthcare system already ranks top in the world in terms of service and availability. If this is true, then we should rank higher than other countries on many key factors that serve as important reflections of the quality of healthcare systems.

America is the only major westernized country that does not offer a government sponsored healthcare plan to all members of its society. Therefore, it is difficult to directly compare specifics of healthcare approaches, as these vary too widely from nation to nation. We can, however, evaluate on some key indicators of the success of any existent healthcare system that can be compared across nations, such as those presented in the following table.

Factor	Source	Year	Value	World Rank
Overall Life Expectancy	NationMaster	2011	78.37	49
Maternal Mortality	CIA World Factbook	2010	0.02%	136
Infant Mortality	United Nations	2012	0.60%	160
Healthcare Cost (%GDP)	WHO	2008	15.20%	1
Healthcare Ranking	WHO	2008	NA	38

A nation that is successful in providing high quality health care to its members should score high in overall life expectancy rates, as these take into account a variety of variables, including availability of nutritious food, medications, medical experts, technologies, and state of the art hospital and clinic facilities. It is also influenced by access to childhood and adult wellness programs, addiction and mental health programs, and funding for research. Unfortunately, the US ranks only 49th in the world in terms of life expectancy, well behind virtually every other industrialized nation on the planet. On other key indicators, however, we fare much better. Maternal mortality rates are extremely low, as are infant mortality rates, stemming from successes in prenatal care programs, advances in medical technology, and medical expertise in obstetrics and gynecology areas. Unfortunately, our healthcare system is also the most expensive in the world and as such is not available to all citizens equally. Taking into account associated factors such as degree of universal coverage, access to advanced healthcare, and other variables that determine when (and if) a given person will seek medical attention, we rank only 38th in the world.

I often hear friends and family members that live in other countries where the medicine is "socialized" complain about how long they might have to wait to have access to certain elective care approaches, like MRIs and PET scans, or to specialized surgical support like transplants or pacemakers. However, I have to ask what is the use of having the world's most advanced healthcare technologies if we cannot afford the insurance required to gain access to them? While we have socialized medicine for the elderly in the form of Medicare and for the poor in the form of Medicaid, these programs often do not fully cover the needs of people who are living on a very limited income. For younger people who are ineligible for Medicaid, many still forgo some forms of medical attention because they have no (or inadequate) insurance coverage, or their deductible is too high and they cannot afford to pay out of pocket. We have become a country where only the very rich, or those who have coverage through their employers, can afford state of the art care. We are exceptional in the scope of *what* we have to offer but not so much in terms of *how* we offer it. Rationally applying your personal process of judgment to these data, it should be clear that the facts do not fully support the concept of exceptionalism in terms of health and wellbeing compared to other industrialized nations primarily because access to high quality care is inequitably divided among socioeconomic classes.

3) Education: Most people would argue that education is one of the most important drivers of a prosperous and thriving nation. Any society that wishes to excel in this global world needs to lead on innovation, science and math, technology, and engineering. Staying abreast of innovation and advancements relevant to the

global market is key to success on the international stage. As a graduate of the American educational system, I share the opinion that we are top notch in our ability to prepare young people for the challenges that face us as a nation. Am I correct or have I simply bought into the cultural cliché? In this section, we will consider the evidence supporting the concept of exceptionalism in terms of our educational acumen.

The following table summarizes key indicators relevant to educational success, focusing both on access to education and performance factors.

Factor	Source	Year	US Value	World Rank
Higher Education Cost	HESA	2010	$13,856	1
Affordability Ratio (% income)	HESA	2010	51.34%	13
Federal Assistance (grants)	HESA	2010	$4,555	2
Federal Assistance (loans)	HESA	2010	$4,678	2
% High School Graduates	OECD	2009	88%	12
% College Graduates	OECD	2009	41%	16
Math/Science Proficiency	OECD	2012	NA	25/17

HESA = Higher Education Statistics Agency
OECD = Organization for Economic Cooperation and Development

The cost of education, and accessibility of programs in place to assist with those costs, are strong predictors of the level of access available to education. The US is notable in ranking #1 in higher education costs in the developed world. Only Japan comes even remotely close to the average cost per person to attend institutions of higher education ($11,865—roughly $2000 less than in the US), and the US is more than double the cost of most other countries. Of course, one must take into account that this is a normalized estimate. Our domestic colleges and universities vary wildly in price, and are influenced by whether they are private or public/state, in state versus out of state, professional or vocational, and even based upon status and/or reputation of the school. We also have a higher per capita income than many other nations that would allow for us to pay higher education costs. However, adjusting for average income, we still rank thirteenth in the world in terms of percentage of income spent on attending college or university. The cost of attending institutions of higher learning in this country thus far outstrips that of virtually every other nation—NOT an achievement that contributes to exceptionalism in the sense we are seeking here.

There is some good news in our favor, however. We are pretty good at trying to help out our young people and those adults seeking continuing education in the form of grants and loans. We are second only to Denmark in the amount of federal money that is spent on educational grants, and second only to Finland in the amount of money available to our students for loans. This is significant as it indicates, in my opinion, a belief in the importance of educational opportunity and thus is at the heart of the exceptionalism we believe is the core of the American ideal.

So, once we get our students in the right institution, how good are we at achieving those educational goals? As we all know, success in this area is directly related to the quality of preparation that went into getting there in the first place. The US only ranks twelfth in percentage of students who complete high school, meaning that we go into the gates with a bit less of a competitive edge than some other countries. Unfortunately, we do not make up that gap while in the higher education realm, slipping to sixteenth in the world in the percentage of students who graduate from college or university. Another way to evaluate our prowess is by looking at how we score on key intellectual skills, such as math and science. The bad news is that we are worse than many other developed countries, coming in at only seventeenth in the world in science and only twenty-fifth in math! Based upon these statistics, we certainly cannot make a claim for educational exceptionalism. The failure to excel in these key educational areas cannot help but make it more difficult for us to compete in innovation and technological areas that are so critical to facing the challenges of the modern world. This will likely have an economic as well as a cultural impact and certainly leaves us shy of earning the right to tout exceptionalism in this particular arena.

4) <u>Military Power</u>: Another way to characterize exceptionalism on a global scale is the scope of military power. America has been viewed globally as the top superpower since World War II, and it is an enormous part of our national mindset and image. It is also the foundation of our current view of American exceptionalism—the ability, and duty, to promote liberty and democracy across the globe, particularly for less prosperous or less advanced countries. So, how do we measure up to this most visible of roles on the world stage?

The following table summarizes some key statistics regarding military power comparing the US to two other nations well known for their military prowess. All data were derived from Globalfirepower.com 2012.

Factor	US	China	Israel
World Rank	1	3	10
Defense Budget	$692B	$100B	$16B
Total Military Personnel	1.48M	2.29M	187K
Total Aircraft	18,234	5,176	1,964
Total Naval Ships	2,384	972	64
Aircraft Carriers	11	1	0
Submarines	71	63	3

This one requires virtually no discussion or debate. When it comes to military power, the US is supreme ruler of the land, air, and sea. We spend more and have more weaponry and technology than any other country. We do come in second in terms of total number of military personnel, but that is to a country (China) with three times our population, so by a per capita basis, we still rank number one. While this factor is not the historic basis for the concept of exceptionalism, it certainly plays an important role now. At the very least, we would not feel either capable or obliged to spread liberty and democracy if we did not have the firepower to back it up.

In the final analysis, the current conceptualization of American exceptionalism is only partially supported by the facts. Applying objective and rational assessment to the data and statistics clearly indicates that a good part of our cultural view of exceptionalism is unfounded. We obviously have positive attributes as a country, but outside of military power, the size of our economy, and our willingness to supplement the education costs of our young people, we do not distinguish ourselves notably from other developed nations in most areas. It seems prudent that we carefully rethink our public mantra of American exceptionalism and take care not to misrepresent ourselves with myopic cheers and jeers and unfounded poster waving. More importantly, our analysis reveals an opportunity for us to address the important areas where we are falling well short of our own expectations.

As a caveat, there are numerous other equally weighty factors one could evaluate in terms of American exceptionalism, as those used here by no means comprise a comprehensive list. Thus we have an excellent opportunity for you to apply the principles of logic and reason to your own list of criteria. As you consider those attributes that you view are the most distinctively American, try to be as objective as possible about how each one supports the concept of exceptionalism, seeking to cast a broad net across a number of areas. Then do some research using accredited statistical sources—make sure those sources are not just the postings of a political or otherwise biased interest group but are the result of careful data collection by organizations without a stake in the game one way or another. If you have applied the principles of empirical investigation appropriately, then once you've tallied up the results, you can make your own judgment about whether America genuinely deserves the title of "exceptional." If the numbers just do not support the sentiment, do not despair! You will simply have identified a list of areas where we as a country could perhaps use a bit of work to improve our game.

The American Gun Culture

America is known the world around as a nation that vigorously embraces gun ownership. It is a fundamental basis of our national identity. We have more guns overall, and more guns per capita (at least recorded gun ownership) than any other nation. Our history is based upon gun ownership, from the earliest days when the British confiscated muzzleloaders in an attempt to quell rebellion, to the days of the Old West where many walked in the open with Colt revolvers (Peacemakers) strapped to their hips and nearly every household had a rifle for hunting and defense. The popularity of guns in this country has led to the stereotype of America as a strong *gun culture* where freedom and the right to bear arms are indistinguishable, and gun rights are protected over some aspects of safety and well-being of our populace.

Certainly, as firearm technology has advanced over the years, so has the public visibility of weapons, and our laws have struggled to adjust while still maintaining our Second Amendment rights. From outlawing Thompson machine guns in the gangster heyday of Chicago up through the assault weapon bans of the 1990's, the gun control advocates have wrestled with the gun rights faction in an often heated and very public confrontation. Not surprisingly, the dichotomous views between these opposing conceptual camps arise from two very differing belief systems around what defines the gun culture and the impact it has on our society.

To gun owners, the Second Amendment of the US Constitution is sacrosanct. It is a right to possess, carry, and use firearms and this right cannot be infringed. They view gun ownership as the means to defend themselves and their families from potential harm, as well as a traditional sporting pastime handed down from generation to generation. Countless times, Second Amendment rights have been upheld in courts of law, from State to Federal. Threats to this right are met with highly charged outrage and swift action from private citizens and national organizations like the National Rifle Association, Gun Owners of America, and the Second Amendment Foundation. There is often resistance to any form of gun control out of fear that it will open to the door to a slippery slope, at the bottom of which will be a government official knocking on the door confiscating weapons in the name of the law.

To gun control advocates, guns represent a threat rather than a personal right, and are directly responsible for the high incidence of violent crime in this country. While they do sometimes attribute gun-related tragedies as stemming from a cultural psyche tainted by gun violence in movies, television, and video games, they also believe that such violence can be avoided by restricting availability to firearms. They do not recognize the right of individual citizens to carry handguns (concealed or otherwise) and do not feel safe in a world that does. Thus, they lobby for bans on guns themselves as well as firearm components like high capacity magazines. They call out for restrictions on ammunition and where (and by whom) it can be purchased. They view the gun culture as the auspice of survivalists, criminals, and nut cases, and look askance at even the average person who professes enjoyment of shooting-related activities.

These two competing views represent a cultural clash of titanic proportions in our society. Both sides are passionate and vocal about their beliefs, and are quick to spout off facts and statistics and examples that support their claims. But like every conflict of this nature, both sides cannot be completely right. Based upon what we understand of the nature of truth, it is likely that both sides attend to that which supports their view while ignoring that which does not. Interpretations are likely biased and slanted. Opinion has likely been confused with empirical fact, and thus the resolution to this ongoing conflict remains elusive.

A variety of factors have been loudly touted as contributors to gun violence, including the very existence of a culture that promotes gun ownership. However, despite the expansive commentary by both sides of the argument, very little factual information has actually been provided to the American public to assist in making a rational judgment around the regulations that would best address the needs and concerns of the public. In essence, most Americans who do not own guns have little or no knowledge of their use and purpose outside of hunting and crime. In this section, we will examine relevant data about guns, their use, and the laws governing such use as a basis for making informed judgments about *popular beliefs* about guns in America.

1) "The Second Amendment means guns cannot be controlled"

At this moment in American history, the standoff between gun lobbies and anti-gun factions in our culture is extremely vocal and visible. At the center of much of the debate are diametrically opposed views about the nature of Second Amendment rights and whether imposing federal restrictions on gun use will constitute an infringement of these rights.

The US Constitution reflects an admirable and unique doctrine upon which this country was founded, and Americans are proud of it for good reason. Nonetheless, not even our astute forefathers could predict every issue and civil liberty that would need to be addressed when the document was first forged. Furthermore, being a living document in an ever changing culture, several additions to the original have been required over the years to account for important emerging issues, such as the abolition of slavery (Thirteenth Amendment) and granting women the right to vote (Ninetheenth Amendment). Perhaps the most hotly contested of all of the amendments, however, is the right to bear arms provision under the Second Amendment.

The Second Amendment to the constitution was adopted in 1791 as part of the Bill of Rights. This amendment grew out of the American colonist's experience with British attempts to restrict their ability to form militia in the buildup to the Revolutionary War, including instituting embargoes on firearms and ammunition. But when it comes to understanding the true intent of the Second Amendment, the truth hangs by a comma!

The wording of the Second Amendment underwent several iterations during its drafting until ratified in its final form, but even then two different versions were passed by Congress and the States.

> Congress: *A well regulated Militia, being necessary to the security of a free State, the right of the people to keep and bear Arms, shall not be infringed.*

> States: *A well regulated militia being necessary to the security of a free State, the right of the people to keep and bear arms shall not be infringed*

In the version passed by Congress, a comma separating the first clause from the second sets apart the reference to militia from that of the people and fosters interpretation of gun rights for both military and individual citizen use. In the version ratified by the States, the punctuation more clearly suggests that gun ownership is the province of the militia and says nothing about individual rights. This has been the source of raging debate throughout our history, but only recently has the US Supreme Court delivered definitive decisions addressing gun rights under the Second Amendment. In 2008, they delivered a ruling supporting interpretation of the verbiage to protect an individual's right to bear arms, rather than restricting that right to formation of militia (*District of Columbia vs. Heller*). This important decision granted gun owners protection from unlawful seizure or restriction of their firearms on a federal level. In 2010, the Court also ruled that States cannot infringe upon gun rights at the State and local level (*McDonald vs. Chicago*), resulting in the loosening of bans and restrictions on certain guns and practices in many states (although challenges to existing state laws continue as a result of this precedent).

Nonetheless, the Second Amendment does not provide carte blanche protection of gun ownership and use within our society. Convicted felons lose their rights to own and use firearms. Private businesses and properties can prohibit guns on their premises. Individual States can control access to firearms based upon age, training, and background checks. Schools, churches, and other public venues can deny licensed gun owners the right to carry firearms on their property. Therefore, it is obvious that regulations can exist that may limit where, when, and how firearms may be used and transported without infringing upon the right of private citizens to possess these weapons. The misconception in the current public debate is that *ANY* regulations are equivalent of infringement of a fundamental right. Certainly, universal background checks that would guarantee access for all legitimate citizens cannot be construed as an infringement, and requiring a license to purchase a firearm does not prevent any legally entitled citizen from exercising his or her Second Amendment right.

2) "Assault weapons and high capacity magazines give rise to mass murders"

In order to fully understand the scope of contention between advocates and opponents of gun rights, it is important to grasp the facts around guns themselves, as much misinformation circulates as the result of confusing basic firearm definitions. The so called "assault weapons" are civilian versions of military firearms that share certain features in common with the military version, but are typically not designed for automatic firing (continuous firing while the trigger is engaged). Guns are frequently labeled as assault weapons by the media solely based upon how they look, not based upon the function or lethality of the weapon. The specific criteria that distinguish an assault weapon from any other standard firearm in the US were defined in the 1994 Federal Assault Weapons Ban (AWB, in effect until 2004). Consider the following list for assault rifles that are currently discussed so liberally in the media:

Assault Rifle Criteria: semiautomatic and two or more of the following:

- folding or telescoping stock
- pistol grip
- bayonet mount
- flash suppressor
- threaded barrel

Note that these criteria can be somewhat confusing to the average gun owner or person looking to buy a firearm for the first time. A semi-automatic weapon is one where the action of discharging the firearm loads the next round so that a bullet or cartridge can be fired with each trigger pull without cocking or racking the slide. While semi-automatic status is required for assault weapon classification, by itself it was not prohibited by the AWB. In fact, a large percentage of handguns and rifles in the US are semi-automatic and this is a factor often inaccurately discussed in the media.

Many of the attributes listed above, while making the gun look like a military weapon, do not actually confer any additional lethality. For instance, a flash suppressor, which reduces muzzle flare so the shooter is not blinded at night, does not affect the firing rate or velocity of the bullet, and the presence of a bayonet mount has never been linked to a gun death in this country to my knowledge. There are also many models of firearms available in this country that cosmetically look like military weapons, but do not have the attributes to be classified as assault weapons, a fact largely ignored by a preponderance of media reporting. Interestingly, no single one of the criteria listed in the AWB contributes more to assault weapon classification than another, so a person could own a semi-automatic rifle with a flash suppressor, or one with a pistol grip, and still be in compliance under the Federal AWB. There does not appear to be any supporting data that any number or combination of these attributes confers any additional threat, and therefore these regulations appear to have been arbitrary and not intelligently applied. It is not surprising that the AWB had little or no discernible impact on the incidence of violent gun crime in this country during its tenure, a fact much touted by gun advocates during the current renewed debate on gun control in the US.

Another hot button around gun control is the number of rounds that a gun can fire before reloading is necessary. One misconception in the public today is that magazine capacity is unnecessarily high. Actual magazine capacity is dictated by the model of gun. For example, with some pistols, eight rounds are the limit whereas for others, sixteen or seventeen might be standard. These are not "high capacity" magazines but rather are *standard* magazines. High capacity more accurately refers to extended magazines—these are magazines that extend below the magazine well in order to accommodate a higher round count. Therefore, restrictions that arbitrarily set the limit at ten rounds actually create a "low capacity" magazine category for many handgun models. This ruling requires the gun manufacturers to create new lower capacity magazines that are not typically available for common models of gun.

There is a concern that restricting magazine capacity might infringe upon the rights of gun owners by making it impossible for them to use their commercially available magazines. For example, the state of New York recently passed a seven round limit for magazines. For almost all handguns on the market today, this is below the lowest capacity magazine available. Thus, use of these guns would be illegal until such time as the individual gun manufacturers are able to market a magazine to meet that criterion. Since some may never do so as the market share might be too low, the New York law has the potential to arbitrarily prohibit the use of firearms that were purchased legally before the ban. As a result, that aspect of the law has been indefinitely suspended until such time as a resolution to the issue can be found, and gun owners are allowed to use higher capacity magazines provide they only load seven rounds or fewer (a law that is obviously very difficult to enforce).

While a restriction on magazine size has a certain emotional appeal, there is little evidence that such a measure would reduce the lethality or frequency of violent crime. For example, there is no limit on the number of magazines a person can carry on their person, and an experienced shooter can reload the gun with a new magazine in a time frame as short as one second, not a long enough period for an unarmed bystander to intervene. In the absence of clear cut data around the impact of magazine size on lethality in violent shootings, there does not appear to be any legitimate legal grounds for the passage of such restrictions. While it is likely that many of the increased gun control measures that are in discussion will meet with legal challenge if passed, it is unclear how magazine capacity restrictions will fare. It can be argued that limiting magazine size does not infringe upon the individual's right to own and use a firearm. However, it can also be argued that any such restriction that results in the prohibition or confiscation of individual property (particularly without recompense) is a violation of Constitutional rights. Magazines are relatively expensive, each ranging from $35-$100 or more, and many gun owners possess multiple magazines. Confiscation of this personal property without recompense, as well as the need to purchase new modified versions, certainly represents a serious financial burden to the lawful gun owner that should be considered in the passage and enforcement of regulations going forward.

Much of the current debate about restricting magazine capacity for home defense is nonsensical and unfounded on any empirical fact. The number of rounds an individual might need to defend their home and family from one or more intruders is highly specific to the situation, the skill of the gun user, the level of fear or anxiety, and a myriad of other factors that cannot be predicted. Even seasoned law enforcement officers can miss their target at close range because of the unpredictable nature of the live situation. For example, nine bystanders were injured by stray bullets when two police officers shot and killed a gunman from no more than ten feet away near the Empire State Building in NYC on August 24, 2012. Furthermore, it has been argued that restricting round counts could lead to more gun-related injury or death, as home defenders would be less likely to fire off warning shots designed to scare the intruders away.

3) "Gun ownership leads to gun violence"

The widespread belief that America is founded upon a strong gun culture is reinforced by the fact that there are nearly as many firearms in the US as there are people. Using data from the comprehensive Small Arms Survey (2007), it is estimated that nearly 270,000,000 rifles, shotguns, and handguns are legally registered in the US, accounting for an incredible 88.8% of the total population and putting the US in the top position for gun ownership. No other country even comes close. The second position in total private gun ownership goes to India with 46,000,000 small arms, albeit in a country with many more people so this number represents only about 4% of the total population. Looking at percentage of total population, Yemen comes in second with only 54.8%.

Factor	USA	Canada	Mexico	Israel	England	Japan	Honduras
Total Firearms *	270M	9.95M	15.5M	500K	3.4M	710K	500K
% Population *	88.8	30.8	15	7.3	6.2	0.6	6.2
Rank (Ownership)	1	13	42	79	88	164	88
Total Gun Homicides **	9960	173	11309	6	41	11	5201
Homicides (per 100K) **	3.2	0.51	9.97	0.09	0.07	0.01	68.43
Rank (Homicides per capita)	26	56	18	97	99	107	1
Total Homicide Rate (/100K)**	4.2	1.6	22.7	2.1	1.3	0.4	82.1
% Gun-Related Homicides	76	32	44	4.2	5.4	2.5	83

* Small Arms Survey 2007
** United Nations Office on Drugs and Crime 2010

With regard to our closest continental neighbors, Canada ranks thirteenth and Mexico forty-second in terms of total number of guns, combined accounting for only about 10% of the market share of the US. At seventy-ninth, Israel, a highly militarized country where all enlisted members of the military typically carry firearms at all times, does not show a transfer of small arms fervor to the civilian population. Only 500,000 registered small arms exist, accounting for only 7% of the total population. This is very similar to England, ranking eighty-eighth with 3,400,000 at 6.2%, which is actually a surprisingly high number considering handguns and many types of rifles have been banned in the UK. At the other end of the spectrum, Japan ranks 164th in guns per capita at 0.6 per 100,000 people, largely arising from an extremely aggressive anti-gun movement that has removed most weapons from civilian access.

It is a belief by many that the American gun culture promotes violence because of the unfettered access to guns. Therefore, one would expect the US to also rank highest in gun violence across countries. However, this claim is not supported by data from the United Nations Office on Drugs and Crime report of 2010, and it appears the linkage between access and violence is much more complicated.

The total number of gun homicides, and gun deaths per capita, is higher for the US than many other developed nations, but is twenthy-sixth across all countries. In general, the highest gun homicide rates are seen in South American and Caribbean countries, with Brazil coming in number one on total annual gun homicides (34,678). Honduras tops the charts on homicides per capita at more than 20 times the rate in the US, despite having only about 500,000 legally owned guns in the country (0.002% that of the US). In contrast, Japan, with its restrictive gun laws, has a startling low incidence of gun related crime, with only 0.01 homicides per 100,000 people. Amongst our close neighbors, Mexico has three times the per capita gun homicide rate as the US, despite having only roughly 5% the number of firearms. Furthermore, Canada, thirteenth in the world in overall gun ownership, has a gun homicide rate of less than 1%.

An added dimension comes to light when we look at the

percentage of violent deaths that are committed using firearms. In both the US and Honduras, more than two thirds of all homicides are committed with guns (76% and 83% respectively), despite the fact that the per capita rate of legal gun ownership in Honduras is less than 10% that of the US. In contrast, Japan, Israel, and England have both low rates of gun-related death but high crime rates, suggesting people utilize other means to perpetuate violence if guns are not readily available. But just to complicate our interpretation, Canada has twice the per capita gun ownership of Mexico, only 5% the homicide rate overall, and a lower percentage of gun-related homicide (33% vs. 44%). Interpretation of these data is further complicated by the likelihood that the gun violence in most countries stems from illegal gun use rather than being directly related to the incidence of lawful gun ownership. Hence, no readily apparent linkage between legal gun ownership and gun violence emerges.

Applying objective and rational analysis, these statistics indicate that it is simply not true to empirically state that access to guns leads to violent crime. Nonetheless, many Americans continue to believe their gut feeling that the number of guns is the root of our problems, a falsehood easily debunked by the process of deductive reasoning.

4) "Tighter regulations will prevent gun violence"
Pressure to implement reform of federal gun laws has received strong public support in light of several highly publicized mass shooting events over the past few years, including the theater massacre in Aurora, Colorado and the particularly heinous murder of young children at Sandy Hook Elementary School in Newtown, Connecticut. In the wake of these tragedies, the Obama administration issued its recommendations for gun control, including restriction on magazine capacity, prohibition of assault weapon style rifles, and requirements for universal background checks. Additionally, some States are taking their own steps,

proposing further restriction on ammunition capacity, putting limits on the number of guns that can be purchased in a year, and levying an additional tax on ammunition and firearm purchases. While the majority of Americans polled support consistent and common sense measures, there is very little agreement about the measures that would actually prevent a repeat of these types of killings in the future, and much of the government response has been criticized as emotional and reactive rather than carefully considered.

From 1994-2004, the AWB sought to limit access to weapons capable of high rates of fire that could be used for mass killings of civilians. This approach was emotionally satisfying to its supporters in that it made reasonable sense that gun violence would decline in the absence of such efficient weapons. However, the facts did not demonstrate that the AWB was a success in reducing mass shootings. Both the National Research Council and the Centers for Disease Control and Prevention complied reports showing no significant impact of the ban on the incidence of violent crime, and expiration of the ban in 2004 did not precipitate an increase in assault weapon crimes in the US. There are a number of reasons why there might be an apparent lack of linkage between access to these weapons and violence. First, the ban only affected the manufacture and sale of weapons during the period of the ban—it did not impact those weapons in that were in circulation before the ban went into effect. Secondly, the incidence of mass killings that employ such weapons is extremely low in the US in general, so it is not easy to lower the bar on a behavior that is already pretty rare. Thirdly, the ban essentially only affected law abiding gun owners who were no longer able to legally purchase these weapons, but was not a deterrent to criminals intent on creating havoc (no criminal ever said "I want to commit a crime but this gun is illegal so I guess I had better not!"). In general, this latter point is at the crux of the problem with trying to understand gun related crime in general, as the people who are regulated by the laws are the ones who are already willing to abide by the laws, while it does nothing to discourage those who want to commit a crime.

Nonetheless, attempts to prevent gun related violence by regulating access to firearms and ammunition occur in almost all countries to some extent. The following table summarizes the regulation of guns and ammunition and the requirements for gun ownership across the same countries we reviewed earlier in terms of gun and crime statistics.

Guns and Ammunition						
Country	Regulation	Semi-Automatic Weapons[1]	Hand Guns	Gun Limit	Ammunition Type Restricted [2]	Ammunition Amount Restricted
US	Permissive	Allowed	Allowed	No	No	No
Canada	Restrictive	Allowed	Allowed	No	No	No
Mexico	Restrictive	Allowed	Partial[3]	Yes	Yes	Yes
Israel	Restrictive	Allowed	Allowed	Yes	No	Yes
England	Restrictive	Prohibited	Prohibited	Yes	Yes	Yes
Japan	Restrictive	Prohibited	Prohibited[4]	No	No	No
Honduras	Permissive	Allowed	Allowed	Yes	No	No

1. Excluding assault weapons
2. Excluding armor piercing
3. Prohibits revolvers above .38mm and handguns above .9mm
4. Except by special permit for competitive sport shooters

Looking first at access to guns and ammunition, we can immediately see that most other countries have more restrictive gun policies than the US. Even Honduras is slightly more restrictive in that there is a limit on firearm ownership to only five weapons, whereas no limit exists in the US. We could argue that this is strong evidence of a link between access and violence, except that Honduras with its limit on guns still far outstrips the US in rate of violence, and Canada, with no limit on gun ownership, ranks well behind the US in gun related violence. Keep in mind that the statistics only reflect legally owned guns whereas the crime rates include those events perpetuated by criminals who obtained guns illegally, and thus it is difficult to draw conclusions about the success of the law.

As previously discussed, access to ammunition is another factor often bandied about in the media regarding gun violence, particularly in the case of mass killings. There are periodic outcries for restrictions on availability of ammunition, with the thought that having access to fewer rounds will lead to fewer deaths. But this argument does not stand up to the principles of logic based on readily available statistics either. Judging by examples from other countries, most mass killings make use of levels of ammunition that would likely be permitted under a restrictive ammunition quota anyway (< 100-200 rounds). People who use more rounds than this on a regular basis (competitive shooters, recreational shooters, etc.) do not typically commit mass murder. Furthermore, there does not appear to be a correlation between rate of gun violence and access to ammunition across countries. For example, access to ammunition is restricted in Mexico to 200 rounds for most types of firearm, yet the per capita rate of gun-related homicides is three times higher than in the US where there are no restrictions on ammunition.

Obviously, we cannot predict likelihood of gun related violence based upon these factors alone, so what about considering behaviors a step upstream? How does the way in which different countries regulate who can legally own a firearm impact the rate of violent crime? The following table summarizes the process for obtaining the right to possess a firearm across various countries.

License/Permit					
Country	License Required	Proof of Need1	Background Check2	References	Safety Training
US	Varies by State	No	Varies by State	Varies by State	Varies by State
Canada	Yes	No	Yes (DV,C,M,A)	Yes	Yes
Mexico	Yes	Yes (SD,H,S,C)	Yes (C,M,A,P)	Yes	Yes
Israel	Yes	Yes (SD,H,S)	Yes (C,M,P)	No	No
England	Yes	Yes (H,S,C)	Yes (C,M,A)	Yes	No
Japan	Yes	Yes (H,S)	Yes (C,M)	No	Yes
Honduras	Yes	No	No	No	No

1. Self-defense (SD), hunting (H), sport shooting (S), collection (C)
2. Domestic Violence (DV), Criminal (C), Mental (M), Addiction (A), Physical (P)

The US is notable in that it is the only country on this list that does not have a federal law requiring a license or permit to purchase and own a gun, nor consistency throughout the country regarding background checks and training (although a change to the law is being considered at the moment). Regulations around licensing vary by state, with many not requiring a permit of any kind to purchase a gun, although most every state does require a permit for concealed carry. The US does not require proof of need for firearm ownership, and the regulations around background checks and training vary from strict to none. This is probably one of the biggest impediments to reciprocity laws in the country, as there are no minimum standards that must be met that would allow for transport of firearms from state to state. Understandably, a citizen of Connecticut where training, background checks, finger printing, and often character references are required in order to obtain a gun permit would not necessarily feel comfortable about someone from Arizona, where no permits are required, driving around their state with a firearm!

Nonetheless, the level of rigor applied for obtaining a firearm across countries also does not directly explain the differences in prevalence of gun related violence. For example, Mexico is the only country on the list that has rigorous standards for all categories of regulation, and yet that does not result in lower levels of gun crime. England with its relatively restrictive laws around gun ownership (prohibiting semi-automatic and hand guns, restricting ammunition, requiring proof of need, conducting mental, health, and criminal background checks, and requiring character references) still does not even require basic safety training for those granted a permit. Furthermore, gun violence has been increasing in England since 2010, despite a total ban on handguns and laws that do not allow individuals to protect their homes and private property from intruders. It should be noted that the increase in gun violence can be attributed to increased criminal and gang activity, all of whom would not submit voluntarily to the gun regulation process even if hand guns were not prohibited. In contrast, Israel maintains a fairly low crime rate without requiring references or basic safety training or restricting access to firearms. Only Japan's approach lends weight to the concept of regulation preventing violence. Firearms in Japan are incredibly rare and the process for obtaining a permit is among the most rigorous in the world. Not only is proof of need, extensive background checks (including a mental health exam), and lengthy firearm training required, but the weapons must be secured in an approved locker (separately from the ammunition) and the location of that locker filed with local law enforcement.

Gun Control—The Continental Divide

In light of recent highly publicized and horrific mass shootings in the US, gun control laws have once again been put in the forefront of the national debate. Emotional and often irrational arguments rage daily in the news and on every street corner. Understandably, there is an outcry for something to be done. But what actions do the facts actually support? The most vocal gun rights advocates (e.g., the National Rifle Association spokespeople) push an agenda of increased gun ownership and an armed presence at vulnerable sites, such as schools. Their premise is based upon meeting might with might. On the gun control side, voices are raised about the need to ban particular types of weapons, and outlaw high capacity magazines that allow for high rates of fire without reloading. They seek to restrict access as a means of controlling use of guns, in the vein of the early twentieth century practice of Prohibition for regulation of access to alcohol.

Our assessment of the available data does not support the concept that violence stems from access to guns or ammunition, as there is no statistical link between the two factors. There is no correlation between legal gun ownership and the incidence of gun-related violence across countries, and there is no consistent evidence that restricting access to particular types of weapons, as during the AWB, has any noticeable effect on the incidence of mass shootings. Furthermore, there is no evidence that limiting the capacity of magazines would result in fewer deaths during a shooting spree. Take for example the shootings at Fort Hood in 2009 when a single individual killed thirteen people and wounded more than two dozen others. The victims were trained military personnel and yet not one of them was able to subdue the shooter while he reloaded. It took the action of armed military police called to the scene to stop the shooting spree.

The belief that the lack of rigor in conducting background checks and references does not explain the phenomenon much better, as most gun related crime is committed by criminals who do not legally own guns to begin with and thus would not undergo background checks or obtain references. In a recent FBI study (*"Violent Encounters: A Study of Felonious Assaults on Our Nation's Law Enforcement Officers"*), it was revealed that most individuals who commit assaults with guns obtained those weapons illegally on the street or black market, not from gun shows or licensed legal transfer. Perhaps these data do not take into account those rare instances where an individual with no criminal record goes on a shooting spree. In some cases, these individuals did obtain the firearms in questions legally, and perhaps better screening on aspects like mental health might have thrown up a red flag and prevented tragedy. In others cases, however, the guns in question were stolen from friends or family members who had obtained them legally, and no amount of background checking would have made a difference. Therefore it is difficult to rationally predict a link between licensing and willingness to commit a violent crime.

However, it is a reasonable approach to require that all individuals who obtain a firearm do so with the same level of scrutiny into criminal records and mental health. This would require some consistency across States with their approaches to gun ownership and also require the same level of stringency for other venues, such as gun shows. It is true that in some States, it is possible for an unlicensed individual who has not undergone any training or background check to obtain a weapon at a gun show. This is akin to allowing someone who buys a car at a used car lot to drive it without a license because of where it was purchased. While this regulation would not likely have an effect on deterring the unbalanced individual from planning massacres, it would at least help solidify the rights of legal gun owners to possess these weapons.

In the final analysis, the facts that best predict the incidence of gun related violence underscore the importance of culture rather than any combination of regulations around access to guns and ammunition. While Japan has some of the most restrictive gun laws in the world, there is also a cultural perspective that promotes adherence to the law and respect for authority. Few people seek to own weapons because it is not within the mindset of the culture to do so. Furthermore, the rigorous training required to obtain the right to own a gun usually involves a need to take time off work, a factor that competes strongly with the cultural work ethic. In contrast, Israel enjoys a fairly low gun related crime rate without heavy handed regulation. It should be noted, however, that military weapons are openly prevalent everywhere in the culture, so it is not the best society within which to attempt mass murder—you would likely be gunned down by bystanders within seconds of firing a shot. And as for our close neighbor, Canada, they manage to maintain a fairly low incidence of gun related crime without restricting access to guns or requiring inordinate regulation around ownership even though roughly about a third of the population own firearms.

Culture is undoubtedly an important factor, but characterizing the key aspects and how to address these influences remains problematic. Certainly there has been much discussion lately in the media about the role of desensitization, a cultural phenomenon of reducing reactivity to violent stimuli through television, videos, and computer games in promoting gun violence. Since the pioneering studies of Albert Bandura in the early 1960's, it has been well documented that children who observe others engaging in violence will mimic the behavior, especially if the violent behavior does not incur negative consequences. It is easy enough to imagine that exposure to violent behaviors through movies and games could have a profound impact on how children and young adults view the nature of violence. However, in the absence of appropriately controlled cross-cultural studies on the relationship between observing gun violence and enacting gun violence, there is little we can do other than speculate at this point.

Thus, when it comes to judging truth around the American

gun culture and its role in promoting violence, there is not a clear judgment that can be made. While a direct relationship might seem intuitively obvious, none of the statistics examined are strong predictors of when guns will be used for violence. It is true that American culture has a strong pro-gun component rooted in the history of the country. It is not true that access to guns alone can explain the tragedies of mass murders and no regulation proposed to date is based upon factual proof that will alter the incidence of such violent crimes. The sad truth may be that our society gives rise to a small number of individuals who want to perpetuate violence regardless of the laws and cultural mandates, and guns are simply an easy and dramatic way to make whatever disturbed point they are seeking to demonstrate. Judging from our analysis of violence across the globe, the gun culture that is unique to America does not appear responsible for a larger portion of gun-related violence than any other potentially contributing factor we might share with other nations.

Bridging the Divide

Real, world application of the process of deductive reasoning is key to being able to both understand current social debates, and well as to identify truth and accuracy within the ever circulating opinions out there. No current issue is immune to the objective probing and the search for trustworthy facts. And furthermore, it is important to remember that those statements made with the most confidence in the public realm are the ones most in need of proper fact checking.

Just a few days ago, a close friend of mine was talking to me about misconceptions around gun violence in America. He made a comment based upon a weblink to an article he had just received in an email—"There are more deaths caused by baseball bats every day than there are by guns." Knowing what I do about firearms related homicides in this country, this immediately sounded off to me. I pulled out my phone, did a quick search, and immediately came upon a Snopes.com story about this issue, stating that it is false and quoting FBI statistics as the source of the evaluation. I then went to the FBI archives on homicide statistics, and saw that, in recent years, approximately 68% of all homicides were gun-related, whereas less than 4% were the result of bludgeoning by baseball bats or other blunt instruments. The whole process took about two minutes to evaluate and I was able to refute the claim as another special interest lobby message circulating the internet. The irony is that my friend should have known better than to lay an unfounded statistic on me, especially since he was very aware of the nature of this book and my efforts to stem the tide of misinformation being passed around the internet.

Whether it is information about politics, current issues, or any national debate, the simple answer is do your own legwork in vetting the information that comes your way. Even more importantly, do not pass on any information as representing the truth unless you are convinced the data included to back up the claim are in fact legitimate and fully accurate. In cases like the ones discussed in this chapter, it is never easy to accept or refute a broad concept without taking a deeper look at multiple aspects of the claim. Nonetheless, great strides can be made by using logic and reason to assess enough aspects of any concept to gain a sense of confidence in the veracity of the claims.

PART 4

Epilogue: Breaking the Cycle

What we have discussed so far throughout this book has been aimed at developing a method of applying deductive and empirical thought processes to the vast array of information to which we are exposed each day, with the goal of being able to sort out the facts from the fiction. We have explored the ways in which falsehoods are created and perpetuated across virtually every facet of our lives. We have applied the principles of logic and healthy skepticism to examples of duplicity and have demonstrated how to debunk and refute false information in a few easy cognitive steps. All that we have discussed has been aimed at protecting us from a dishonest world and given us confidence in our ability to sort through the information we receive in a rational and empirically valid manner.

However, the world in which we live would be a much better place if the need to apply our skills of judgment around the truth were not so necessary. In other words, the ability to tell fact from fiction on its own has little or no impact on the prevalence of lying in our environment. For there to be any real impact on the decay of honesty in our society, we need to be able to implement consequences for false behavior that shift the balance of behavior in our society.

The final section of this book will therefore summarize the ways in which consumers of information can react to dishonesty with an eye towards minimizing the behavior going forward. As I have stressed throughout the scope of this book, the spread of false and misleading information will not stop until the negative consequences for such behaviors far outweigh the benefits.

CHAPTER 13

Mechanisms for Modifying
Dishonest Behavior

Throughout this book, one obviously emerging theme should be the importance of creating and implementing consequences for lying. So much of the disingenuous behavior described throughout these chapters is met with little or no push back, despite the existence of numerous fact checking and empirical knowledge-based resources. Politicians lie to potential voters with impunity. Pundits distort information and mislead their audiences without a qualm. Special interest groups spread doctrines based upon false evidence to skew the opinions of the uninformed with hardly an outcry from the public. In fact, only those who impede the justice system directly, financially defraud the public, or make unsubstantiated claims in advertising regularly meet with any retribution at all for their actions.

The very principles of learning theory tell us that those behaviors that are rewarded are likely to be repeated, whereas those that meet with negative consequences are less likely to occur in the future. The trick to succeeding in dishonesty is balancing out the scale between those two outcomes. It is easy to see how those who escape punishment for behaving dishonestly would seek to continue to reap the benefits of misbegotten gains. There simply is no incentive to behave differently, particularly in the absence of conscience or any other moral compass mediating one's actions. But is also becomes clear that, even in those cases where dishonest behaviors have the potential for punishment, the perpetuators are seldom dissuaded from misleading or scamming the public.

One approach to better discourage such behavior could certainly be to up the ante in terms of punishment. In some cases, fines and imprisonment are accepted forms of retribution for behaviors like fraud, false representation, and perjury, but with limited success. For example, companies are held accountable for false advertising all the time, often paying out millions in settlement costs, and yet false claims continue to be put before the American public. Obviously, the costs of being caught do not appear to outweigh the benefits realized in the short term for these commercial enterprises, suggesting that the current remedies are largely ineffective. One would imagine that a scenario where a harsh consequence such as a stint locked in the stocks in the center of the public square, on view to all as rotten tomatoes find their target, would very quickly discourage disingenuous behaviors from politicians, pundits, and other public figures.

While such blatant corporal forms of punishment are typically discouraged in a civilized society, some judges and law enforcement agents have embraced a similar approach of punishment whereby perpetrators of wrong doing are required to stand on a street corner wearing a sandwich board that tells everyone about their crime. It is unlikely that we will see disingenuous politicians put on display in such a manner, but the point remains that public embarrassment (and subsequent loss of votes) would certainly be one mechanism by which to modify their behavior.

Public humiliation aside, what then can you, the average consumer of information, do to help stem the tide of lies, distortions, and outrageous claims that come your way on a regular basis? I have stressed throughout the book the importance of being able to apply the principles of rigorous deductive logic in order to make accurate judgments about the information to which we are exposed. This is a critical first step and obviously cannot be emphasized enough. Only by first identifying the falseness in information can we put ourselves in a position to make a difference within our immediate life circumstances.

But the responsibility on each individual consumer goes beyond just piecing apart fact from fiction. It becomes a moral obligation to call attention to instances of abuse within our information sharing system and to bring real consequences to the bad actors, thereby improving the overall accuracy of information out there. There are numerous simple approaches that each and every one of us can employ to start dissuading the expression of dishonesty in our society. And the good news is that the more of us who make the effort, the more noticeable the impact of the collective will be on the nature of information shared across the broad spectrum of daily life.

Teach Our Children Well

First and foremost among the weapons available to the information-consuming public is to put more effort into teaching our children the difference between lying and honesty, and to provide consistently applied punishment and reward in order to appropriately mold behavior. From the time we are born, we are veritable sponges for information, yet without the ability as children to assess the factual basis of that which we are absorbing. The role of parents, teachers, and caregivers here cannot be overestimated. Children not only learn actively by direct instruction, but also by modeling their behavior based upon what they observe around them.

Obviously, children who are rewarded for honest behavior and punished for lying are being provided with a consistent framework for judgment, and will likely be discouraged from lying in adulthood. But a system of reward and punishment alone is not sufficient to solidify a full understanding of acceptable behavior. Learning by example is perhaps even more important than direct instruction. Children who see parents lie to each other are going to have a difficult time understanding why dishonesty is an undesirable behavior. And children who are made complicit in those lies have no solid ground upon which to develop a concept of right and wrong. Ask yourself how a child who is told by one parent to hide information from the other can possibly develop a belief system that promotes a truthful approach to social interaction. There is quite simply no way to reconcile such a "do as I say, not as I do" kind of approach to child rearing. Therefore, adults need to be more cognizant of the example they set for developing children, particularly when it comes to understanding the negative consequences of lying.

Children also need to understand the nuances in social interaction in a way that helps them form appropriate flexibility in their world views. As mentioned elsewhere in this book, there are social situations where most individuals would agree that a certain measure of evasion when it comes to telling the truth is required by social convention. For example, a purely honest approach to life means that truthful answers to ego-related questions will result in hurt feelings and social tension. It is thus an accepted social more that dishonesty is ok in some situations where the truth will only be hurtful and serve no positive purpose. One could argue that we should eradicate such social "fibs" from our repertoire of behaviors, but those who do are usually viewed as being socially inept and unlikeable. Thus every child will need to find a way to balance honesty with discretionary lying to get along in many social situations. The answer here is to explain to children when and where it is appropriate to fudge the truth. Show them by example when possible. Discuss the pros and cons, the potential consequences in either direction, of telling the truth versus telling the "little white lie" and help them understand how to draw boundaries around such behavior. Let us face the truth; everyone lies in social situations to maintain the peace on occasion. As such, it behooves us as child-rearers to help children understand the function of such behavior in a way that does not simply bleed across all social interaction.

Make Your Vote Count

We have all become somewhat numb and jaded to the extent of lying displayed by our modern politicians in the public arena. Campaign ads are famous for skewing or misrepresenting information, taking things out of context to paint a picture quite different from the facts, and in some cases, telling outright falsehoods in the name of promoting the candidate's chances at the ballot box. Although we all know political duplicity is rampant, we do little or nothing to try and institute consequences for such behavior. There is little evidence for a negative impact of deceptive practices on our willingness to vote. Since we view all politicians as dishonest, spreading false information during a campaign is not much of a deterrent to casting our ballot. Therefore, we certainly cannot expect the level of honesty in political debate to increase while there is no cost to the behavior.

The first thing you can do is actually make your vote count. Do not vote for those that promote falsehoods, and be public about your decision. This might mean that there are no candidates you can vote for, since dishonesty is so rampant, but at the very least, withholding your vote from those who do not tell the truth will send a message that can have impact down the road, as long as you are public about your reasons.

Secondly, demand accountability for dishonest behavior. Establish community action groups to monitor the truthfulness of candidates and incumbents alike. Demand alternative candidates if the current field does not meet the bar for honesty. Inspire recall elections for incumbents who try to dupe the voting public with their words and actions. Promote commissions and investigations into potential falsehoods and dishonest behaviors, and require politicians to answer for their actions in a public forum. In short, stop accepting the fact that politicians lie to us with impunity and start driving for active consequences to dishonest behavior.

I do not mean to imply that such actions will be easy to take in our current culture. We have become way too complacent about political behaviors and it will take effort and a great deal of courage to try and turn the tide. But the bottom line is that nothing will change while we, the information seeking public, stand idly by and allow the disingenuous behaviors of politicians to occur without raising our voices in protest. At the very least, support, publicize, and build upon information fact-checking resource sites on the internet where the facts can be displayed for the general public's consumption. Share links to relevant postings with family and friends, helping to educate them on the accurate information as a counter to the political rhetoric. While you might not consider any single action you might take to be more than a drop of truth in the ocean of political lies, you might be amazed at what the concerted effort of a growing movement toward honesty could do in terms of impacting political behavior going forward.

Hit Them In Their Ratings!

With everything we have learned about applying the principles of deductive reasoning, it should be easy to tell fact from fiction in the emanations of pundits from both sides of the philosophical arena. But the purpose of being able to ascertain truth in the media is not just to tell right from wrong, it is also to give us the power of choice over which source we turn to for information and news. Pundits cannot survive without an audience. As a public consumer, it is your right to choose who you tune in to as your eyes and ears on the world. Therefore, if members of the media are regularly found to be supplying false or misleading information to their viewers or listeners, it is then the public consumer who is at fault for continuing to listen to them.

If you want to lobby for more honest and straight line news media, hit the worst offenders in their ratings by refusing to engage with their shows. Furthermore, make public statements about your opinion of pundits who abuse the truth by means of blogs, editorials, and letters to the broadcasting management. Decry their lack of professionalism to their managers. Send letters or tweets or post comments on Facebook that let these pundits know you do not care for their lack of truthfulness. Discourage advertisers from associating with disreputable news sources by boycotting their products until they revoke their sponsorships. Companies are very sensitive to the level of popularity of those individuals whose shows they choose for advertising time and you can have a very big impact with minimal effort by rallying consumers around such boycott efforts.

Believe it or not, there is growing interest (and possibly increased market share) in the concept of cleaning up our news networks to make things more realistic and above board. Recently, WDRB TV, a FOX affiliate in Louisville, KY, made a strategic decision to move away from misleading and disingenuous public relations techniques and to embrace a more honest approach to the news. For example, the station has rejected the use of phrases like "Breaking News" applied to anything other than urgently emerging stories about actual news. Here are some highlights from a promotional advertisement announcing the station's change in philosophy:

> *You hear the term, 'Breaking News' quite frequently these days. It is a marketing ploy to convince you that at television station is better at bringing you the news first, as it happens. The problem is, It is just not true...Breaking news is seldom actually*

*breaking, and quite often, isn't even news. ..We
believe the relationship you have with your television
statement shouldn't begin with a deception.*

Some programmers, networks, and newscasters are getting the message. News is supposed to be about journalism, not sensationalism (leave that up to the rag sheets!). Consider for a moment the growing popularity of the HBO series "Network News" that portrays the struggles of both the network and the staff to maintain a high standard of journalism against the ever present pressures of ratings and advertising support. The plight of the moralistic journalist struggling against the company machine is one that resonates with the viewing audience in a very compelling fashion. Furthermore, the growing appetite for shows that put the spotlight on misinformation and contradictions in the mainstream news (like *The Daily Show* with John Stewart or *Last Week Tonight* with John Oliver) suggest that the world is ready to take a harder look at the information being broadcast to us from skewed sources. These examples illustrate that the voice of the general public can be a potent force in determining the quality and nature of the nonstop information that blares out at us from electronic devices of all shapes and sizes.

In short, if you know a given pundit or journalist has a reputation for stretching the truth or even misrepresenting information directly, and you still tune into their show, you are as much a part of the problem as they are. Much of the dishonest behavior so common in our modern culture is the result of acceptance and apathy by the consuming public. We have become lazy about our expectations, unwilling to put out any effort to alter the environment in which we live, content instead to sit back and complain amongst ourselves about what nonsense is served up to us on a daily basis. There is little to be gained from applying objectivity and rationality to public sources of information if we are willing to accept the lies and inconsistencies without action.

Don't Fad Away

Fads are an unfortunate reality in modern society. Everyone wants results the easy way, and many are willing to pay for it. It would seem clear that enough compelling evidence exists to prove that a thing that seems too good to be true probably is. Nonetheless, millions of people worldwide are duped into purchasing useless remedies, technologies, or health aids every year solely on the basis of false advertising claims. And although legal action is brought against many companies for misleading or false advertising claims, many more go undetected and/or unpunished. With such a record of success, why would companies worry overly much about class action lawsuits?!

Under such conditions, it becomes the responsibility of the consumer to make educated purchases and follow up where service or product quality does not meet the advertised standards. Any investment should always begin with the process of deductive reasoning discussed throughout this book. Search the internet, read consumer reports, look for blogs or reviews or other postings that warn of scams and problems with the product or company. It is also helpful to explore unbiased sources of information to determine whether there is a sound basis to expect that the product works. And if you remain concerned about any aspect of the product advertisement, do not hesitate to contact the company directly for more information, and ask them to provide evidence to support their claims.

If, despite all of your best efforts, you do become the victim of false advertising, do not meekly accept your fate. Companies rely upon the tendency for most people to avoid confrontation. In general, the average consumer shuts up and goes away after one or two attempts to reconcile an issue with the offending distributer. Do not give up—continue to make your voice heard with the company, seeking to go higher up the food chain with each complaint. And do not restrict your scope to the company itself. Publish reviews about the product and the problems on requisite product review websites. Participate in blogs and scam alert sites. Contact the Better Business Bureau, Federal Trade Commission, Food and Drug Administration, or any other oversight agency that is relevant for the product or service in question. The governance and enforcement system can only function properly if consumers are willing to share information about their experiences in a timely fashion.

In some cases, it might be advantageous to pursue legal action against the purveyor of false advertising, either individually or as part of a community (e.g., class action law suit). While such a response may be expensive in terms of time and finances, it is certainly the best way to both draw public attention to the issue and to put in place serious negative consequences to curtail the activity. In part, many companies push the edge in terms of misleading advertising because it is still relatively rare for complaints to go the legal route and result in substantive impact on sales and/or revenues. Consider that for every person who sucks up their losses and decides not to press the issue legally, many other people may fall victim to the same scam or sales trick.

Putting Brakes on the Information Highway

The current generation of humans is extremely lucky to have access to the internet with its enormous potential for information sharing, archiving of knowledge, and avenues for global discussion. However, as previously discussed, it is a tool that is easy to pervert as a means of spreading false and unsubstantiated information. While we have discussed in depth the ways in which we can ascertain the validity of information we find through the internet, the global scope of this largely unregulated electronic tool makes it difficult to combat campaigns based upon false facts and data. Many websites already exist to evaluate the validity of information and debunk those circulating rumors and stories that are incorrect or misleading. These are extremely valuable resources and go a long way toward uncovering cases of lying and fraudulent claims. Unfortunately, not enough people make it a habit to use these sites, at least as a starting point for investigation in the course of coming to their own conclusions about a theory, an event, or given statement.

In this case, the individual consumer of information is the most valuable weapon against the perpetuation of falsehood. It is up to you to apply the principles of reason and logic in order to arrive at a well informed decision about the nature of information to which you are exposed. But it is also up to you to share your conclusions with others. You already know not to take the claims of special interest groups at their word without doing some fact checking first. If you find factual inconsistencies or false information, it is your civic duty to share those findings with others. At the very least, do not become part of the problem by forwarding the suspect information on without first doing a bit of a dive into the factual grounds upon which it is supposedly based. If the information is based upon lies and false information, pass it on with an alert or disclaimer at the top so that the issues are brought to the attention of the next individual in the chain. I regularly receive emails from loved ones alerting me to potential scams or fraudulent activity circulating on the internet. This is incredibly helpful if for no other reason than the benefit of being forewarned of a potential issue before I get tricked by it myself.

Or you can take it a step further and share your conclusions farther afield. You can post comments on websites that contain questionable information pointing out inconsistencies or inaccuracies. You can participate in blogs or tweets or Facebook postings that warn others of the issue. You can even start a counter campaign—do your own research about a circulating claim or theory and start a website or email chain that gets the contrary information out there for others to see. The possibilities are practically endless, once you decide to harness the power of the information highway in an active way rather than as a passive recipient of whatever undocumented information comes your way.

Be Part of the Solution

The most important way in which you can combat the prevalence of lying, disingenuousness, and misinformation in our society is to teach other people how to make judgments. Feel free to take the process of rational judgment that you have learned from this book and share it with others. Help your children better understand how to make factual and informed judgments and reward them for their efforts. Provide your parents with mechanisms for properly evaluating information about everything from political promises to health aides to automobile purchases. Provide facts and figures and alternative ways of thinking to your friends and co-workers in a way that challenges them to think about the basis of the so-called facts they are sharing with others.

No matter how you decide to approach the line between truth and falsehood, be active, be vocal, and demand factual, high quality information as a consumer. Make political candidates back up their claims with real facts and empirical data. React to pundits and members of the news media with healthy skepticism until they deliver truthful unbiased information to the consuming public. Be creative in how you promulgate the truth. Express your opinions about lying by word of mouth, in blogs or tweets or editorials, or even consider writing a book—I did! Whatever you decide to do, I hope you will be part of the solution and not simply a part of the culture that sits back and buys whatever bridge the latest trickster has to sell.

A Parting Comment

I have tried to cover as many of the potential opportunities to tell truth from falsehood as I could with this work. Unfortunately, the nature of society and human psychology is such that the propensity for deception is rampant across all aspects of social interaction. Luckily, there are certain general red flags that can clue us in to a potential issue across any number of situations. For example, be wary of words and phrases that imply more consistency than is perhaps warranted. For instance, "always," "never," and "100% of the time" are often misleading. Few things in life are that black and white, so claims to the contrary should be suspect until investigated further.

Claims and statements that include numbers and figures usually provide a sense of comfort and confidence in their authenticity, but keep in mind that numbers are just numbers unless there is empirical evidence to back it up. In other words, anyone can provide numerical statistics to back up any point, but that does not mean those numbers are accurate. It is in the best interest of every consumer to think logically about what they hear and apply deductive reasoning to fully evaluate any piece of information.

For example, I was recently struck by a TV commercial airing at the moment about how shipping freight by rail is more economical and environmentally friendly than other forms of transportation. The actual statement made in the ad was "CSX moves one ton of freight 450 miles on a single gallon of fuel." These numbers did not sit comfortably with me. A single loaded freight car weighs upwards of fifty tons. Did the statement in this ad mean that the fuel used to transport a fifty ton car would be fifty times that needed to ship a single ton? If so, I could not see how shipping by rail would be an economical proposition at all! So I contacted the company. Much to their credit, they responded quite quickly with the following statement that helped clear up the issue for me.

Our ad states "trains can move a ton of freight nearly 500 miles, on average, per gallon of diesel fuel," and it is correct. The 500 is calculated by dividing the total tons hauled by a single freight train by the total gallons of fuel used. So, on a per mile, per ton basis, the amount of fuel needed is extremely low. In fact, it is so low that trains are between three and four times more fuel efficient than trucks. Even though it takes more than one gallon of fuel to power a train for nearly 500 miles, the train actually uses less fuel than the more than 280 trucks it would take to haul the same amount of freight.

The point here is that not every action designed to probe the validity of a statement uncovers a lie. Sometimes the truth is clarified and we learn something by looking a bit deeper into any explanation. The purpose of the principles and approaches I have shared in this book is not for you to become a habitual debunker of myths and lies, but rather to give you a better framework from which to tell the difference between truth and fiction when it is relevant for you. The exercises I have provided in this book are relatively easy to grasp, can be employed across a wide range of situations, and are virtually immune to cultural perspective or mindset. Quite simply, the search for empirical facts works across virtually all circumstances, barring the quest for religious truth, and thus is an incredibly valuable tool for each and every one of us on a daily basis.

One final point to consider, however, is not how to apply the principles described in this book, but whether any of you will be motivated to do so at all. Since we are all capable of fact checking but seldom do so on a regular basis, we have to consider whether the American public actually wants to be told the truth. It is a very simple thing to question a speaker about the evidence they have to support their claim, or to look up information from valid sources to confirm or refute any statement or theory. Yet most of us choose to employ others means for determining whether we believe information is true or not—the identification with the source of the information, how well the information fits in with pre-existing beliefs and ideas, or whether there is a certain emotional comfort to the claim we are considering. These factors often preclude our willingness to delve any deeper into the information and thus we become complicit in the falsehood itself. Perhaps we prefer a fiction of our own choosing that requires neither proof nor evidence to support our beliefs over that which challenges our preconceptions and common mindset.

About this last possibility, I can provide no recourse. Without a willingness to challenge the status quo, to seek truth wherever it may be found (whether the outcome suits you or not), the principles and examples in this book remain interesting tools with which we can philosophically agree but not bother to take down and employ when the need arises. The answer to that conundrum rests with each and every one of you who has journeyed through these pages with me. The process of deductive reasoning is a powerful tool if employed with a goal of increasing accountability and honesty in our society, but it is up to you to decide whether or not to wield it. I certainly hope you will.

Made in the USA
Middletown, DE
26 August 2022